GCSE (9–1)

RELIGIOUS STUDIES A

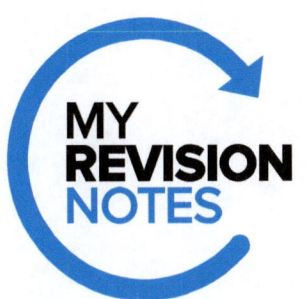

MY REVISION NOTES

AQA

GCSE (9–1)

RELIGIOUS STUDIES A
CHRISTIANITY, BUDDHISM AND THE THEMES

UPDATED

HODDER
EDUCATION
AN HACHETTE UK COMPANY

Every effort has been made to trace all copyright holders, but if any have been inadvertently overlooked, the Publishers will be pleased to make the necessary arrangements at the first opportunity. Although every effort has been made to ensure that website addresses are correct at time of going to press, Hodder Education cannot be held responsible for the content of any website mentioned in this book. It is sometimes possible to find a relocated web page by typing in the address of the home page for a website in the URL window of your browser.

Hachette UK's policy is to use papers that are natural, renewable and recyclable products and made from wood grown in well-managed forests and other controlled sources. The logging and manufacturing processes are expected to conform to the environmental regulations of the country of origin.

Orders: please contact Hachette UK Distribution, Hely Hutchinson Centre, Milton Road, Didcot, Oxfordshire, OX11 7HH. Telephone: +44 (0)1235 827827. Email education@hachette.co.uk Lines are open from 9 a.m. to 5 p.m., Monday to Friday. You can also order through our website: www.hoddereducation.co.uk

ISBN 9781398324503

© Jan Hayes and Lesley Parry 2021
First published in 2021 by
Hodder Education (a trading division of Hodder & Stoughton Limited),
An Hachette Company
Carmelite House
50 Victoria Embankment
London EC4Y 0DZ

www.hoddereducation.co.uk

Reprinted with amendments in 2026

The authorised representative in the EEA is Hachette Ireland, 8 Castlecourt Centre, Dublin 15, D15 XTP3, Ireland (email: info@hbgi.ie)

Impression number   10 9 8 7 6 5

Year   2026

Cover photo © Beboy - stock.adobe.com

Illustrations by Integra Software Serv. Ltd

Typeset in India by Integra Software Serv. Ltd

Printed in CPI Group (UK) Ltd, Croydon, CR0 4YY

A catalogue record for this title is available from the British Library.

My Revision Planner

Introduction

REVISED   TESTED   EXAM READY

My Revision Notes: AQA GCSE (9–1) Religious Studies A: Christianity, Buddhism and the Themes

2.2 Buddhism: Practices

Key terms from the Specification

General teachings of the six major religions

Theme A: Relationships and families

Theme B: Religion and life

REVISED   TESTED   EXAM READY

My Revision Planner

4

	REVISED	TESTED	EXAM READY

My Revision Notes: AQA GCSE (9–1) Religious Studies A: Christianity, Buddhism and the Themes

Find Now Test Yourself and Exam Practice answers at **https://www.hoddereducation.co.uk/myrevisionnotesdownloads**

Introduction

It is very common practice for schools to recommend to students that they get a revision guide to support their final revision for GCSE (and in fact any formal exams). The point being that you, the student, can do some reading and studying at home with a set of reliable notes. This is crucial to GCSE success – just working in school is not enough. This book is to help you revise, covering the whole Specification.

Of course, revision guides are just shortened forms of the textbook (which is a shortened form of what you should be covering in class). They don't give you every detail and do expect you to have some knowledge to start with. This guide is no different, though it should give you enough detail and clues to be able to revise effectively. It is meant to support your revision, not teach you anew.

Doing well in exams is about knowing and understanding the subject content in a course. It is also very much about being able to understand the questions you are faced with and what they want of you. This usually means you have to apply your knowledge, and demonstrate clear understanding and insight. This guide gives you lots of exam advice, practice questions and practice answers to think about.

Hopefully your teachers have taught you a few revision techniques. Make sure you try them out, bearing in mind that some people use the same method effectively for every subject, while others use a variety of methods depending on the subject they are revising. Your revision programme will be unique to you – just make sure you have one! This guide suggests a small number of revision strategies which have been effective for GCSE students in the past – feel free to try them, use them as described or tailor them to your style.

How does it work? REVISED ⬤

+ Each topic lists the **key terms** you need to know so that you can answer questions. Knowing key terms is the bedrock of your success.
+ A **glossary of key terms** gives you the words used in the Specification itself – questions use these terms, so they are the most important.
+ Each topic is written in bitesize chunks – read and learn them all. There are three religions in this book – revise only the two you studied in school. All six Themes are here, but in the exam you answer four.
+ Key teachings are found throughout the book. Those prescribed by the Specification are there, but we have added quite a few extras. It always impresses examiners if you use teachings that are specific to a question.
+ At the end of each section there is a page of exam practice questions – great practice for you. And as a bonus, you will gain increased familiarity with exam question wording, reducing anxiety and confusion in the exam.
+ There is a section on revision techniques. Try them all – you never know what might work for you. Try them in other subjects, too.
+ Throughout the book we have scattered quick tips and hints – tips for revision, for the exam, and common mistakes.
+ We also give you a checkpoint page which doubles as the contents page. Track your revision progress and grow your confidence as you tick the boxes.

Good luck!

Get the most from this book

These revision notes will help you to revise for AQA's GCSE (1–9) Religious Studies Specification A. It is essential to review your work, learn it and test your understanding.

Tick to track your progress

Use the revision planner on pages 3 to 6 to plan your revision, topic by topic. Tick each box when you have:

+ revised and understood a topic
+ tested yourself
+ practised the exam questions and gone online to check your answers

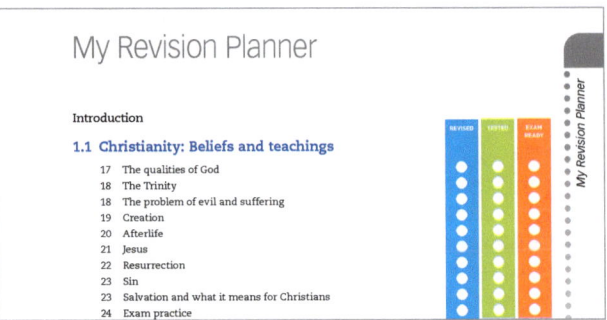

Features to help you succeed

Exam practice

An Exam Practice page is provided for each topic. Use these to consolidate your revision and practise your exam skills.

Religious teachings

It is crucial that you can write about religious teachings in your exam. Almost all the questions demand this. This book includes many teachings to use, but you should look to add your own.

Now test yourself

This is a series of quick questions to check your knowledge. You could do them before or after you revise the information from the page. Some suggested answers to these questions can be found online at www.hoddereducation.co.uk/myrevisionnotesdownloads

Exam tips

Throughout the book there are tips to help you boost your grade. They can also be used with other topics and Themes.

Key terms

Key terms are highlighted and defined throughout the book. There are lists of Specification-specific terms at the end of each section, but you should familiarise yourself with all the highlighted terms.

Revision tip

Throughout the book there are tips to help you improve your revision.

Activities

Activities consist of sample questions and answers for you to use to improve your technique. A number of these are evaluation tasks, and will give you ideas of arguments as well.

Find Now Test Yourself and Exam Practice answers at https://www.hoddereducation.co.uk/myrevisionnotesdownloads

Full Course and Short Course outlines

If you have this book and you are revising for the **Full Course RS GCSE** check the following:

+ You have studied **two** world religions. This book covers Christianity and Buddhism.
+ You know both the **beliefs** and the **practices** for the two religions you have studied.
+ You have studied **four Themes** – there are six covered in the book so make sure you are revising the ones your teacher has taught you. The attitudes of all six world faiths are referred to in each Theme.

You will have one exam paper for the religions. This is Paper 1.

+ Religion 1 – Beliefs = 24 marks + 3 SPaG
+ Practices = 24 marks
  Total for Beliefs and Practices 51 marks
+ Religion 2 – Beliefs = 24 marks + 3 SPaG
+ Practices = 24 marks
  Total for Beliefs and Practices 51 marks
+ Total marks for Paper 1 = 102. You will have 1 hour 45 minutes.

You will have one exam paper for the Themes. This is called Paper 2.

+ You will answer four full questions, each worth 24 marks.
+ Total marks for Paper 2 = 99 marks (96 + 3 SPaG). You will have 1 hour 45 minutes.

The questions within each religion (both beliefs and practices) and Themes have a common structure made up of five part-questions of 1, 1, 4, 6 and 12 marks.

If you have this book and you are revising for the **Short Course RS GCSE**, check the following:

+ You know the **Beliefs** for the two religions you have studied. **Do not** revise the Practices sections for either religion.
+ You also need to have studied **two Themes** – there are six covered in the book so make sure you are revising Theme A Relationships and families and Theme B Religion, peace and conflict.
  Note: Theme B for the Short Course is actually Theme D in this book.
+ You will have one exam (called Paper 1), split into three mini-papers.
  + Mini-paper 1 – Religion 1 – Beliefs = 24 marks (+ 3 SPaG)
  + Mini-paper 2 – Religion 2 – Beliefs = 24 marks (+ 3 SPaG)
  + Mini-paper 3 – Theme A – Relationships and families = 24 marks plus Theme B – Religion, peace and conflict = 24 marks

Total marks for Paper 1 = 102. You will have 1 hour 45 minutes.

The questions within each religion (beliefs) and Themes have a common structure made up of five-part questions of 1, 1, 4, 6 and 12 marks.

The exam for Full Course GCSE

All of your work for Religious Studies is summed up in your performance in two exam papers. You can look at each paper as being four sets of 24 marks; the mark breakdown in each 24 set is rigid, that is always the same.

	Four sets	Questions	Total marks
Paper 1	Religion 1 – Beliefs and teachings	Questions worth 1, 1, 4, 6, 12 marks	24 × 4 plus 3 marks for SPaG
	Religion 1 – Practices	Questions worth 1, 1, 4, 6, 12 marks	
	Religion 2 – Beliefs and teachings	Questions worth 1, 1, 4, 6, 12 marks	
	Religion 2 – Practices	Questions worth 1, 1, 4, 6, 12 marks	
Paper 2	Theme choice 1	Questions worth 1, 1, 4, 6, 12 marks	24 × 4 plus 3 marks for SPaG
	Theme choice 2	Questions worth 1, 1, 4, 6, 12 marks	
	Theme choice 3	Questions worth 1, 1, 4, 6, 12 marks	
	Theme choice 4	Questions worth 1, 1, 4, 6, 12 marks	

To reach the higher grades, aim to score at least 14 marks per set. Evenly scoring across all of the sets works best for this. If you know you have a weaker set – for example, you hate the fourth of your Themes – then do extra revision work to bring that weak set up to the level of your stronger ones. Eradicate the weakness!

Command phrases in the exam – what they are and what they mean

REVISED ●

The wording of the exam questions is fixed and examiners have to write questions which fit into the prescribed wording. The wording is specific for Religion Beliefs (RB), Religion Practices (RP) and the Themes (T). So what are they seeking?

Which section?	Wording	Explanation	Marks
All	Give/name one …	For 1-mark questions you just write one idea. This could be one word, a short phrase or a sentence.	1
RB	Explain two ways in which … influences _____ today	You must give and explain two ways, but you must show the impact on behaviour/thinking of people in that religion today.	4
RP/T	Explain two different _____ in contemporary British society	You must give and explain two beliefs/teachings/practices, but they must be contrasting or different. In the Themes, there are only three 'contrasting' topics to know about per Theme and you must answer from a Christian perspective for one view.	4
T	Explain two similar …	You must give and explain two beliefs/teachings/practices. Can be from any aspect of the topic.	4
T	Explain two different …	You must give and explain two teachings/practices. Can be from any aspect of the topic and any religion.	4
RB	Explain two (religion) teachings about …	You must give and explain two teachings. Stating and applying the source of authority gains two marks. It is easier to get the marks by using clear, specific teachings.	6

➡

Find Now Test Yourself and Exam Practice answers at https://www.hoddereducation.co.uk/myrevisionnotesdownloads

Which section?	Wording	Explanation	Marks
RP	Explain two different ways in which …	You must give and explain two ways in which something is done. Using and applying a source of authority will earn the fifth and sixth marks.	6
T	Explain two religious beliefs about …	You must give and explain two beliefs. Giving and applying the source of the belief earns two marks.	6
All	Refer to sacred writings or another source of _____ authority in your answer	You must refer to and apply a source of authority, for example a holy book or a religious leader, to get the fifth and sixth marks available.	6
RB/RP	Refer to (religion) teaching	Your answer must include clear and repeated reference to the teachings of the specified religion in order to reach higher levels.	12
All	Give reasoned arguments to support of this statement.	You must support the statement and explain the reasons you give.	12
All	Give reasoned arguments to support a different point of view.	You must provide a different point of view and explain the reasons you give for it.	12
T	Should refer to religious arguments	You must use religious arguments in your answer – it can't be entirely non-religious (that will limit you to fewer than half the available marks).	12
T	May refer to non-religious arguments	You could – but don't have to – use non-religious arguments.	12
All	Should reach a justified conclusion.	This is where you say which point of view is stronger/better and why it is. You should not just be repeating arguments you used earlier.	12

How examiners mark your work – question by question

REVISED

Question mark	Wording examiners follow	What that means to you
1	Award a mark for choosing the correct option	Right answer gets the mark.
1	Award a mark for a correct answer	One correct point gets 1 mark.
4	**First belief/way/etc.** Simple explanation of relevant and accurate point – 1 mark Detailed explanation of relevant and accurate point – 2 marks	First set of 2 marks comes from first making the point or giving the relevant teaching, second explaining that point/teaching and showing how it is relevant to the question.
	Second belief/way/etc. Simple explanation of relevant and accurate point – 1 mark Detailed explanation of relevant and accurate point – 2 marks	Second set of 2 marks is given for doing the same thing for a new point.
6	**First teaching/belief/way/etc.** Simple explanation of relevant and accurate point – 1 mark Detailed explanation of relevant and accurate point – 2 marks	First set of 2 marks comes from first making the point or giving the relevant teaching, second explaining that point/teaching and showing how it is relevant to the question.

➡

My Revision Notes: AQA GCSE (9–1) Religious Studies A: Christianity, Buddhism and the Themes

Question mark	Wording examiners follow	What that means to you
	Second teaching/belief/way/etc. Simple explanation of relevant and accurate point – 1 mark Detailed explanation of relevant and accurate point – 2 marks	Second set of 2 marks is given for doing the same thing for a new point.
	Somewhere in the answer, you must use a relevant religious teaching/quotation. You must also state the source of this authority, for example by naming a holy book or religious leader.	You get a mark for naming a relevant source of authority, and another mark for applying it to the question (showing how it is relevant).
12 (in four levels)	Level 4: 10–12 marks A well-argued response, reasoned consideration of different points of view. Logical chains of reasoning leading to judgement(s) supported by knowledge and understanding of relevant evidence and information.	You give several arguments from at least two points of view. These are mostly/all explained and expanded in a clear and effective way. Your points are all clearly relevant to the statement. There is a strong element of religious argument in your answer. There is clear evidence of a conclusion regarding the relative strengths of the points of view you have presented. The examiner won't have to think about what you are trying to say because you have argued logically and coherently.
	Level 3: 7–9 marks Reasoned consideration of different points of view. Logical chains of reasoning that draw on knowledge and understanding of relevant evidence and information.	You give several arguments from at least two points of view. You explain/expand some of these. Most of them will be obviously relevant to the statement, so that your points are clear. You will have put more than just a hint of religious argument in your answer. You will be evaluating the statement, not just writing attitudes about the topic of the statement.
	Level 2: 4–6 marks Reasoned consideration of a point of view. A logical chain of reasoning drawing on knowledge and understanding of relevant evidence and information. Or Recognition of different points of view, each supported by relevant reasons/ evidence.	If you write about only one point of view, you cannot achieve a higher level than this one. It might be one-sided. If it is, it will have several arguments which are explained and expanded well, and which clearly weigh up the statement. Or You give a series of arguments for more than one point of view with limited explanation of any argument.
	Level 1: 1–3 marks Point of view with reason(s) stated in support.	You are unlikely to have explained very much at all; just listed reasons to support what you think.

NB: while the wording of the 4- and 6-mark questions may vary, essentially the awarding of marks is as above (idea – explanation – idea 2 – explanation = 4 marks; idea – explanation – idea 2 – explanation – source (holy book, religious leader, etc) = 6 marks). 'Point' means place of belief/teaching/way, etc.

Your written English (SPaG)

REVISED ⬤

You will be judged on your written English in certain 12-mark questions you answer. This is worth up to 3 marks for the whole paper and is based around the quality of your spelling, punctuation and grammar. When your paper is marked, you will be provisionally awarded up to three marks for each of the four 12-mark evaluation answers. The highest of these four provisional SPaG marks is what you will be awarded for the whole paper; a maximum of 3 marks.

Find Now Test Yourself and Exam Practice answers at **https://www.hoddereducation.co.uk/myrevisionnotesdownloads**

So how are the marks awarded? Here is a simple guide.

0	You haven't written anything, e.g. not answered any of the 12-mark questions.
	You have written answers which have nothing to do with the question, so don't answer it.
	What you wrote doesn't make sense, so can't be understood or marked.
1	Called 'threshold performance'.
	You will have used only a limited range of specialist words.
	While probably making a lot of errors in grammar, what you write is still understandable.
	Your punctuation and spelling are reasonably accurate.
2	Called 'intermediate performance'.
	You will have used a good range of specialist terms and used them in the right context.
	You are generally accurate with grammar.
	Your spelling and punctuation are good, with few mistakes.
3	Called 'high performance'.
	You use lots of specialist language, in the right context and showing clear understanding of how to use it very appropriately.
	Your grammar is almost always correct and you use complex grammar (extended sentences and paragraphs, high-level grammatical constructions, etc.).
	Your spelling and punctuation are almost flawless, again beyond simple constructions.

You can improve your SPaG by paying attention to your English the whole time you are studying. It isn't something you can fix overnight as it is about your habitual way of writing. Learning and using key language as well as using connectives to make more complex sentences helps. Ask your teacher what you need to do to hit a better performance descriptor and get better marks.

Using specific religious teachings

How well you are able to learn and to use religious teachings in your exams will determine the grade you achieve. The wider the range of teachings you can refer to, the better your answers will be.

The exam Specification refers to the following teachings in the four religions covered in this book.

The exam questions can refer specifically to the content of these quotes, so be aware of their content. They are all explained in the relevant section of this guide.

You can use them in your answers, which will show your direct understanding of the religion.

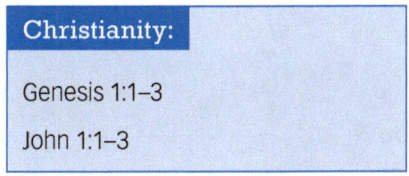

Christianity:

Genesis 1:1–3

John 1:1–3

Buddhism:

Jataka 075

Dhammapada 190-191

Will it really make a difference to an exam grade to learn teachings?

On the **Religions** paper the 6- and 12-mark questions specifically instruct you to 'refer to religious teachings in your answer'. This means that 18/24 marks are reliant on you using teachings to explain your answers. Over the whole paper: 72/102 marks! Probably the 4-mark questions will be easier to answer if you have teachings you can refer to as well. You need the teachings to use as the core of your answers for the 4- and 6-mark questions or to support ideas in your 12-mark evaluations.

On the **Themes** paper the 6- and 12-mark questions specifically instruct you to 'refer to religious teachings in your answer'. Again 18/24 marks are reliant on you using teachings to explain your answers. Over the whole paper: 72/99 marks! Also, in the 4-mark questions where you are asked to comment on 'similarities or differences' in beliefs, quotes will really help you, so add another 16 marks to your 72 – total 88/99 marks!

By knowing the teachings, explaining them in relation to the topic of the 4- and 6-mark questions, and using these to build arguments in your 12-mark evaluations, your answers will be able to access higher marks.

It is well worth the effort in your revision to learn teachings.

There are two ways to do this

On page 84 you will find 'general teachings' that can be used again and again across the Religions paper and the Themes paper. They are called general because they can be applied to many topics, but as they aren't specifically linked it will take more work, exam time and writing for you to make them relevant to the question. For example:

'Explain two religious beliefs about why fighting a war may be wrong.'

Two teachings – 'Love your neighbour'; 'Those who live by the sword, die by the sword.'

Using the first teaching you would need to explain that loving your neighbour means not to harm others and that as most wars include killing others (clearly harming and not loving others) then wars must be wrong to fight. Most wars are also fought against neighbouring countries, so this would not follow the teaching, etc.

The answer would be rather rambling, a little contrived – you would have to make the link more obvious. If you wrote it any more briefly, the examiner might not get the point you are making (they can only mark what you write, after all, not what you were thinking when you wrote it).

Using the second teaching you can simply say that 'war is wrong because those who take up arms will end up dying by them too so war is futile to fight'. The second is far more concise and direct, making clear sense for the examiner.

Good advice from an examiner would be to learn three teachings from two religions for each theme.

So four themes = 12 quotes each from the two religions studied. The revision guide provides those teachings for you. They are simple to learn and they do not have to be absolutely exact – as long as your examiner can tell which quote/teaching you are referring to, that will be enough. Hopefully you have been using these throughout your course so you should be familiar with many of them. If not, it's not too late – learn six per week for the month leading up to your exam … job done! It's never too late.

Remember that teachings/quotes you revise for the Themes might also be useful to you on the Religions paper. For example, teachings about helping those in poverty could be used as reasons why street pastors in Christianity carry out their work.

Once you begin to see how the teachings can be used across Themes and Religions, then your revision is going well and you are getting nearer to being ready to take the exam.

Top tips for writing good evaluation responses

+ Make sure you give more than one point of view. (Giving only one point of view will limit your potential mark to half of those available.) You can avoid the mistake by giving 'agree' and 'disagree' arguments. Spell it out for the examiner by using this kind of language:

  One point of view might be to agree because …

  Another point of view which also agrees is …

  There are points of view which disagree, for example …

  You are clearly telling the examiner you are giving different points of view, and even if you could only answer from agree or disagree and not both, your language shows you have still given different points of view (different people can share agreement or disagreement but have very different reasons, that is different points of view, for their agreement).

+ Make sure you write arguments for/against the statement, and don't just write about the topic of the statement. A good way to avoid this trap is to ask yourself 'Is this statement true/valid?'

+ The best answers include a justified conclusion. This is where you say which point of view is the strongest one and *why* it is. You can show the examiner you are doing this by using phrases like 'most compelling', 'most persuasive', 'easiest to attack/defend' and so on. Don't forget to explain and back up these evaluative phrases though, as the explanation of them is what counts as 'justified'.

+ Try never to leave points without explanations – the detail is important for achieving higher levels/marks. When you write a new point, ask yourself – what example could I give to demonstrate that?

+ Don't forget that this is a Religious Studies GCSE. You need to include religious ideas and arguments. In the Themes paper, it can be easy to forget to do this – after all, the Themes are social issues. Avoid this trap by asking yourself – would religious believers agree with the statement? – and then checking your answer for religion.

From the start of revision to the exam itself

Doing GCSEs is like running a race. You do the preparation and training (your study and revision), then you turn up to the race putting yourself in the right frame of mind (that is, your last-minute revision, and getting focused for the exam itself), and finally you run the race (the exam itself). You don't see the outcome when you finish the exam, as you would with a race – that comes later. However, better than a race where only one person gets to win, in GCSEs everybody who meets the grade gets to be a winner.

On your marks ...

REVISED

Make sure you have good notes covering all the topics – you can't have anything missing. You can revise only what you have studied already (otherwise it is study, not revision). Use your class and other notes to make a set of revision notes, in a style that suits you (check out the revision strategies in the back of this guide if you don't know any). This book could be the start of your notes – if it belongs to you, write on it. Then use your notes along with revision techniques to fix the information in your head/memory.

Where there are questions in the book, do them all – it is good practice. Also check out the AQA website for further assessment materials you could use for practice. Always do timed practices – that helps you in the exam where time is precious. Work to a minute a mark, perhaps allowing a couple extra for the 6- and 12-mark questions.

Get set ...

REVISED

+ Prepare yourself for the specific exam.
+ Get a good night's sleep beforehand.
+ Have breakfast (your brain needs fuel). If it is an afternoon exam, avoid a stodgy lunch (it will put you to sleep when you need to be alert).
+ Any revision now should be light, as it really should only be a case of refreshing your memory.
+ Be in good time for the exam – rushing and arriving at the last minute encourages panic.

Go ...

REVISED

+ Sitting in the exam room, breathe slowly and relax yourself (carefully reading every word of the exam paper cover is a good way to do this). Focus on your space, not the big room. Make sure you can see a clock so you can keep track of time.
+ Read the exam paper and decide which questions are best for you. Answer your strongest first to give yourself confidence – if you started with your weakest, you could undermine your confidence and thus not perform so well.
+ Within the exam, take mini-breaks. After completing a question take a moment to clear your head so you can get your focus clearly for the next. If you feel yourself panicking, just give yourself a breathing break to calm yourself down.
+ If your mind goes blank on a question, just leave it, move on and come back to it later. Mark the question paper to remind yourself that you need to do that.
+ Finished? Check your answers. Do this by reading the question, thinking of an answer, **and only then** reading your answer – you stand more chance of spotting any gaps. Also remind yourself of technique. What does the 4-marker require? Check you have done it.

On the podium ...

REVISED

It is a big podium for GCSE. With the right revision, you will be on it and receiving a good grade in the summer.

Let's get going then.

1.1 Christianity: Beliefs and teachings

The qualities of God

There are many qualities of God. This course seeks that you recognise and can explain a number of them, so questions could be asked specifically about these terms. The key qualities you must know are omnipotence, all-loving and just. If you know other characteristics that is good as you can use that knowledge in some of your answers.

Qualities of God evidenced in the Bible

1 Omnipotence means God is all-powerful. God can do anything because of this power. It does not mean God can do the impossible (such as create a mountain that God could not then move). Evidence includes:
   + the creation of the world (Genesis)
   + miracles performed by Jesus, for example calming a storm on the sea, raising Jairus' daughter from the dead
   + the resurrection of Jesus, which shows power over death.

2 All-loving means what it says – God loves all, without exception and without prejudice. Even a bad person is loved by God, which suggests that even bad people can be redeemed and reconciled to God. Evidence includes:
   + sacrificing his own son to make atonement for the sins of humans
   + parable of the Prodigal Son (Luke 15:11–32)
   + Jesus' teachings, for example Sermon on the Mount (Matthew 5: 43–45, 48).

3 Just means that God is fair and will not act unjustly. God will give everyone equal value and rights, without prejudice or favour.
   + For Christians, it is important to believe God is just because they believe all will be judged after death. In the Parable of the Sheep and Goats (Matthew 25:31–46), Jesus talks about that just judgement.
   + In the Book of Job, it states that God will not act unjustly. 'God is fair and just' (Psalm 25:8).

Other characteristics

Other characteristics of God include that he is all-knowing (omniscient) – God is the supreme being so must be omniscient. St Anselm said that if God exists, he must be the 'greatest conceivable being', which means the most intelligent. Being all-powerful and all-knowing means God could create the world.

God is also eternal – he created the world, so must have existed before it did, and is outside space and time, controlled by neither, so must be eternal as time does not impact on God. This also makes him transcendent, which emphasises how different God is to humans and how humans cannot hope to fully understand the nature of God.

Finally, God is immanent – involved in the world. Jesus is an example of this, as are miracles, which are a sign of God at work within the world.

Influences

As a Christian my belief in God influences my life because I know he has the ability to do anything so he can look after me in all situations and as he is all-loving I know he won't give me more than I can cope with and everything has a reason.

All-loving: God's love is without prejudice and without limit; the sacrifice made through Jesus evidences this love.

Just: fair; God is always fair in his treatment, he will be fair at the Judgement.

Omnipotence: all-powerful; God created the world, revealing his power. Nothing can ultimately defeat God's power.

Revision tip

Learn all key terms – you could be asked what they mean, or find a question which relies on you knowing one of them. There is a glossary on page 61, which gives all the Specification key terms – the minimum you should know.

Activity

Fix it!

A student wrote this answer. Improve it for them.

Explain how believing that God is omnipotent might influence a Christian today. (4 marks)

They might say that it makes them feel safer because they know God loves them so much, he will look after them. In a difficult situation, they would know God was by their side and helping them.

17

The Trinity

Like some other religions, Christians believe there is only One God; however, Christians fundamentally differ from other monotheistic religions in believing that God is revealed in three distinct ways, eternally as a unity of three 'Persons'. This is called the Trinity, or Godhead:

+ God the Father – loving creator and sustainer of the universe.
+ God the Son – saviour who became incarnate (human), lived, was crucified and then resurrected, namely Jesus Christ.
+ God the Holy Spirit – source of strength which Christians find at work in their hearts.

The Trinity is referred to in all Christian ceremonies, for example baptism (I baptise you in the name of the Father and of the Son and of the Holy Spirit). It is part of basic statements of belief, such as the Apostles' Creed. Many hymns and prayers mention it.

> **Trinity:** the belief in God the Father, God the Son and God the Holy Spirit.

Why is the Trinity important?

It is God, and the religion is based on that concept. Symbols, such as the shamrock and triskelion, demonstrate the concept in an easy way.

It helps Christians gain some understanding of God, who really is beyond the understanding of humans, and it makes best sense of what is written in the Bible.

> **Influences**
>
> As a Christian, believing in the Trinity influences my life because I have a way to visualise God in my mind when actually God is a really hard concept to describe. Also the act of God sending his son – showing this ultimate act of love encourages me to try to always show love to others even when it might put me at a disadvantage.

> **Now test yourself** 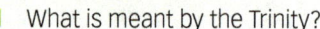 TESTED
>
> 1 What is meant by the Trinity?
> 2 Why is it important for Christians?

The problem of evil and suffering

What is the problem?

Christians believe that God is omnipotent, omniscient, benevolent and absolute. They believe this as a fact – God does exist. Christians, from their experience and knowledge, realise that there is suffering in the world. Some of the suffering is caused by humans (deliberately and accidentally), which is moral evil. Some is caused by nature – suffering is a fact of the world humans live in – which is natural evil.

The problem is why, if God exists, he allows humans, especially seemingly good and/or innocent ones, to suffer. He must know about it, has the power to prevent/end it, and loves humans unconditionally. So why does God allow the evils which cause suffering?

> **Absolute:** unchanging, eternal.
>
> **Benevolent:** all-loving; unconditional love.
>
> **Omniscient:** all-knowing; knowledge without limits.

Some solutions

Some suggestions that have been offered up to explain this dilemma include:

+ Moral evil: the devil tempts people (e.g. Adam and Eve); humans have free will, which they abuse and so hurt others.
+ Natural evil: suffering is allowed as a punishment for wrong-doing; it is a test of faith to strengthen the soul, for example the story of Job; it is needed so that we can appreciate good, that acts as a balance; it is an education – we learn to help others and look after our world by seeing/experiencing suffering.

No attempt at a solution solves the problem completely. Most Christians say that humans must just accept the suffering, as humans cannot possibly understand God and his purposes, but he does provide ways of understanding and living with it. God is just, so the fairness of all will be made clear at the end of days. Most important is that humans respond positively to suffering, for example by helping others, as Jesus told in the Parable of the Sheep and Goats (Matthew 25:31–46).

Now test yourself   TESTED ○

1 Give two solutions to the problem of evil and suffering.
2 Explain two ways in which a belief in evil and suffering influences Christians today.

Creation

REVISED ○

Christians hold various beliefs about creation:

+ God pre-existed the world, hence being able to create it.
+ God is transcendent (outside space and time). As such he created the world and is not controlled by it.
+ Genesis describes the creation: 1:1: 'In the beginning, God created the heavens and the Earth.'
+ John 1:1–3 opens with: 'In the beginning was the Word, and the Word was with God, and the Word was God. He was with God in the beginning. Through him all things were made; without him nothing was made that has been made.'
+ God created through his word – 'Let there be light', for example; 'Let there be space between the water and the heavens' and so on.
+ The term Word is linked to Jesus: 'The Word became flesh and lived for a while amongst us.' This second person of the Trinity is being referred to as both the Word and the Son of God (Jesus). Hence God and Jesus are ONE.
+ The Trinity is also part of the creation: 'the Spirit of God hovering over the face of the waters.' This is the third person, the Holy Spirit. So God, Son and Holy Spirit are ONE.
+ To conclude, therefore, all parts of the Trinity were involved in creation, so must have pre-existed it.

> **Genesis creation story**
>
> Genesis 1 teaches us that in the beginning there was nothing. He created (in order) - light, sky, land/sea/vegetation, sun/moon/stars, fish and birds, animals and humans. On the seventh day he rested. He saw that all 'was good'.

Genesis and its importance

The key points are that Christians believe the message within Genesis 1 is true. The world was planned, ordered and sustained by God. Human lives have purpose and meaning because God created those lives and humans are made in the image of God so all humans are of value.

Humans have a responsibility to treat each other equally. Humans were made stewards of the world to look after it.

Different interpretations

1 Genesis is literally true – every word is the word of God; God dictated the book and is totally correct. It happened as it says it happened. God is all-powerful and all-knowing, capable of doing all this in seven days.
2 Genesis does contain truth but it was not dictated. God inspired the writers – so if there are errors in the story, they are human errors. While generally correct, within the story, elements can be reinterpreted – does 'day' mean 'our day' or 'a period of time', for example?
3 Genesis was written by a person whose sense of God in the world inspired them to write. It is a man-made document. The point of the story is to give the messages that God is a loving God, we have a place in the world, and the world is a good place. It is a myth with an important message.

Each one of these has religious truths. Each way may influence a Christian slightly differently but essentially the messages are the same.

> **Influences**
>
> As a Christian, knowing that God created the world for us influences me to feel really special that he made me in his image. It also lets me understand my world is ordered and planned and I believe I have a purpose to being here and I must make the most of being here … sort of making God proud of me.

Afterlife

Death separates life on earth (temporary) from life with God (eternal) – it is not something to be feared. Christians believe they will reunite with the dead, thus easing the pain of bereavement.

The Book of Revelations says God will wipe every tear – there will be no more death or crying or pain.

Afterlife for Christians

Belief in the resurrection is important to Christians. Resurrection means that the dead will be raised to life because of what Jesus taught and that he himself overcame death. St Paul said this was central to Christian belief.

What Christians mean by resurrection

Christians believe God will resurrect them before Judgement Day. Jesus told people that the new mode of existence would be different from the earthly one. On earth it is perishable; it is raised imperishable (a spiritual body). There is continuity between the person's earthly life and the resurrected life.

Roman Catholics believe in purgatory, a state between death and the afterlife. After death of the body, the soul goes to purgatory if it is destined for heaven, where it is purified enough to enter heaven.

There are different views about resurrection. Many Christians simply say humans have no answers – only to trust in God. Without scientific evidence it is all a matter of belief based in Bible teachings and Jesus' words.

Judgement

Jesus taught that God's love and mercy are unconditional and that God is just. At the end of time on the Day of Judgement all souls (Christian or not) will be judged by Jesus. The parables – the Rich Man and Lazarus, and the Sheep and Goats – are Judgement teachings. Jesus will come to judge both the living and the dead. A person needs to personally accept God's offer of mercy.

Others reject the idea of a second coming of Christ. Jesus was just trying to express something that humans simply cannot understand. Humans will account for their actions, but no one knows how or when.

Heaven and hell

Christians use earthly images to explain their understanding of heaven.

People often see heaven in a way they see their present lives. It is often described in a way that would appeal to them now, for example those in poverty describe it as a land of milk, honey and plenty.

The Bible paints a picture of hell via the metaphor of an unquenchable fire. This idea was historically used to frighten people into obeying Church rules. Hell is now seen as eternal separation from God. It is neither decided by God nor what God wants – humans choose it by turning away from God.

Some Christians embrace universalism – they believe everyone will eventually respond to God's love, having repented and been forgiven.

> **Resurrection:** the physical return of Jesus on the third day after he died.
>
> **Roman Catholic:** the largest Christian group based in Rome and led by the Pope.

> ### Influences
> The afterlife for me as a Christian influences my life in that I know that God will be my ultimate judge. If I live a Christian life and believe in Jesus then heaven is open to me. Secondly, as there is an afterlife, it gives me hope and comfort that this life is not the end and God is waiting for me.

> ### Now test yourself
> 1 How does belief in Judgement Day affect people in their lives today?
> 2 How might the existence of heaven and/or hell influence Christians in their lives?
> 3 Give two reasons why Christians might disagree about judgement.
> 4 What do Christians mean by the word resurrection?
>
> TESTED

Find Now Test Yourself and Exam Practice answers at **https://www.hoddereducation.co.uk/myrevisionnotesdownloads**

Jesus

His incarnation – Jesus the Son

Central to Christian belief is the idea that God the Son took on human form as Jesus. John 1:14 says 'the Word became flesh and lived amongst us'. Christians believe Jesus was fully God and fully human – truly the Son of God. If Christians acknowledge Jesus as the Son of God, God lives in them.

> **Incarnation:** God in human form; Jesus.
>
> **Messiah:** the anointed one who is seen as the saviour by Christians.
>
> **Salvation:** the saving of the soul from sin; includes through grace and spirit.

Jesus: Son of God	Jesus' knowledge	Importance of belief in incarnation
+ The title 'Son of God' is used about Jesus in the New Testament. + Mary was a virgin who conceived through the power of the Holy Spirit. + Some Christians accept the virgin birth as true whereas others suggest it is more a metaphor to show that Jesus was both human and divine.	+ If fully divine, Jesus should have had full knowledge of what was happening, yet at times his knowledge was limited – e.g. he said he didn't understand fully about the end of the world. + This can be explained by saying that to become fully human he had to give up some of his divine knowledge – a great sacrificial act. He came as a servant but was still fully God in his relationship with and understanding of God.	+ It helps Christians understand the extent of God's love for humanity – Jesus had to become human to be able to make reconciliation with God possible through his life being sacrificed as a payment for human sin. + It shows how Christians should live – as God so loved us so we should love one another (1 John 4:11). + Many Christians have taken on this act of selfless love – consider Mother Teresa.

Crucifixion

+ Jesus' work on earth lasted about three years, then he was arrested, tried and crucified.
+ Convicted of blasphemy by the Jewish authorities, he was put to death for treason under Roman law.
+ He was crucified at Golgotha – the place of the skull. It took six hours for him to die. Mark records that for three hours the Earth was dark, perhaps symbolic of the judgement on Israel for its rejection of the **Messiah**.
+ Matthew and Mark's Gospels say that Jesus questioned: 'God, why have you forsaken me?' (this is also a quotation from Psalm 22:1)
+ Mark says that at the point of death, the temple curtain tore in two – believed by some to show that Jesus' death had destroyed the barrier of sin that separated humans from God, therefore making it possible to access God.

Why he had to die

+ At the time – Jesus' teachings gave a new understanding of the Torah, which brought him into direct conflict with Jewish leaders.
+ At the time – the Roman governor was under pressure to keep a peaceful land, so came down hard on any religious rebellion. When Jewish leaders implied Jesus was stirring up trouble, the governor had to act.
+ In Christian thought – Jesus had to die to fulfil God's plan. Without his death humans could not be reunited with God and enter heaven. Jesus atoned for the sins of humanity, bringing God and humans back together.

Salvation and reconciliation

+ God gave his only son so that humans could be saved in eternal life (**salvation**).
+ Jesus' death atoned (made up for) human sin by bearing its just penalty on the cross.
+ This was God reconciling with his people. He is so loving and merciful he made forgiveness possible through his own son.
+ Christians work for reconciliation with others in the world today.

Now test yourself

1 What is the incarnation?
2 Why did Jesus have to die?
3 What is salvation?

Resurrection

What happened to Jesus?

This is recorded in the New Testament in the Gospels of Matthew, Mark, Luke and John.

Joseph (of Arimathea) was given permission to take Jesus' body down from the cross. Joseph was allowed by Pontius Pilate (the Roman governor) to bury Jesus in a rock tomb he owned. However, the burial rites were delayed as it was the Sabbath day of rest. When the women returned on the Sunday morning, they found the stone rolled away. All three Gospel writers say that the body had gone and the women were told Jesus had 'risen'.

Mark says a man in white tells the women to return to Galilee to meet the risen Jesus.

John says a man reveals himself to Mary Magdalene as Jesus himself come back to life and she returns to the disciples to say 'she had seen the risen Jesus'.

All this is followed by 'resurrection appearances' recorded in Matthew, Luke and John only. During the next 40 days when he appeared he was not always recognised at first but the physical nature of his 'appearances' is always stressed.

The impact of the Resurrection

The disciples turned from men in hiding to going out spreading Jesus' message. This put them in great danger, indicating that something significant had happened. Peter, for example, went from being terrified, so that he denied he even knew Jesus to teaching his message openly. Seeing the risen Jesus was what caused these transformations.

What happened next?

On the 40th day after the resurrection some texts describe 'the Ascension of Jesus'. At Bethany, Jesus blessed his disciples before being taken up to heaven – 'a cloud received him from their sight' (Acts). This was the successful completion of his mission and return to God.

How does Jesus' resurrection influence Christians today?

It is the central element of Christian belief – if Jesus simply died then he is no different to others who may have died for their beliefs or as punishment for going against the authorities. Christians believe resurrection is the proof Jesus is the Son of God – showing how God triumphed over evil and death.

This victory over death opens up heaven for Christians. Jesus' sacrifice overcame sin, reconciled humanity with God and offered eternal life.

> **Revision tip**
>
> It is more important to know why the resurrection was important and questions raised about it than knowing the narrative. There is some debate about whether Jesus actually 'rose from the dead'.

> **Ascension:** Jesus being taken up to heaven on the 40th day of Easter.

> **Influences**
>
> This for me makes my faith complete. Jesus' resurrection makes him different to anyone else and so I know this is the true faith. I also know that if Jesus can overcome death as a human, like me, then so can I and I can enter heaven as Jesus did. Jesus showed us his Father's power by what he did.

Sin

The story of 'original sin' is in Genesis – Adam and Eve are tempted by the devil to eat from the tree of good and evil (the only tree in the whole garden to have been forbidden). Adam and Eve were evicted from the Garden of Eden as punishment.

Many Christians believe humans were all descended from Adam and Eve. Tainted by this act, all humans have an inbuilt tendency to disobey God and to face God's just penalty for sin.

Sin separates humans from God, bringing eternal punishment. As humans are full of sin, so only God can rectify this problem. Christians believe God offered salvation through the sacrifice of Christ.

Most Christians do not take the Genesis story literally. To many, it conveys the message that humanity has the inclination to do what they are told *not* to (hence disobeying God), which damages their relationship with him.

Influences

I always know that God loves me, even though often I don't deserve it. So I show love to others regardless. I feel that I have the Holy Spirit within me. I try to act in a way that reflects this gift in me. But I know sin is so easy to do and often the right way is the most difficult so I have to be conscious of this.

Salvation and what it means for Christians

Salvation means being forgiven by God and being assured of eternal life.

1 Salvation through law:
   + In Jesus' time, Jewish teachings emphasised that 'obeying the law' was the way to salvation.
   + Some Christians believe in salvation through work – the idea that a right relationship with God has to be earned.
   + Some Christians think salvation can be earned through obedience to God's laws; others take on Jesus' idea that God was more pleased with the thoughts in our minds and the love in our hearts for him and others. Christians need to put these thoughts into action in their lives.
2 Salvation through grace:
   + Grace is the unconditional love that God has for all humans. God's love is there despite everything humans do – it need not be earned.
   + God shows his love in the gift of salvation to all who believe in Jesus as the Son of God.
   + Salvation through grace and spirit is made possible through Jesus' atoning death. Jesus' actions made possible the forgiveness for the sins of the world, leading to reconciliation.
   + Christians believe they receive God's grace through the presence in their hearts of the Holy Spirit. This allows them to try to show love as Jesus did.
   + Many people today believe that 'the grace of God' helps them every day and that 'acts of God's grace' are seen in the world daily.

Atonement: means making amends for sin. Christians believe that Jesus' death was the atonement for humankind's sins. It allowed God and humans to be reconciled, so humans could go to heaven. Jesus had a role in salvation – to die as atonement, or sacrifice, for the salvation of all souls.

Original sin: belief that everyone born carries the sins of their forefathers.

Activity

Continue the answer

This is half of a 4-mark answer. Write the other half giving a second way. Use it as a model in answering these types of questions in your exam.

Explain two ways in which belief in 'salvation through grace' might influence Christians today. (4 marks)

One way that belief in salvation through grace could influence Christians today is to try and help others that are in need. This shows their love for others as Jesus showed his love for them. It is by the grace of the Holy Spirit in their hearts which enables them to carry out such actions.

Try another:

Explain two ways in which belief in 'sin' might influence Christians today. (4 marks)

Exam practice

What questions on this section look like:

Christianity: Beliefs and teachings

This page contains a range of questions that could be on an exam paper. Practise them all to strengthen your knowledge and technique while revising. Check back to pages 11–12 to see the marking grids that examiners use: this will help you to mark your answers.

1 Which part of Jesus' life is referred to by the term 'incarnation'?

  (a) his baptism   **(b)** his birth   **(c)** his death   **(d)** his rising from the dead   [1]

2 Which of the Gospels refers to the 'role of the word' in creation?

  (a) John   **(b)** Luke   **(c)** Mark   **(d)** Matthew   [1]

3 Give one Christian teaching about the Creation.   [1]

4 Give one Christian belief about heaven.   [1]

5 Give one reason Jesus' death is important for Christians.   [1]

6 Explain two ways in which belief in the resurrection of Jesus influences Christians today.   [4]

7 Explain two ways in which belief in God being just influences Christians today.   [4]

8 Explain two ways in which belief in the creation story influences Christians today.   [4]

9 Explain two ways in which belief in heaven influences Christians today.   [4]

10 Explain two Christian teachings about the role of Christ in salvation. Refer to sacred writings or another source of Christian belief and teachings in your answer.   [6]

11 Explain two Christian teachings about the Incarnation. Refer to sacred writings or another source of Christian belief and teachings in your answer.   [6]

12 Explain two Christian teachings about the nature of God. Refer to sacred writings or another source of Christian belief and teachings in your answer.   [6]

13 'For Christians, the crucifixion of Jesus is more important than his resurrection.' Evaluate this statement. In your answer you should:
+ refer to Christian teaching
+ give reasoned arguments to support this statement
+ give reasoned arguments to support a different point of view
+ reach a justified conclusion.   [12]

14 'God cannot be all-loving because evil and suffering exist.' Evaluate this statement. In your answer you should:
+ refer to Christian teaching
+ give reasoned arguments to support this statement
+ give reasoned arguments to support a different point of view
+ reach a justified conclusion.   [12]

15 The 'Creation was so long ago it does not matter what actually happened.' Evaluate this statement. In your answer you should:
+ refer to Christian teaching
+ give reasoned arguments to support this statement
+ give reasoned arguments to support a different point of view
+ reach a justified conclusion.   [12]

Exam tip

Level 2 students write in a very limited way. They often write only a few words or a single sentence – no matter how many marks a question is worth. They also miss out questions. If this is you, then part of the problem is having too little knowledge – get notes which work for you, learn revision techniques which work for you, and use them. You will then have more to be able to say in the exam.

Level 5 students write in sentences and paragraphs. They usually try to extend their writing in all their answers. However, they may write less fluently than higher grade students and so the quality is not so good. If this is you, you need to learn and understand the topics better – that gives you more to write from, and when we have confidence in our understanding, we write better and fuller answers.

Level 8 students write fluently and in good, detailed English. Their work flows, using connectives and paragraphing well to give an impression of having good command of the subject.

Find Now Test Yourself and Exam Practice answers at **https://www.hoddereducation.co.uk/myrevisionnotesdownloads**

Worship

There are many forms of informal worship across the different Christian groups.

Worship is an act devoted to God to show love and reverence for God. Christians believe that when they worship God, God speaks back through the Bible, sermon and sacraments. Most Christians hold acts of worship, or services, on Sunday of every week as a communal show of devotion. There are different types of worship.

What is liturgical worship?

Liturgical worship is found in the Roman Catholic, Orthodox and Church of England (Anglican) churches. The services follow a liturgy – a set pattern – usually from a printed book. The liturgy has an established structure (order) of set prayers and readings, with the congregation repeating key phrases.

Hymns are sung at set times (hymns vary) and a sermon (speech) is given. Some of the prayers, the hymns chosen, the Bible readings and the sermon differ from service to service.

The ordered nature makes worshippers feel comfortable and part of the process.

What is non-liturgical worship?

Non-liturgical worship is a more informal way of worship. It follows a pattern or order but the elements are tailored to each service. Prayers are often in the leader's own words, the sermon on a topical theme and Bible readings chosen to fit.

Without set words, worshippers feel it comes more from the heart.

What is charismatic worship?

Charismatic worship is a kind of informal worship. Evangelical worship is often in this style.

The service has recognisable characteristics (hymns, prayers, sermon, readings) but is very free-flowing. Charismatic is 'Spirit inspired' – people often speak in tongues or feel the Holy Spirit at work within them.

How is the Bible used in worship?

The Bible is always the focus of any act of worship because it is considered either the 'word of God' or 'inspired by God'.

The Bible can be processed into church, many hymns are based on it, portions are often read out loud and the sermon often explains a Bible passage.

Key quotes

'Humble yourselves in the sight of the Lord, and he will lift you up.' James 4:10

'But the hour is coming, and now is, when true worshippers will worship the Father in spirit and in truth, for the Father is seeking such to worship him.' John 4:23

Charismatic worship: (informal) worship that is free-flowing and lacks structure.

Evangelical worship: worship stressing the teaching of Jesus, personal conversion experiences, scripture and evangelism to others.

Liturgical worship: worship that follows a set pattern (liturgy).

Non-liturgical worship: worship that follows a changeable structure.

Orthodox: a branch of the Christian church with its origins in Greece and Russia.

Private worship

This is just as important as public worship for Christians. It can be liturgical – for example, Roman Catholics may say the Angelus (a series of short meditations performed three times a day) – or non-liturgical – for example, a simple prayer at a time of need. Worshipping alone allows the person to feel close to God in exactly the way they want. It is a time to 'be with God', say things from the 'heart' and build a 'relationship' with God.

A rosary is a set of beads on a string with a crucifix on the end. Believers thread the beads through the fingers while saying set prayers (the Lord's Prayer, the Hail Mary, etc.).

Meditation, meanwhile, is mainly silent thought. It could be reflection on a Bible passage or religious truth. A sense of peace and calm is a key characteristic, alternating with the hustle of daily life.

> **Lord's Prayer:** the prayer Jesus taught his disciples to show them how to pray.

Prayer

Prayer is both talking and listening to God – to be open to guidance from the Holy Spirit. It should include praise, confession, thanks, prayers for others and then the self.

Jesus spoke about prayer – humility and honesty are essential. He stated that an all-loving God would always respond to sincere prayers. Outcomes are not always in the way Christians seek, however – God knows best.

Set prayers (e.g. the Lord's Prayer) are used both publicly and privately.

Why it is important to worship

God wants people to worship him. Worship can bring a sense of connection/togetherness with God to a community and/or an individual. It is an external expression of internal faith.

Through worship people gain a deeper understanding of their religion or of their faith in God. It strengthens the worshipper's faith and deepens their understanding, making them spiritually fit for what they do.

> **Revision tip**
>
> Questions with 4 marks should focus on differences or contrasts in religious practice. Make sure you know the differences:
> 1 Between the different types of worship – liturgical/non-liturgical/charismatic or informal/formal.
> 2 Between public and private prayers – what they are/how they are done.
> 3 Between the importance for the believers of the types of worship/prayers.

The Lord's Prayer

This is important as it is the prayer Jesus taught his disciples when he was asked by them 'Master, how should we pray?'
1 Know what each line of the prayer means (find a copy and jot down notes against each line).
2 You don't need to learn it off by heart, as any questions based on this prayer should give you the part you need to comment on.
3 It has praise, thanks, confession and asking God for the things the worshipper and others need – so it's a 'perfect prayer'.
4 As it was given by Jesus, it links back throughout the history of Christianity.
5 It can be used in public or private worship, out loud or silently.
6 It is usually part of all types of worship.

> **Now test yourself** TESTED
>
> 1 Describe the three different types of Christian worship.
> 2 Why is prayer important for Christians?
> 3 Explain why the Lord's Prayer is so important to Christians.

Sacraments

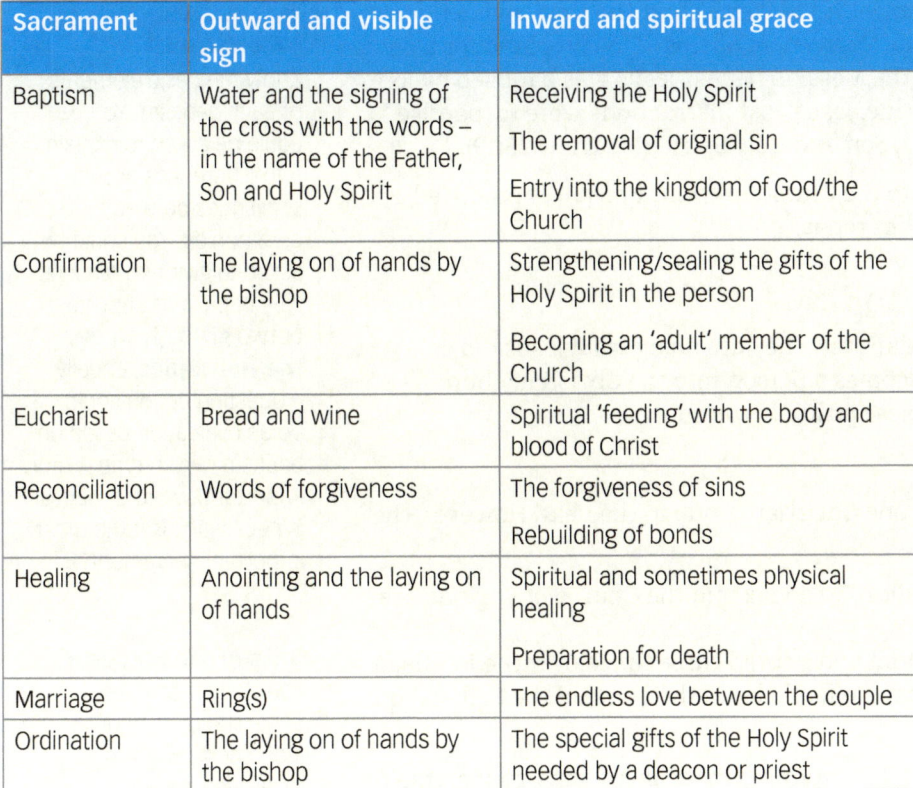

Sacrament	Outward and visible sign	Inward and spiritual grace
Baptism	Water and the signing of the cross with the words – in the name of the Father, Son and Holy Spirit	Receiving the Holy Spirit The removal of original sin Entry into the kingdom of God/the Church
Confirmation	The laying on of hands by the bishop	Strengthening/sealing the gifts of the Holy Spirit in the person Becoming an 'adult' member of the Church
Eucharist	Bread and wine	Spiritual 'feeding' with the body and blood of Christ
Reconciliation	Words of forgiveness	The forgiveness of sins Rebuilding of bonds
Healing	Anointing and the laying on of hands	Spiritual and sometimes physical healing Preparation for death
Marriage	Ring(s)	The endless love between the couple
Ordination	The laying on of hands by the bishop	The special gifts of the Holy Spirit needed by a deacon or priest

Baptism: the sacrament by which people become members of the Church.

Eucharist: bread and wine ceremony in the Anglican church.

Protestant: a branch of the Christian church that broke away from the Roman Catholic Church.

Sacrament:
+ The external and visible sign of an inward spiritual grace.
+ Can be experienced with the senses.
+ Has a deeper meaning which is not experienced through the senses.

Protestants acknowledge two **sacraments: baptism** and the **Eucharist**. They are known as Gospel sacraments because they were authorised by Jesus and there are many references to their use in much of the New Testament.

Roman Catholics, Orthodox Christians and some Anglicans have seven sacraments, all of which are implied through Jesus and the early church.

The importance for those who observe them

Christians believe God imparts gifts through the sacraments. They are offered at appropriate times in a person's life (like rites of passage) – baptism, confirmation and marriage.

In the Eucharist the bread and wine unites Christians with the risen Christ. Reconciliation helps Christians realise what they have done wrong, show penitence and then receive forgiveness through the priest's words.

Healing can be given during a long illness or when a person is near to death to give strength and peace of mind.

Ordination separates those who devote their lives to God in the priesthood, giving them gifts to carry out this role.

Why some Christians do not believe in sacraments

Quakers and members of the Salvation Army reject all sacraments – no direct reference is made to most of the seven in the Bible.

They believe Jesus did not intend either baptism or his words and actions over the bread and wine at the Last Supper to become prescribed rituals. They believe that God speaks directly to the believer's heart so there is no need of any form of 'go-between', and that symbols and ritual distract from true religion.

Revision tip

Definitions of these words could be required as a 1-mark multiple-choice question.

For the 1-mark short-response question you might be asked to name a sacrament, or give a reason why Christians see them as important.

There are many differences to refer to if you are asked about how different groups view the sacraments as a 4-mark question.

Some Christians do not believe in sacraments so this could be the focus of an evaluation ('The sacraments are not important'). Or it could focus on which is most important.

So this topic could appear in a variety of question types – it is worth learning carefully.

Baptism

According to Christian tradition, John the Baptist was the first Jewish figure to use baptism to symbolise the 'forgiveness of sins'. This prepared for a new way of life with the coming of the Messiah (Jesus). Jesus was baptised by John and the Holy Spirit entered his life. Jesus' last instructions were to 'baptise them in the name of the Father, Son and Holy Spirit' (Matthew 28:19).

Baptism welcomes a person into the Christian community. It is practised by almost all Christian communities today.

Baptism ceremonies today

Baptism is important as Christians feel they are doing what Jesus did so it connects them to him. It welcomes a person into the Christian church. Baptism removes sin and enables spiritual growth.

Infant baptism

Actual ceremonies differ from one Christian group to the next. However, the services have core similarities.

Key elements for Roman Catholics, Orthodox and the Church of England are:
+ baptism of a baby
+ use of holy water from the font and poured three times over the forehead
+ the sign of the cross made on the forehead in the name of the Father, Son and Holy Spirit.

Many baptism services also include promises made by parents/godparents on behalf of the child to reject evil, repent sins and turn to Christ; the lighting of a pascal candle, which symbolises receiving the light of Christ; the use of holy oils to symbolise strength (to fight evil) and salvation; and readings and prayers.

Believers' baptism

This is a ceremony for older children and adults, which takes places in a baptistery. The central rituals are the use of water and the Trinitarian formula (Father, Son and Holy Spirit).

The subject testifies to why they seek baptism, then declares the repentance of sin and their intention to follow a Christ-centred life, avoiding evil.

Walking down three steps symbolises the end of the old life of sin. Then there are three full submersions in the name of the Father, Son and Holy Spirit. The person then leaves by three other steps to start a new life as a Christian.

> **Revision tip**
>
> Know the basic elements of each baptism. You could be asked to explain two differences or two similarities between ceremonies. You could be asked to give two reasons why baptism is important or two **gifts given by the Holy Spirit**. Equally, a question option could be an evaluation based on baptism (which type is more important, whether baptism is necessary, is it the most important sacrament?).

> **Gifts of the Holy Spirit:** knowledge, courage, understanding, right judgement, wisdom, reverence, awe and wonder in God's presence – 1 Corinthians 12.
>
> **Holy Water:** used in the Roman Catholic, Orthodox and Anglican Churches, this is water that has been blessed by having a prayer said over it by a religious leader.

Support for infant baptism	Support for believers' baptism
Natural for parents to want to bring their child into the Christian faith	Only those old enough to understand should take this step – should be able to make their own promises
Gifts of the Holy Spirit to allow the child to grow up strong in God's love	A child might grow up to resent the promises made for them so they need to decide for themselves
Enables the child to receive the other sacraments	Jesus was an adult when baptised
Brings comfort to the family of an ill child that if it dies then it will be with God	God's love is not dependent on human actions – so baptism is unnecessary
Removes original sin and purifies the child	How can a child even have sins to remove?

The Eucharist

The Last Supper

The Last Supper is the basis of the 'bread and wine' service. Jesus took bread, broke it – 'This is my body which is given for you; do this in remembrance of me.' Jesus took wine – 'This is my blood, do this in remembrance of me.'

Some say the Eucharist is a taste of heaven, unites the worshipper with Christ, and is food for the soul, giving strength to live every day as a Christian.

Christians today re-enact the Last Supper in different ways. It can be done daily, weekly or monthly, as part of, or in addition to, a normal service.

The Orthodox Divine Liturgy

'Divine' is a reminder of the sacred mystery of the service and 'liturgy' means 'work of the people' in the praising of God.

Bread and wine are prepared on the altar behind the iconostasis. It is divided into four – the Eucharistic prayer said to consecrate three of them so that they coexist with the actual body and blood of Jesus.

The service includes Bible readings, sermon, prayers and the Bible processed through the Royal Doors. The cherubic hymn is sung. The bread and wine are carried through the Royal Doors. The priest invites all baptised members to participate. From one chalice of bread soaked in the wine, spoonfuls are given. The fourth unconsecrated piece of bread is broken up to be taken home.

The Roman Catholic mass

In a Roman Catholic mass, worshippers confess sins and forgiveness is given. The service includes Bible readings, sermon and prayers, and the Nicene Creed is recited. Bread and wine are brought to the altar and the Eucharistic prayer is said to consecrate them.

The people stand before the priest to receive the bread, which is placed on the tongue or in their hands. Only the priest drinks the wine. The post-Eucharistic prayer and blessings are said.

Anglican Holy Communion

This follows a similar pattern to that of the Roman Catholics. However, wine is taken by the congregation from one single chalice and the bread is placed on crossed hands – all participate in both bread and wine.

The Lord's Supper – other Protestant groups

These tend to be much simpler services, with people gathering at the front of the church. The Last Supper story is read out; bread and wine are shared. Often the wine is non-alcoholic and given in little individual cups. Hymns may be sung and the Lord's Prayer and additional prayers may be said by all.

The meaning and significance vary for different Christian groups:
+ Orthodox: the consecration of bread and wine remains a mystery but they believe that Jesus is mystically present in the elements.
+ Roman Catholic: believe in transubstantiation – the bread and wine are invisibly transformed into the actual body and blood of Jesus.
+ Anglicans: some believe the same as the Catholics but most believe that the bread and wine hold the spiritual presence of the body and blood rather than becoming it.
+ Other Protestants believe the bread and wine are purely symbolic of Jesus' death, which brought salvation.

> **Elements:** bread and wine used in the Eucharist.
>
> **Last Supper:** the last evening meal Jesus shared with his disciples before he was arrested.
>
> **Transubstantiation:** the change in the bread and wine to become the body and blood of Jesus.

1.2 Christianity: Practices

29

Pilgrimage

A religious pilgrimage is a visit to a holy place. These places often have a feeling of spirituality and of closeness to God. The journey can be as important as the visit.

Lourdes (France) – history and significance

Bernadette in Lourdes	Pilgrimage to Lourdes	Healings in Lourdes
Here Bernadette Soubirous claimed she had seen a woman, the Virgin Mary, in 18 visions.	Many pilgrims visit Lourdes today – taking part in processions, saying the rosary and mass, touching the walls of the cave (grotto).	Since the first cure in 1858, 69 more Lourdes healings have been miracles declared by the Catholic Church.
In a cave near the River Gave she was told to dig away the growth clogging the spring and drink the water.	Water is often taken home and statues of the Virgin Mary bought.	Most pilgrims not experiencing physical healing still feel as though they have been healed spiritually.
Her friend bathed her dislocated arm in the water and it was healed.	People with sickness or disability go hoping for healing.	Pilgrims also describe feeling peace of mind.

Iona – history and significance

About Iona	Pilgrimage to Iona today
This is known as the cradle of Christianity in Scotland, as Columba, an Irish monk, settled there in 563CE.	Iona has a very long history, making pilgrims want to visit.
The Gaelic rulers of Ireland gave him Iona to build a monastery and spread the Christian message.	Individuals or groups often go home renewed in their faith to live and work in the modern world.
Columba died in 597CE but the monastery continued, leading to new monasteries in Ireland and Lindisfarne. Many came on pilgrimage via a system of Celtic crosses and processional roads which were built.	A stay at Iona means work as well as worship (and study).
The Book of Kells, an illuminated manuscript of the Gospels, was produced.	
Iona fell into disuse, but in 1938 George Macleod had the monastery rebuilt and set up the foundation of the ecumenical Iona Community – open to all Christian groups.	
Their way of life was founded in the Bible – daily prayer, Bible reading, stewardship of time and money, regular meeting with other members and the active promotion of justice, peace and the environment.	

Importance

A pilgrimage allows focus on faith and a renewed energy to cope with the demands of life, as well as offering time for spiritual growth. Some pilgrimages include very simple living, being closer to the way Jesus led his life. The experience might bring healing, either physical or spiritual.

However, the money could be better spent in helping others, and some people cannot afford to make a pilgrimage. The renewal while on pilgrimage quickly wears off when pilgrims return home. Spiritual development can be gained at home in prayer and reflection – prayers and healings can happen anywhere as God hears all prayers.

> **Revision tip**
>
> This is a good topic for evaluative questions. List reasons for and against the following:
> 1 Lourdes is the best place for pilgrimage.
> 2 Pilgrimage is the greatest act of devotion in the life of a Christian.
> 3 Pilgrimage is just an excuse for a holiday.
> 4 All Christians should make a pilgrimage to a holy site.

Festivals

> **Key quote**
>
> 'For unto us a child is born, to us a son is given, and the government will be on his shoulders. And he will be called Wonderful Counsellor, Mighty God, Everlasting Father, the Prince of Peace.' Isaiah 9:6

Christmas

Christmas celebrates the birth of Jesus. The specific date is unknown but the Western church chose 25 December and the Eastern church chose 6 January.

The story of Jesus' birth is found only in the Gospels of Matthew and Luke. These accounts are slightly different in detail if you read Matthew Chapters 1 and 2 and Luke Chapter 2.

The general outline of the story is that Jesus was born in Bethlehem (there because of the Roman census) in a stable as the town was overcrowded. Mary gave birth, laid him in a manger and he was visited by kings/shepherds who had been told that the new King of the Jews/Messiah had been born.

Christians disagree over the accuracy of what happened but the message is key – that the incarnation of God the Son (Jesus) had humble beginnings, thus showing humility.

Celebration and importance

Christmas is a state holiday in the UK, showing the importance of this event in a 'Christian country'. It is celebrated in a secular way with cards, gifts, food and parties, and in a religious way with the four weeks of advent, the Christingle service, Christmas Eve mass and a Christmas Day service. Christmas carols are sung throughout the period, the birth stories are read and nativities are acted out. Believers often send religious cards (e.g. with a nativity scene, religious wording, etc.). Christians also celebrate with gifts and food.

Christians thank God for his gift of Jesus. They focus on family, children, people in poverty and who are lonely to make Christmas a time of warmth, love and togetherness. It is common for churches to set up shelters, host meals and distribute gift parcels for/to the most needy.

It is a time of giving, receiving and of love to symbolise the love that God showed. It is also a time for hope – for peace, reconciliation, love to our fellow humans – and for Christians to show their faith to the world.

> **Revision tip**
>
> Remember, you will not need to recall every detail of the Christmas story, just its key elements. Questions at 4/6/12 marks will focus around the symbolism, importance and influence of the festival, or an evaluation of it.

> **Revision tip**
>
> Read the stories and jot down some similarities and differences between the birth stories from the Gospels. Also look at the ways the birth stories are celebrated by different Christians today. A simple description of the festival stories or celebration is unlikely to be asked for, but knowing both will help make evaluations much easier to discuss. By writing notes, you are helping your brain retain the information, so it is easier to recall it later.

> **Activity**
>
> **Fix it!**
>
> Read this answer and improve it.
>
> *Explain two ways in which Christians celebrate Christmas* (4 marks)
>
> Christians go to church. They also send cards to each other.

Easter

Easter remembers the death and resurrection of Jesus.

Holy Week begins with Palm Sunday and ends with Easter Sunday. Each day remembers the events that led to Jesus' death, his actual death and then resurrection.

The stories can be found in Matthew Chapters 21–28, Mark Chapters 11–16, Luke Chapters 19–24 and John Chapters 12–21. From this you can see how much of each Gospel refers to this last week – thus its importance.

The key events are:
1 Palm Sunday – Jesus' entry into Jerusalem.
2 Maundy Thursday – the Last Supper and Jesus' arrest.
3 Good Friday – Jesus' crucifixion and death.
4 Easter Sunday – the resurrection.

Celebration and importance

Special church services run throughout the week remembering the lead-up to 'the greatest sacrifice ever made'. In a secular way people send cards, gifts, Easter chocolates and have family meals. In a religious way for Christians Palm crosses are given out, church services take place for each of the special days, including Easter vigils, and special Easter prayers and hymns are said. Believers send Easter cards.

Christians move from a period of great sadness to great joy knowing what God has done for them (sacrifice of his son to bring about reconciliation). The human suffering of Jesus and his obedience to the will of God are emphasised.

Christians believe that God reunited himself with humanity by the actions of Jesus so that they can once again be reunited with him relationally when we accept Christ and physically in the new heavens and earth – the new covenant.

> **Revision tip**
>
> Remember, you will not need to recall every detail of the Easter story, just its key elements. Questions at 4/6/12 marks will focus around the symbolism, importance and influence of the festival, or an evaluation of it.

> **Crucifixion:** capital punishment used by the Romans which involves nailing a person to a cross to kill them; Jesus died this way.

> **Revision tip**
>
> Festivals could be a topic for 6-mark questions, focusing on two ways in which a chosen festival is important to Christians. You need to be able to back up these ideas with Christian teachings as you have to refer to both teachings and the source of the teaching in your answer for a 6-mark question.
>
> *Explain two ways in which Easter is important for Christians today. Refer to sacred writings or another source of Christian beliefs and teachings in your answer.*

> **Now test yourself**   TESTED ◯
>
> 1 What is a sacrament? Name two.
> 2 Why are sacraments important?
> 3 What is a pilgrimage? Name a Christian place.
> 4 Why is pilgrimage important?
> 5 Name a Christian festival. Say what it celebrates.
> 6 Name another Christian festival. Say why it is important.

> **Activity**
>
> Which bit of Jesus' life was the most important? Evaluative questions could easily focus on this, for example *'Christmas is more important than Easter'*. You would need to refer to the events of his life to answer this. Complete this chart to prepare yourself for any question like that.
>
> | Reasons why it is ... | Christmas (birth) | Easter (death) | Easter (resurrection) |
> |---|---|---|---|
> | Most important | | | |
> | Not most important | | | |

The role of the Church in the local community

Christians have always been involved in working to make communities better places to live. They work in support groups for the young and old, support charities that help the needy, welcome immigrants, and work as street pastors and at food banks.

The parable of the sheep and goats teaches that if people fail to help those around them, it is as though they fail to help Jesus himself.

1 John says, 'If anyone has material possessions and ignores his brother in need, how can he love God?' Also, 'Let's not love with words or thoughts but with actions and in truth'.

Jesus spent much of his time helping people in society who were needy or outcasts or simply those who were looked down on by others. He said, 'It is not the well that need a doctor but the sick', showing how we should help those that need help in any way possible. Many Christians use the phrase 'What Would Jesus Do?' as motivation to go and help those in need.

> **Food banks:** places in local communities where people can go and have food if they are in need.
>
> **Street pastors:** a Christian organisation where people work on the streets at night to help people in need.

Food banks and street pastors

At food banks people volunteer to collect and distribute food. In 2005, the Trussell Trust launched its UK-wide network with a vision to end poverty and hunger, show compassion and give practical help.

Many food banks are centred in churches or church halls. People in need are identified by police, schools or social services and given vouchers to exchange for food parcels. The 2020 pandemic saw Food Banks become even more important to even more people.

Street pastors are Christians who go out on city streets at night to care for the physical and spiritual needs of young people who might be affected by excessive drinking, drug use, fighting, etc. They care for, listen and try to help, regardless of the young people's behaviour. Following training, they ask for God's blessing on this difficult type of ministry.

Over 270 towns now have street pastors. Their governing body is the Ascension Trust, which works with local councils, the police and other official bodies. The work is based in places where there may be anticipated issues.

> **Revision tip**
>
> Knowing the religious teachings and examples on which Christians base their work will be useful for this topic. Also the emphasis here is on the value of Christians using their faith as a basis for action and the action itself showing that faith. High marks require the use of teachings in an answer.

The Salvation Army

Founded in 1865 in East London, as a result of the deprivation people lived in and the apparent unconcern shown by many Christian churches. The Salvation Army works with those in poverty and who are disadvantaged, setting up, for example:

+ food kitchens and hostels for the homeless, including emergency assistance
+ toy collections at Christmas
+ training and employment help and advice.

St Vincent de Paul Society

This is a Roman Catholic society whose aim is to provide for the great needs of people in society. Its motto is to help the homeless, visit the sick, befriend the lonely and feed the hungry. The society is involved in, for example:

+ setting up support centres and counselling services
+ providing work training
+ helping refugees, released prisoners, people with disabilities and mental health problems.

Church growth

Christianity has always been a missionary religion, spreading all over the world. African Christian membership is on the rise but in Europe it is in decline. In recent years there has been a renewed focus on preaching to make the Gospel relevant in a modern world. Many churches are trying to find fresh approaches to worship while maintaining their key beliefs.

The Church Army – committed to Christian mission

Church Army members are trained and licensed by the Church of England to work throughout the UK. They aim to help people find faith, showing their love of God as revealed through Christ. They focus their work on vulnerable and marginalised people in society – for example, providing projects for young children and families, working with drug addicts, as chaplains in prisons and hospitals, visiting elderly people, and providing access to worship outside of church.

SIM – Serving in Mission

SIM has a worldwide scope to follow Jesus' instruction to send people out on mission. Members work chiefly in areas where it appears Christianity is under attack – for example, in Nigeria where Christians are often the target for terrorist groups. Churches have been destroyed, vicars killed and people left traumatised by what they have suffered. SIM supports the rebuilding of these communities.

The Ichthus Fellowship

This is a group of new 'churches' linked to already established churches which are 'planted' so that the church continues to grow. They offer more evangelical than traditional worship, to appeal to a modern audience who are not enthused by traditional forms of worship.

Fresh Expressions

This organisation offers 'different churches', set up in pubs, cafés, schools and even skate parks or beaches. These gatherings take religion directly to people who would never think about going to church. They are all planted to suit the needs of that group and help them become and develop as Christians.

> **Evangelical:** spreading the word by way of preaching the Gospel of Christ.
>
> **Mission:** 'a sending' – being sent to do something.

> **Revision tip**
>
> Mission has become popular because there is a discussion as to whether religion can still be as relevant to people in a modern world as it was centuries ago. It is possible for evaluation questions to look at this issue with a statement to discuss, such as 'Religion is not relevant in the modern world'. Knowing examples of how people are making it relevant could help with such a question.

Activity

Fix it!

Read the answers below, each of which is worth 2 marks, and improve each to 6 marks.

Explain two ways in which mission is important to Christians today. Refer to sacred writings or a Christian source of authority in your answer.

(6 marks)

Mission is important to Christians today because in Matthew's Gospel, Jesus told his disciples to go and make everyone a Christian follower. It is also important because it means that people in non-Christian countries get to hear the Christian message.

Explain two ways in which mission is important in showing faith in action for Christians today. Refer to sacred writings or a Christian source of authority in your answer.

(6 marks)

Mission shows faith in action because a Christian knows Jesus told them to 'Go make disciples of all nations' (Matthew). They could just read the Bible and think about it, but this is an instruction, so they have to actually get out and do something active. In other words, they aren't just believing in their heads, but showing their belief by their actions (faith into action).

Persecution and reconciliation

Persecution is hostility and ill-treatment, usually because of prejudice. It can be brief or long-term; it can be by one person or many; it can be by a government, or against the law in a country; it can be recently begun or historic in nature and spanning many years; it can be mild or life-threatening.

The Church has faced persecution as far back as Jesus himself. The Roman and Jewish authorities persecuted him and his disciples. Many early Christians suffered death as a result of spreading the Christian message. For nearly 300 years after Jesus' death it was illegal to be a Christian, carrying a likely death sentence as punishment.

Christian reaction to this has been to trust God in times of need ('all things will pass', 'God knows best', 'blessed are the persecuted'), react with forgiveness and love rather than hate, and for those not suffering persecution to support the persecuted (irrespective of faith or no faith). This is still the case in the world today.

There have been individuals and organisations involved in support for the persecuted, from Brother Andrew who smuggled Bibles into communist countries, to James and Stephen Smith who set up the Aegis Trust, which encourages people to challenge all types of discrimination (now working extensively in Rwanda following genocide there), and the work of Open Doors, an organisation which fights for justice and freedom, raises awareness of persecution issues, trains people to work with those affected by persecution and offers practical help to rebuild communities.

Reconciliation means bringing people together to be friendly again. When Jesus made reconciliation with God possible through his death, it was the ultimate sacrifice. Christians should be able to reconcile with each other after dispute, whether as families, communities or nations.

Corrymeela in Ireland and the international Community of the Cross of Nails are two communities working for reconciliation. There are also individuals with similar aims, such as Archbishop Desmond Tutu in South Africa who spent his whole life trying to reconcile the black and white communities there after years of discrimination. He also worked with the Israeli and Palestinian communities.

The Quakers do not believe in the use of violence. Many Quakers have worked as mediators to bring reconciliation to opposing sides in the pursuit of peace.

> **Persecution:** hostility and ill-treatment, usually because of prejudice.
>
> **Reconciliation:** coming back together after a falling out, so that no grudge is held.

> **Revision tip**
>
> Reconciliation is a key Christian concept so make sure you: (**1**) know a clear definition; (**2**) can give examples of why it is necessary and examples of how it works; (**3**) know similar and different ways that Christian groups work to reconcile people; (**4**) can explain two ways in which reconciliation is important to Christians and two teachings to support this, and (**5**) can evaluate the need for reconciliation and the outcomes if the world was reconciled (and indeed if this is even possible).

> **Now test yourself**   TESTED
>
> 1 What are mission and evangelism?
> 2 Why do Christians evangelise?
> 3 What is persecution?
> 4 How have Christians fought persecution?

1.2 Christianity: Practices

35

Poverty

 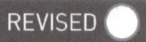

Why the need for help and the Christian response

LEDCs are the poorest countries in the world and the people suffer generally through no fault of their own. Often one or more of these contexts applies: they are at war, debt ridden, suffer natural disasters, have corrupt governments, have few natural resources, employment/pay is low, and they are exploited by rich countries. They are not in an economic position to raise the standard of living for all their people.

Christians have links to many countries and they are moved with compassion at media coverage of disasters and crises that some people face. Many see helping as putting their beliefs (faith) into action. In the poorest countries even the smallest response can make a massive difference. Jesus worked among people in poverty and so Christians are copying his example and re-enacting his work.

The Parable of the Sheep and Goats clearly states that whoever a believer helps, it is as if they are helping Jesus himself and that they will gain the reward of heaven.

The Parable of the Good Samaritan clearly shows the need to help where help is needed, regardless of who the victim is – this encourages Christians to help in all situations.

The Specification names three religious agencies at work in LEDCs – Christian Aid, CAFOD and Tearfund. You must study at least one. All three provide emergency, short-term and long-term aid. They are all part of the UK's Disasters Emergency Committee (DEC) and work with partner organisations when a disaster occurs.

All three work in the UK to campaign for the government to raise issues to secure justice for LEDCs. They increase public awareness through the media and educational programmes which keep the issues in the minds of the public. They all fundraise so that the public keep giving money, ensuring these charities can continue to meet the needs of many people in poverty.

All encourage Fair Trade. This means that producers get a fair amount for the goods produced and in turn can pay their workers fairly. It helps raise the economic status of people throughout the system, but crucially the producers who are usually paid least.

CAFOD

The Catholic Agency for Overseas Development has more than 500 partners in LEDCs. The organisation works in disaster areas providing relief and disaster risk reduction strategies. Long-term projects are carried out with local groups. It is essential that the communities themselves see the value of what is being done.

The idea is that projects can breed self-belief and self-reliance, which often then lead to much greater change, as communities gain confidence and see more ways to develop and improve what they have.

Christian Aid

This organisation was set up to deal with the refugee crises in Europe after the Second World War, but since then it has extended its work worldwide, providing a response to disasters and promoting long-term development. It works with partner agencies and will support all of them, regardless of race, religion, etc. It assesses projects in a country, then supplies experts and materials for the projects to be completed.

CAFOD: a charity (Catholic Agency for Overseas Development).

Christian Aid: a charity working in the UK and developing world providing emergency and long-term aid.

Emergency aid: immediate response to a disaster with urgent medical and survival provisions.

LEDC: less economically developed country.

Long-term aid: development of communities to become self-sufficient, through projects which usually last for at least a year.

Poverty: the absence or paucity of the basic needs of life – food, water, shelter, healthcare, education and employment.

Short-term aid: start of the rebuilding process after emergency response, or development projects which usually last a few weeks or months.

Tearfund: a Christian charity working to relieve poverty in developing countries.

Revision tip

Notice the similarities here in reasons to help and the way that help is achieved. As there are plenty of religious teachings that cover the requirement to help, this lends itself to a 6-mark question. It is also good to have in mind a couple of real examples of what has been done in aid projects.

Find Now Test Yourself and Exam Practice answers at **https://www.hoddereducation.co.uk/myrevisionnotesdownloads**

The key focus since 2012 has been to see an end to poverty and to generate global justice by empowering those who are currently exploited and disadvantaged.

Every year 'Christian Aid Week' envelopes are delivered to all households to collect money to continue the organisation's work.

Tearfund

This began as a fund collected for the 40 million refugees caused by wars worldwide. The money was given to evangelical agencies caring for such refugees.

Prayer is key to the organisation's work, as well as the principle of following Jesus to where the need is greatest. Money is raised from evangelical churches and young people are encouraged to join gap year projects or mission trips.

All types of aid are given but Tearfund does emphasise people's spiritual as well as physical needs – 67,000 churches have been created or helped in the past five years. The agency claims to have changed 15 million lives.

It promotes self-help projects so that people are empowered to help themselves out of poverty, for example loans given for small business start-up, so that money is community produced rather than from charity.

Exam tip

When you give a teaching remember to also say where it is from. Most Christian teachings you use come from Jesus or the New Testament, for example, 'Jesus said 'Love your neighbour' so Christians help those in need.' Make sure it is clear how the quote/teaching you use is relevant. You will get a mark for showing how it applies to the topic in question – and it isn't always obvious!

> **Now test yourself** TESTED ⬤
>
> 1 Explain why Christians help those in poverty.
> 2 Explain the ways in which aid agencies might help those in poverty.

Activity

Support or challenge?

'Religious people should make helping people out of poverty their most important duty.' Evaluate this statement. Refer to Christianity in your answer. You should agree and disagree, and come to a justified conclusion. (12 marks)

Use the list of arguments below to help you write a strong answer to the question. They are mixed up though, so first you need to work out which ones agree (support) and which disagree (challenge) with the statement. You may have other arguments as well. Remember that a conclusion should not just be repeating what you have already said, so it is worth keeping back one argument to use as your reason for agreeing or not. Your conclusion must say which point of view is stronger, and why.

Argument	Supports statement in question	Challenges statement in question
Jesus said 'Give up what you own to the poor, and follow me.'		
Religious people should worship God as their priority.		
Religious people need to look after themselves and their families before they look after anyone else.		
Most Western Christians can afford to give to those in poverty, so they should.		
Love thy neighbour – the Good Samaritan helped.		
Money is no good when we die, but using money to help others now might help on Judgement Day.		

Check back to pages 11-12

Exam practice

What questions on this section look like:

Christianity: Practices

This page contains a range of questions that could be on an exam paper. Practise them all to strengthen your knowledge and technique while revising. Check back to pages 11-12 to see the marking grids that examiners use: this will help you to mark your answers.

1 What does the term 'eucharist' refer to?

   (a) Bread and wine ceremony   **(b)** Last meal   **(c)** Praise   **(d)** Thanksgiving   [1]

2 Which of the following remembers the resurrection of Jesus?

   (a) Christmas   **(b)** Easter   **(c)** Good Friday   **(d)** Palm Sunday   [1]

3 Give one type of Christian worship. [1]

4 Give one Christian teaching about evangelism. [1]

5 Give one reason why Christians pray. [1]

6 Explain two different ways in which Christian aid agencies help those in poverty. [4]

7 Explain two different Christian beliefs about mission. [4]

8 Explain two different forms of Christian worship. [4]

9 Explain two different beliefs about non-liturgical worship. [4]

10 Explain two ways in which the Eucharist is important to Christians. Refer to sacred writings or another source of Christian belief and teachings in your answer. [6]

11 Explain two ways in which the Bible is used in Christian worship. Refer to sacred writings or another source of Christian belief and teachings in your answer. [6]

12 Explain two ways in which pilgrimage is important for Christians today. Refer to sacred writings or another source of Christian belief and teachings in your answer. [6]

13 'Worship should always be liturgical.' Evaluate this statement. In your answer you should:

  ✚ refer to Christian teaching
  ✚ give reasoned arguments to support this statement
  ✚ give reasoned arguments to support a different point of view
  ✚ reach a justified conclusion. [12]

14 'The sacraments are just excuses for celebrations.' Evaluate this statement. In your answer you should:

  ✚ refer to Christian teaching
  ✚ give reasoned arguments to support this statement
  ✚ give reasoned arguments to support a different point of view
  ✚ reach a justified conclusion. [12]

15 'The churches should focus on the worship of God rather than helping the community.' Evaluate this statement. In your answer you should:

  ✚ refer to Christian teaching
  ✚ give reasoned arguments to support this statement
  ✚ give reasoned arguments to support a different point of view
  ✚ reach a justified conclusion. [12]

Exam tip

Level 2 students answer questions simply and not always in the way asked. They mix up the 'command words', which are the key instructions of a question. They also fail to provide required information, especially the religious teachings. If this is you, you need to practise so that you are really clear on what the questions are asking. You also need to have a few teachings which you can use – don't bother learning them word for word, an approximation is usually good enough.

Level 5 students do as the questions ask but often not in enough detail and also without providing enough teachings. This course demands them all the time, so you have to know some. If this is you, get a teacher to help you rewrite the teachings in a way that you can understand and learn, then learn them. Write them on the front of the exam paper before you start answering to help you as you do the exam.

Level 8 students know and use a lot of teachings. This is part of how they demonstrate their very good subject knowledge and why they are worth the highest grades.

2.1 Buddhism: Beliefs and teachings

The Buddhist religion originated in India in the 5th century BCE, begun by a man named Siddhartha Gotama (the Buddha). It is called the Middle Way. It is very influential in Asia and the Far East, but is found in most Western countries as well. Buddhism is a way of living, not just a religion.

The Dhamma (Dharma)

REVISED

This is the teaching of the Buddha. The Dhamma (Dharma) is the way the universe operates, like 'cosmic law'. It existed before the Buddha. The Buddha put it into words and explained it for others to understand. So what the Buddha taught is, to Buddhists, a form of law. The Buddha's teachings include the Three Marks of Existence, the Four Noble Truths and the Noble Eightfold Path (aka the Threefold Way).

> **Key quote**
>
> 'Cease to do evil, learn to do good, purify the mind – this is the teaching of the Buddhas.' Dhammapada 183

The nature of reality

There are two basic beliefs in Buddhism about the nature of reality: first, the Three Marks of Existence and second, 'dependent arising'.

The Three Marks of Existence

REVISED

These are also known as the Three Universal Truths. The Buddha taught that:

+ everything is impermanent and illusory. Everything changes and is constantly in flux – this is anicca
+ since everything is constantly changing, there can be no permanent self or soul, as the elements which might make this are in constant flux – this is anatta
+ everything is constantly changing, which causes unsatisfactoriness, which leads to suffering – this is dukkha.

Dependent arising (Paticcasamupada)

'If this exists, that comes to exist': Buddhists believe that we have many thousands of rebirths – we are each a changing bundle of elements (skandhas) born into many lifetimes, each time trying to attain enlightenment. Together these elements are enough to keep the illusion going, but the chain of existence comes from paticcasamupada, or *dependent arising* (that there are interdependent events which cause the existence or occurrence of other events).

This is usually described as 12 links:

+ Links 1–2: relate to past existence and are what makes the present.
+ Links 3–10: relate to this existence and are shaping the future.
+ Links 11–12: relate to the future, based on links 1–10.

Enlightenment (nirvana): ceasing to be bound by the wheel of samsara; full realisation of the true nature of things.

Paticcasamupada: dependent arising, meaning there are interdependent events which cause the existence or occurrence of other events.

Rebirth: belief that the skandhas are reborn into new lifetimes, shaped by the karma of previous ones, until enlightenment is achieved.

Skandhas: the Five Aggregates which make up each person (form, sensation, perception, mental formations, consciousness).

> **Now test yourself**
>
> TESTED
>
> 1   What are the Three Marks of Existence? What does each mean?
> 2   What is 'dependent arising'?

39

Human personality

Theravada

There are two schools of Buddhism – Theravada and Mahayana. In Theravada Buddhism, enlightenment is a personal goal, sought by monks who become arhats (perfected beings); in Mahayana, individuals can support others to achieve enlightenment. So, while both forms show everyone can become a Buddha (eventually), the journey may be very different.

The ultimate goal and ambition is to become Buddha. This can be done in many ways, particularly by following the Buddhist Path, namely living according to the teaching of the Buddha, the path of Dhamma. This means having faith in the Buddha, showing determination to achieve enlightenment and not give up, cultivating wisdom in oneself, and perfecting compassion and loving kindness towards others.

The skandhas

According to Buddhism, a person is made up of five elements (aggregates), known as skandhas. These are constantly changing even from second to second – which is why Buddhists believe in anatta. All skandhas are impermanent, so lead to dukkha.

+ Physical form (rupa) – made up of the elements of air, earth, fire and water – anything we perceive through our senses.
+ Sensations/feelings (vedana) – caused when the eye sees, ear hears, mouth tastes, nose smells, body touches, or mind thinks. For example, we taste something (feeling) which we decide is not pleasant (sensation).
+ Perception (samjna) – perceptions of sense.
+ Mental formations (samskara) – our mental and emotional habits, which make us say/think/do something.
+ Awareness/consciousness (vijnana).

Consider this: are you exactly the same person as the person that woke up this morning? Or have you learned something new? Since then, you have certainly shed skin cells. So you are not the same – this is an example of anatta.

Sunyata

Sunyata means 'emptiness'. To realise sunyata is to end attachment and craving. To realise sunyata, a person must be dedicated to ethical living and to meditation. This dedication purifies the mind, and brings wisdom. It leads to enlightenment. Meditation is a means to that understanding, which is why meditation is believed to be able to deliver enlightenment (as for the Buddha).

Buddha described sunyata as 'void', 'no rising and falling', 'calmness' and 'extinction'. Without having this, he would not have been able to attain enlightenment.

Attaining Buddhahood and the Buddha-nature

Mahayana Buddhism believes that everyone has Buddha-nature – that is, the potential to become Buddha, to become enlightened. It is the practice of Buddhism which helps us to realise our Buddha-nature for ourselves.

Arhat: in Theravada Buddhism, a perfected being (the stage before enlightenment).

Attachment: upadana/clinging/not wanting to be separated from someone or something.

Buddha-nature: the belief that everyone possesses the capacity to become Buddha.

Mahayana: major tradition within Buddhism (53 per cent), mainly found in China, Japan, Korea and the Himalayas.

Meditation: practice of focusing; samatha (concentration), vipassana (achieving insight); includes zazen form (self-focus) and visualisation exercises.

Sunyata: emptiness, void.

Theravada: oldest form of Buddhism, based around the Sangha.

With any concept, it isn't enough to 'understand' something; 'realising' it means you have both understood and experienced it – it is full understanding based on knowledge, a form of wisdom.

Now test yourself	TESTED

1   What are the five skandhas?
2   Explain sunyata.
3   Why do Buddhists believe it is possible for everyone to become Buddha?

Human destiny

Buddhahood

Buddhists believe that every person has within them the potential to become Buddha. This means there are an infinite number of Buddhas now and to come. The different groups within Buddhism see our capacity for this slightly differently.

Arhat

Found in Theravada Buddhism, arhat means 'perfected being', one who has gained insight into the true nature of existence and has achieved nibbana. Being an arhat is the goal of Theravadins and takes absolute dedication.

Realistically, one is unlikely to become an arhat unless a monk in a monastery. Monks follow the sila (Ten Precepts), developing their morality, discipline and insight to become arhats. Most importantly, they develop wisdom (prajna).

Bodhisattva

Found in Mahayana Buddhism, this means 'one whose essence is bodhi (enlightened)'. Siddhartha Gotama (the Buddha) was a bodhisattva in life prior to his enlightenment.

Mahayanans believe the bodhisattva has made a vow to postpone their full enlightenment in order to help other beings. They see this as a higher being than the Theravadin arhat (who is focused on their own enlightenment). Compassion (karuna) comes ahead of wisdom (prajna), because this is what drives them to put off full enlightenment.

The bodhisattva can transfer their own merit to their followers, thus helping them move nearer to achieving enlightenment.

Stages of being a bodhisattva are:
+ first, declaring the intention to put off Buddhahood to help others
+ second, taking vows to show determination – a vow to become a Buddha, and one to help others achieve enlightenment
+ third, living as a bodhisattva, so working hard to develop and perfect the Six Perfections (charity, morality, patience, energy, meditation and wisdom)
+ fourth, becoming enlightened and attaining Buddhahood. This is really the realisation that the person has been Buddha all along because everything they have done has been selfless.

Bodhisattvas include Avalokiteshvara, Maitreya and Manjushri.

Pure Land Buddhism

Amitabha Buddha was a monk who vowed that after he achieved his own enlightenment, anyone male or female who called his name could live in his heaven (Sukhavati, or Western paradise) until they attained enlightenment for themselves. Sukhavati heaven is a beautiful place free from pain and need/want.

The Pure Land school of Buddhism, formed in Japan in the 12th–13th centuries CE, emphasises faith in Amitabha. However, a version existed in China from the 4th century CE. In Japan this form of Buddhism is known as Jodo.

Influences

If I believe that everyone can become Buddha, I know that following the Buddha's teachings will help me achieve that, so I follow them. Also that wisdom and compassion are important, so I try to show these qualities in my daily life when dealing with others.

Amitabha: the Buddha of infinite light; the most important form of Buddha for Japanese Buddhists, who resides in the Pure Land heaven (Sukhavati).

Bodhisattva: a being who has postponed enlightenment after taking a vow to help others.

Buddhahood: the realisation of perfect enlightenment.

Human destiny: the potential we all have; in Theravada to become an arhat (perfected being), then achieve Buddhahood (full enlightenment); in Mahayana, to become a bodhisattva (an enlightened being who has chosen to put off full enlightenment in order to help others), or to achieve enlightenment.

Pure Land: Sukhavati heaven, the residence of Amitabha.

Sila: moral principles that inform behaviour and attitudes.

The Buddha – his birth and life of luxury

Siddhartha Gotama was the man born to be the Buddha in 563 BCE. Stories of his life were written after his death, some many centuries later.

Special birth

Queen Maya, his mother, dreamed that an elephant with six tusks and a head coloured like rubies came down from heaven, entering her womb from the right side. The King sought advice from Brahmin priests about this dream – it meant Maya would have a holy child who would achieve perfect wisdom.

Siddhartha was born in the gardens of Lumbini, as his mother walked. A sala tree bent its branch for her to hold and from her side came Siddhartha. He immediately walked seven paces and from each footprint grew a lotus flower. He said this would be his last rebirth and that he would end the sorrow of birth and death.

Shortly after his birth, a holy man, Asita, told the King that Siddhartha would become either a great king or a great holy man. His father wanted him to rule, so he shaped Siddhartha's life and experiences around that aim. He was given a life of luxury, but he was kept ignorant of death, illness and other suffering in order to prevent him from becoming concerned about the meaning of life.

Points of importance

+ Even before conception, Siddhartha Gotama was special.
+ Prophecies were made saying Siddhartha Gotama would become a holy man and renounce his life of extreme wealth, and these prophecies later came true.
+ His statements at birth show that we are driven by past lives.

The Four Sights – illness, old age, death, holy man

Asita had said that Siddhartha would become a great religious leader if he saw the Four Sights. Siddhartha grew curious about the world outside the palace. Jataka 075 tells the story. Aged 29, during four visits outside the palace, Siddhartha encountered an old man (realising that aging happened to all regardless of wealth), then a sick person (realising that illness is an unavoidable part of life) and then a dead body (realising that we all crumble to dust eventually). These sights troubled and saddened him greatly and made him totally dissatisfied with his extreme wealth, but he had no solution – until he saw a holy man. This man had renounced the material life to find the truth, and seemed content. It inspired Siddhartha to try for himself, vowing to find a solution to suffering.

Points of importance

+ The encounter with death shows the impermanence of the material world – no amount of money can stop this.
+ Seeing the Four Sights with no comprehension of them beforehand was mind-blowing – it resulted in Siddhartha renouncing his life of extreme wealth, rejecting it as not being satisfactory. This was the trigger for his spiritual journey to enlightenment.
+ The last of the Four Sights (the holy man) gave him a potential solution to the dissatisfaction caused by the other three – a religious path.

Revision tip

Know the story of the Buddha's life so that you can refer to it in your answers. It is perhaps more important to know why each aspect was important in itself and any symbolic features, as these are more likely to be the basis of questions.

Revision tip

Watch the film 'Little Buddha', starring Keanu Reeves as the Buddha. It has really good depictions of the key elements of the Buddha's life. Seeing this visually will help you learn the story to use in answers.

Four Sights: illness, old age, death, holy man: seeing these made Siddhartha begin his search for enlightenment.

Now test yourself

1 What was the human name of the Buddha?

2 What dreams and prophecies suggested Siddhartha was special?

3 What were the Four Sights?

4 Why did Siddhartha's father not want him to see the Four Sights?

TESTED

Ascetic life

Having seen the Four Sights, which made him realise that suffering was unavoidable, Siddhartha left the palace and his luxurious life. He rejected them as unsatisfactory. He spent the next few years learning meditation techniques from different Hindu masters. He wanted to gain insight into the problem of suffering. He also lived a very austere life, denying himself the things he craved, especially food. This period of his life lasted six years, during which he almost starved to death – but he did not find the solution to suffering.

One day, while meditating, he heard a man telling his son about stringing an instrument – fasten the strings too tightly they snap, too loosely they will not play. Either way, no music is made. Siddhartha saw this as a metaphor for what he was doing – his life of luxury had not worked, and neither did the extreme austerity he now practised. He washed and ate proper food for the first time. His companions deserted him, seeing him as a failure.

Points of importance

+ This was the opposite extreme to Siddhartha's life of luxury – he had now experienced both extremes, neither of which worked. To him, this meant the solution had to be between these – hence Buddhism is a Middle Way.
+ Siddhartha reflected on the Four Sights as he saw them, then learned to meditate from masters. He later reflected that as a child he had meditated, though he had not known that was what he was doing. Meditation became a central theme in his life and in his teachings.

Enlightenment

Siddhartha sat beneath a bodhi tree and vowed to meditate without stopping until he achieved enlightenment. At first, the demon Mara tried to stop him – he tried to frighten him with fierce armies, then sent his daughters to tempt Siddhartha and so distract him from his purpose. Finally, Mara challenged his very right to achieve enlightenment. Siddhartha called on the earth goddess Vasundhara to act as witness that he was fit to achieve enlightenment. Mara left. Four periods were then marked out in the actual enlightenment:

1 Siddhartha recalled all his past lives, thus being able to see that he was ready to become enlightened.
2 He understood how all living things come to exist – paticcasamupada. He understood that everything is impermanent.
3 He realised that suffering comes from a desire or craving for things to stay as they are, or for the better. Overcoming those cravings was the key.
4 With these realisations, he attained nibbana – the three poisons (greed, hatred and ignorance) stopped within him, so no longer controlling him, and he was left with a sense of calm and happiness.

> **The three poisons:** the three causes of suffering: ignorance, greed and hate.

Points of importance

+ We are reminded that it takes many lifetimes to attain enlightenment – and we learn in each one.
+ Even with great determination, a person can be distracted and have doubts. These have to be seen for what they are, illusions.
+ Enlightenment comes from the power of the human mind, not a divine intervention.
+ Siddhartha's realisations form the basis of Buddhist teaching (paticcasamupada, Three Marks of Existence, Four Noble Truths). These teachings have the status of 'law' to Buddhists – the Dharma (Dhamma).

After enlightenment

The Buddha was not sure that he could teach others, so he did not turn to teaching immediately. However, the god Brahma spoke to him. He likened people to the lotus flower, a plant that grows in water – while some see only their mundane lives (like the roots of the plant in mud), others are ready to be taught (like the flower bud breaking the surface of the water) and others are ready to attain enlightenment (like the flower bursting open in the sun). The Buddha sought out the ascetics who had left him as a failure. He taught them first and thereafter anyone who came to listen.

> **Ascetic:** a life spent in extreme self-discipline and denying oneself any indulgence.

Points of importance

+ The lotus is one of the symbols of Buddhism – for example, a statue of a seated Buddha will be sitting on an opened lotus flower, while a standing Buddha may be holding out a closed flower to the worshipper. In many Buddhist countries it is the norm for worshippers to give lotus flowers as offerings at the temple.
+ Having taught the ascetics – who were close to enlightenment – Siddhartha taught anyone. This shows Buddhism is for anyone, regardless of gender, age or creed, which reflects the Buddha's compassion and concern for all.

Activity

Which bit of the Buddha's life was the most important? Evaluative questions could easily focus on this, for example *'Seeing the Four Sights was the most important part of the Buddha's life'*. Complete this chart to prepare yourself for any question like that.

Reasons why it is …	Birth	Four Sights	Ascetic life	Enlightenment
Most important				
Not most important				

Influences

As a Buddhist, the Buddha is my role model. That he became enlightened by his own efforts tells me that I can as well. From him I learn compassion for others – because he became a teacher of the Middle Way. So I work hard in my religion and try to be kind to others always.

The Four Noble Truths

This teaching flows from the Three Marks of Existence, as it explores suffering and impermanence. During his enlightenment, the Buddha realised these Truths. The Four Noble Truths are the essence of the Dhamma.

The Buddha was known as the 'great physician' and the Four Noble Truths can be seen as following a medical model of diagnosis (First Truth), cause (Second Truth), cure (Third Truth) and prescription (Fourth Truth).

Dhammapada 190–191: He who has gone for refuge to the Buddha, the teaching and his Order, penetrates with transcendental wisdom the Four Noble Truths – suffering, the cessation of suffering, and the Noble Eightfold Path leading to the cessation of suffering.

First Noble Truth

Since all existence is impermanent, all existence must involve suffering (dukkha). Three forms of dukkha are everyday pain and unpleasantness, that caused by the experience and realisation of impermanence (anicca/anatta), and that caused by what has gone before leading to the feeling there must be something more.

Dukkha is caused by desire/craving, our attitude, and attachment. It is also caused by the Three Poisons (or 'fires') – greed, ignorance and hatred.

In Buddhism, there is no value to suffering, though suffering is endless until a person can cease attachment (and hence achieve enlightenment).

> **Dhammapada:** collected sayings/teachings of the Buddha.
>
> **Nirodha:** cessation of suffering.
>
> **Tanha:** craving.

Second Noble Truth

Dukkha is caused by craving (tanha). We suffer because we continue to crave – we want bad things to stop, we want good things to never end, we want more of what makes us feel good. This may all sound fine, but it perpetuates the craving, which is itself suffering.

Paticcasamupada (dependent arising) explains how tanha comes about because it explains how all things come to exist. 'He who perceives paticcasamupada perceives the Dhamma,' said the Buddha. Essentially, our past lives shape our present and future, but in the present life desire and attachment build to keep us bound to the cycle of rebirth (samsara).

This is considered to be the core of the Buddha's teaching and its realisation was the trigger for his enlightenment.

> **Key quote**
>
> This being, that comes to be;
>
> from the arising of this, that arises;
>
> this not being, that ceases;
>
> from the ceasing of this, that ceases.
>
> (Samyutta Nikaya)

Third Noble Truth

End tanha by achieving non-attachment (nirodha) – stop wanting = stop suffering. This is also nibbana (cessation of suffering) – when a person stops being attached to the material world and what is in it, they have the calm of enlightenment and are not affected by the Three Poisons because of non-attachment.

Nirodha is described in many ways in Buddhist scripture – the destruction of the skandhas, supreme happiness, the stopping of becoming, the ending of craving, the end of suffering. It can be seen as a state of being (peace, blessing, purity), or a place (the unborn, the unbecome, the eternal).

Fourth Noble Truth

The way to nirodha is by the path (magga). This is Buddhist practice, known as the Noble Eightfold Path. It is the Middle Way.

Magga has eight elements, all of which are important – a Buddhist cannot focus on just one or two. Think of the Buddhist wheel (Figure 1). The eight spokes (Noble Eightfold Path elements) lead to the hub (enlightenment) and those not following the spokes are on the outer rim (wheel of rebirth, samsara). This is one reason the wheel (Dharmachakra) is such an important symbol for Buddhism.

Wheel of rebirth – samsara

Enlight-enment

Figure 1 The Buddhist wheel

The eight elements are Right View, Right Thought/Intention, Right Speech, Right Action, Right Livelihood, Right Effort, Right Mindfulness, Right Concentration.

Magga can also be understood as the Threefold Way – this still uses the elements of the Eightfold Path but grouped into three aspects of wisdom (Right Thought/View), morality (Right Action/Speech/Livelihood) and meditation (Right Effort/Meditation/Concentration).

> **Magga:** the path, the Fourth Noble Truth.

Influences

These teachings affect my life every day. I try to always see things – good and bad – as transient, they will pass. This helps me get through difficulties, but also means I try not to hold on to good happenings. The important thing is not to hold on, because that attitude causes me angst on top of the hurt already felt – if I get ill, for example, the illness makes me suffer, so I accept it; moaning on about it only makes it worse (for everyone!). So I suppose a side effect of believing these Truths is to be determined to be detached.

Now test yourself　　　　　　　　　　　**TESTED** ⚪

1　Which of these is not one of the Four Noble Truths?
　　(a) Nirodha　　(b) Tanha　　(c) Samsara　　(d) Dukkha
2　Which of these is the First Noble Truth?
　　(a) Magga　　(b) Nirodha　　(c) Tanha　　(d) Dukkha
3　How many parts are there to the path of Buddhism (Magga)?
　　(a) 3　　　(b) 4　　　(c) 8　　　(d) 5
4　Explain the Four Noble Truths.
5　Explain how belief in the Four Noble Truths might influence a Buddhist in their daily lives.

The Noble Eightfold Path

Magga – the Fourth Noble Truth – is the Noble Eightfold Path. It is the eight-part system for living for a Buddhist. The Dharmachakra ('wheel symbol' for Buddhism) reflects the idea that we are on the rim of life, but by following the Eightfold Path (spokes) we reach enlightenment (hub).

Each part of the Eightfold Path must be followed as the eight elements are linked. A Buddhist would not try to perfect just one element at a time, they would be working on all of them.

It can also be split three ways: wisdom (panna) – Right Thought, Right View; morality/ethics (sila) – Right Speech, Right Action, Right Livelihood; and meditation (samadhi) – Right Effort, Right Mindfulness and Right Concentration (Figure 2). This is called the Threefold Way and is seen in Dhammapada 183 – to avoid all evil, to cultivate good, and to cleanse one's mind – this is the teaching of the Buddhas.

Panna: wisdom; insight into the true nature of reality.

Samadhi: meditation.

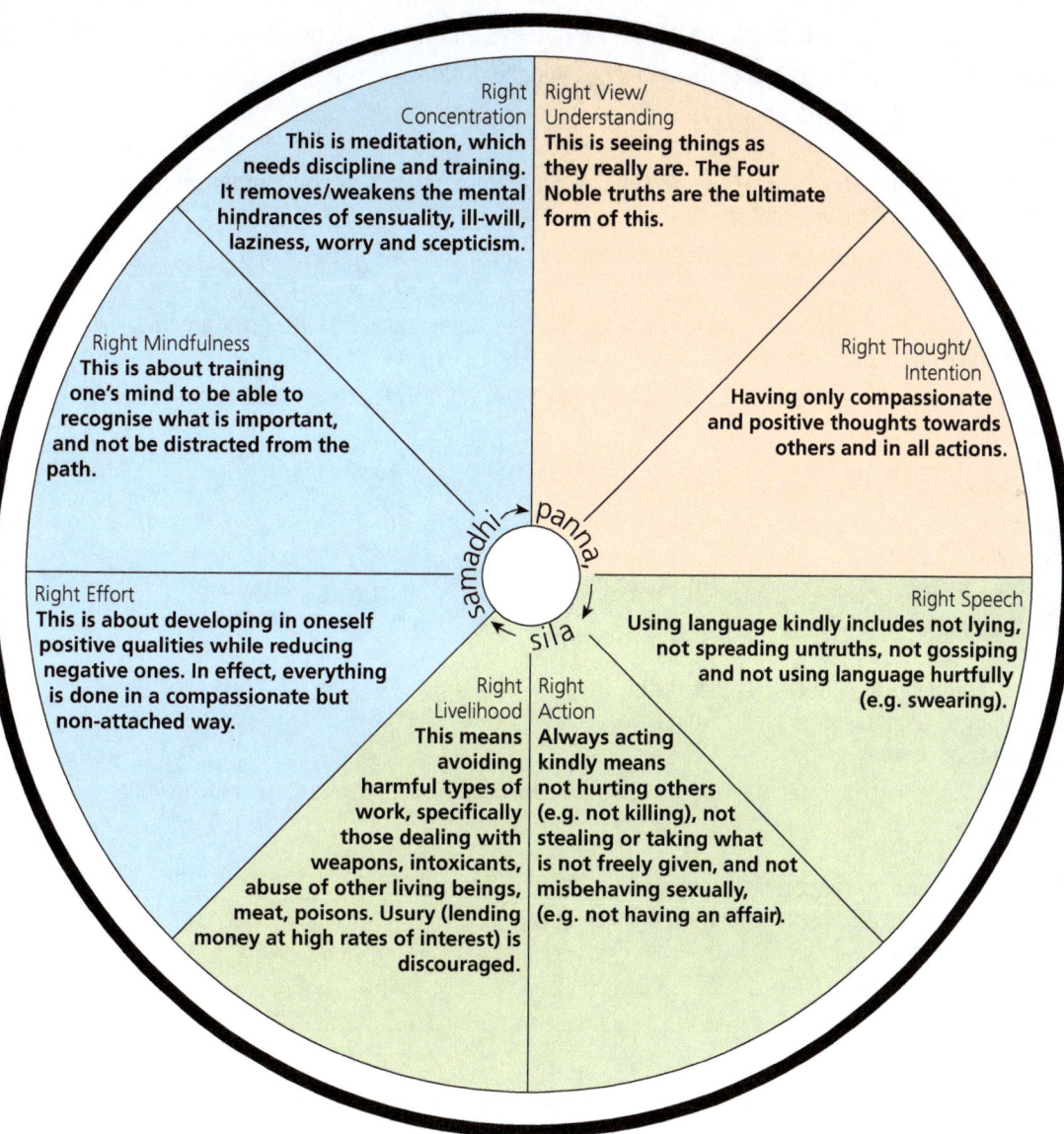

Right Concentration
This is meditation, which needs discipline and training. It removes/weakens the mental hindrances of sensuality, ill-will, laziness, worry and scepticism.

Right View/Understanding
This is seeing things as they really are. The Four Noble truths are the ultimate form of this.

Right Mindfulness
This is about training one's mind to be able to recognise what is important, and not be distracted from the path.

Right Thought/Intention
Having only compassionate and positive thoughts towards others and in all actions.

Right Effort
This is about developing in oneself positive qualities while reducing negative ones. In effect, everything is done in a compassionate but non-attached way.

Right Speech
Using language kindly includes not lying, not spreading untruths, not gossiping and not using language hurtfully (e.g. swearing).

Right Livelihood
This means avoiding harmful types of work, specifically those dealing with weapons, intoxicants, abuse of other living beings, meat, poisons. Usury (lending money at high rates of interest) is discouraged.

Right Action
Always acting kindly means not hurting others (e.g. not killing), not stealing or taking what is not freely given, and not misbehaving sexually, (e.g. not having an affair).

samadhi panna sila

Figure 2 The Noble Eightfold Path

What questions on this section look like:

Buddhism: Beliefs and teachings

This page contains a range of questions that could be on an exam paper. Practise them all to strengthen your knowledge and technique while revising. Check back to pages 11–12 to see the marking grids that examiners use: this will help you to mark your answers.

1 What is meant by dukkha?
   (a) Charity   **(b)** Craving   **(c)** Loving kindness   **(d)** Suffering   [1]

2 Which one of the following is **not** one of the five skandhas?
   (a) Consciousness   **(b)** Form   **(c)** Mental formations   **(d)** Wealth   [1]

3 Give one of the Four Noble Truths. [1]

4 Give one teaching about the Dhamma (Dharma). [1]

5 Give one of the Three Poisons. [1]

6 Explain two ways in which belief in Buddha-nature influences Buddhists today. [4]

7 Explain two ways in which belief in the cause of suffering (samudaya) influences Buddhists today. [4]

8 Explain two ways in which belief in enlightenment influences Buddhists today. [4]

9 Explain two ways in which a belief in dependent arising (paticcasamupada) influences Buddhists today. [4]

10 Explain two Buddhist teachings about the human personality. Refer to sacred writings or another source of Buddhist belief and teachings in your answer. [6]

11 Explain two Buddhist teachings about sunyata. Refer to sacred writings or another source of Buddhist belief and teachings in your answer. [6]

12 Explain two Buddhist teachings about the importance of the Buddha. Refer to sacred writings or another source of Buddhist belief and teachings in your answer. [6]

13 'The enlightenment of the Buddha was the most important event in his life.' Evaluate this statement. In your answer you should:
   + refer to Buddhist teaching
   + give reasoned arguments to support this statement
   + give reasoned arguments to support a different point of view
   + reach a justified conclusion. [12]

14 'Buddhists cannot expect to become enlightened if they are not a monk.' Evaluate this statement. In your answer you should:
   + refer to Buddhist teaching
   + give reasoned arguments to support this statement
   + give reasoned arguments to support a different point of view
   + reach a justified conclusion. [12]

15 'Dependent arising is the most important part of the Buddha's teachings.' Evaluate this statement. In your answer you should:
   + refer to Buddhist teaching
   + give reasoned arguments to support this statement
   + give reasoned arguments to support a different point of view
   + reach a justified conclusion. [12]

Grade 2 students have limited knowledge of the course content, writing very short answers and sometimes giving no answer at all. If this is you, get notes that you can revise from and learn effective revision methods that can help you tackle the exam.

Grade 5 students have general knowledge of the topics, but their answers often aren't detailed enough. They might also be be great on one question and poor on another, showing patchy knowledge and understanding. If this is you, make sure you have notes that make sense to you and cover every bit of the Specification and make yourself explain everything as this comes from having a good understanding of the content.

Grade 8 students have a strong understanding of the content – their answers are detailed and clear. Through their writing they demonstrate an understanding of the connections between the different elements they have studied.

Find Now Test Yourself and Exam Practice answers at **https://www.hoddereducation.co.uk/myrevisionnotesdownloads**

2.2 Buddhism: Practices

Buddhist ethics

REVISED

Buddhists follow the Noble Eightfold Path to attain enlightenment. The Path is also known as the Threefold Way. One of these is sila or morality/ethics, covering Right Speech, Action and Livelihood. Let's face it – if everyone behaved compassionately in all these three 'Rights', the world would be much nicer, since they provoke most problems.

Karma and rebirth

Karma/kamma means 'action'. Buddhists believe that all intentional actions/thoughts/words have consequences. Actions are skilful (kusala) when done with positive intention, bringing happiness to self and others. Actions are unskilful (akusala) when done out of a negative state of mind, bringing suffering. The consequence can come in this lifetime, the next one or many lifetimes away, but Buddhists believe it will happen as an automatic outcome, without someone giving a judgement or sentence. A current lifetime is a result of karma from previous one(s). Since the key is 'intention', having generally good morality can outweigh unskilful action to some extent (i.e. one unskilful action does not necessarily define a future lifetime, and may even have no consequence). Many Buddhists believe in merit-making – building good karma by good deeds – which offsets previous bad karma. Essentially, our rebirth (samsara) – positive or negative – is defined by our karma.

> **Now test yourself** TESTED
>
> 1 What is karma? How does it bind us?
> 2 What is rebirth? How does it link to karma?
> 3 What are karuna and metta?

Karuna

This is mercy or compassion. It is one of the four sublime states (Brahma-viharas) which Buddhists are constantly urged to develop in themselves. It is a virtue or state of mind which leads to a sense of selflessness. The bodhisattva exemplifies this virtue, as a bodhisattva has vowed to help others. Amitabha welcomes Buddhists into his heaven as an act of karuna. The Buddha is the model of compassion and wisdom – compassion without wisdom can lead to harmful actions. The whole point of the Noble Eightfold Path is to develop wisdom and compassion.

Metta

Metta is loving kindness. It is selfless – kindness not done for personal gain. It is another of the Brahma-viharas. It is a concern for the well-being of others – actions flow from that concern. The act of kindness can be small or large, done for those near or for those far away.

The Metta Sutta says, 'Whatever beings there may be … may all beings, without exception, be happy-minded.' Mettabhavana meditation makes the meditator think loving thoughts to push out to the world in stages from those closest to us to those we dislike to those we do not even know. The Dalai Lama once said, 'My religion is simple, my religion is kindness.'

Brahma-viharas: four sublime states – living kindness, compassion, sympathetic joy and equanimity.

Karma/Kamma: the ethical quality or value of all intentional actions/words/thoughts.

Metta: loving kindness.

Samsara: cycle of birth, death and rebirth.

Activity

Develop the notes

A student ran out of time in their exam and had to write their answer in notes. Use them to write a well-argued, detailed answer. Remember it needs a conclusion.

Metta and karuna are the most important Buddhist virtues. (12 marks)

Agree – Buddha's example – did not keep what he learned to himself; helped many to achieve enlightenment; selfless = non-attachment; Dalai Lama – 'compassion is my religion'.

Disagree – wisdom more important; misguided compassion causes more trouble; being faithful to Dharma more important; metta/karuna not always possible in a situation.

The Six Perfections (paramitas)

In Mahayana Buddhism the Six Perfections (paramitas) are the virtues perfected by a bodhisattva in the course of their spiritual development and journey towards enlightenment. For a bodhisattva, they are often seen to replace the Noble Eightfold Path. They are considered to be perfected when even the most difficult actions can be carried out with a mind free of discriminatory ideas, without reference to self, without ulterior motives and with no thought of reward. As with the Noble Eightfold Path, practice is the key to perfecting these. However, any person can try to be better at any of them – they neither have to be Buddhist nor bodhisattva.

Five Moral Precepts:
panca sila – five guidelines which all Buddhists must follow in order to live compassionately.

Six Perfections:
paramitas – six virtues which bodhisattvas work to perfect in themselves.

Perfection (paramita)	How to cultivate this in oneself
Giving/generosity (dana)	Someone who practises perfect giving sees no difference between the giver and the receiver. This includes giving guidance on the Dhamma, material items, accumulated merit and his/her own life, if necessary (the Buddha in one lifetime gave his life to a she-tiger who had no food for her cubs).
Morality (sila)	Keeping all the Ten Precepts. It is also the understanding of how one can break a Precept yet still be acting for the greater good, for example killing someone to prevent them murdering another person.
Patience (ksanti)	Non-anger/non-agitation. This is going beyond enduring suffering, but rather accepting any difficulties one has. Accepting sunyata means that the bodhisattva sees no difference between themselves as sufferer and the cause of the suffering.
Effort/energy (virya)	This means never getting bored/tired of working for one's vows. It is unrelenting energy in overcoming one's faults and cultivating the virtues of the bodhisattva.
Meditation (bhavana)	Following all forms of meditation. This is about cultivating the energised calm and the brahma viharas, becoming able to always see things as they are so as to help others more effectively.
Wisdom (prajna)	Realisation of sunyata. This is perfect wisdom.

The Five Precepts (panca sila)

The Five Precepts are five guidelines for living which all Buddhist laity (ordinary people) must keep to. They are not laws. They are followed in skilful (kausala) or unskilful (akusala) ways. To follow them in skilful ways results in good karma, while following them in unskilful ways results in bad karma being generated. Keeping them in a skilful way is also a good counter to the Three Poisons (greed, hatred, ignorance). Unskillful means ignoring Precepts, as well as deliberately breaking them. Buddhism emphasises intention, so thoughts and words matter just as actions do. A Precept can be kept or broken in mind as well as in practice.

Skilful example	Precept	Unskilful example
Looking after someone in need, for example because they are homeless	First Precept Abstain from harming sentient beings (any form of feeling life)	Beating someone up
Being kind with one's possessions so as to share them with others	Second Precept Abstain from taking that which is not freely given (including not forcing others to give)	'Borrowing' something from someone with no intention of returning it
Being faithful in marriage	Third Precept Abstain from sexual misconduct (physical or emotional)	Making unwanted sexual comments to someone
Being honest but kind in speech	Fourth Precept Abstain from using false speech (including being untruthful or unkind with language)	Telling hurtful lies about someone to make yourself look good
Not drinking alcohol so as not to be unaware of actions	Fifth Precept Abstain from using intoxicating drinks and drugs causing heedlessness (not being concerned about consequences)	Taking drugs not prescribed as medicines

Monks keeping the Precepts

Monks are required to follow ten Precepts (dasa sila), as are any non-monks who are focused on their religious path. As well as the Five Precepts, these are abstaining from taking untimely meals, abstaining from dancing/ music/singing, abstaining from the use of garlands/perfumes/jewellery, abstaining from use of high seats/luxurious beds and abstaining from accepting gold/silver (money). All these things are focused around luxury and pleasing the senses. The Ten Precepts effectively separate monks from others and prove they have renounced the world. Essentially, the monks are giving up all sensual attachments – the things we take for granted in daily life.

Activity

Use the answer starters to write a strong answer to this question:

Explain two ways in which a Buddhist might act in skilful ways. Refer to Buddhist teachings in your answer. (6 marks)

Buddhists follow the Five Precepts. The Buddha gave these five guidelines for living compassionately. Following these guidelines in a positive way is skilful means. First, they might ...... which keeps the _____ Precept (to abstain from _____) in a skilful way because ......

Second, they might ...... which keeps the _____ Precept (to abstain from _____) in a skilful way because ......

Activity

Show your understanding

1 Come up with your own example of each of the Five Precepts followed in a skilful and an unskilful way.

2 How much more difficult is it for monks to keep the Ten Precepts than for the laity to keep the Five Precepts?

Influences

As a Buddhist, I start my day by reciting the Five Precepts. In the day I try to remain mindful of them as I go from task to task – I want to be aware of my impact on others, so that it can be positive. At the end of the day, I use the Precepts to think about how I could have done something better, and resolve to do so next time.

51

Worship in Buddhism

Places of worship

There are a number of different names for places of worship in Buddhism. Buddhists do not worship the Buddha; they venerate the Buddha, that is, they show respect and gratitude to the Buddha because he found the Middle Way. The Specification uses the term 'worship', so you need to be able to manage questions using that term.

Name	Use
Temple	Buddhist laity attend the temple whenever they wish to. Most attend every festival day. Temples include worship halls and shrines. Many have gardens for reflection and spaces for meditation. Many also have rooms for consultation with the monks based at the temple. Pujas (acts of worship) are held here daily.
	Many temples are built near stupas, which are relic houses (contain religious artefacts such as a tooth from the Buddha). Stupas are dome shaped.
	There are bodhi trees at many temples, reminding people of the Buddha's enlightenment. Many of these trees are said to be descended from the original tree sat under.
Shrine	A shrine is a small or large sacred place dedicated to the Buddha; it can be at home. It is centred around at least one **Buddha rupa** (statue of the Buddha). Each temple has a shrine room as its most important place for worship. Acts of worship take place and offerings are made to the Buddha here.
Vihara (monastery)	All have a temple within their compound. Pujas (acts of worship, but NOT services) are held here daily. Since the monks live here, there will be living quarters, as well as kitchens, meeting rooms, etc.
Gompa (hall for learning)	This is the name given to Tibetan Buddhist shrine rooms. In Tibetan Buddhism there is a long tradition of training for monks to attain a degree in Buddhist philosophy, hence a hall for learning.

Some differences

Depending on the country, the name for the temple varies – a pagoda in China is a stupa in India is a wat in Sri Lanka.

In Theravada Buddhism, many temples are also homes to monks, that is they are also small or large monasteries. In Mahayana Buddhism, monasteries are less common and many temples have only a single religious leader based at them.

The importance of Buddhist places of worship

+ Place of learning – laity or monk, anyone can learn more about the Dhamma from the religious leaders based there via lessons, individual discussions, or services (Dhammapada 276).
+ Place for reflection/meditation – Right Meditation.
+ Place to pay tribute to the Buddha – making offerings in thankfulness for his gift of the teaching of the Dhamma and for his example of attaining enlightenment – the act of dana (giving).
+ Advice – many Buddhists will discuss personal and life issues with the monks to learn the correct Buddhist response as per Dhammapada 276.
+ Centre of the community.

> **Revision tip**
>
> It is always easier to recall the elements of this page when we have a visual image. Collect images of all the things mentioned here and annotate them. The act of annotating helps your brain to take in and retain the information.

> **Buddha rupa:** a statue of Buddha.
>
> **Places of worship:** temple, shrine, vihara (monastery), gompa (hall for learning/meditation.

> **Key quote**
>
> 'You yourselves should make the effort; the enlightened ones are only teachers.'
> Dhammapada 276

Key features of Buddhist places of worship

 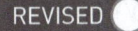

The table shows the key features of places of worship in Buddhism.

Feature	About	Importance
Buddha rupa (statue of Buddha)	Can be sat in meditative pose, reclining, or standing. One focal Buddha rupa, usually centrally positioned (might be part of a trio). Often many rupas in a shrine room – different sizes, materials, etc.	Buddha is central to religion, so central to shrine. Symbols within rupa help worshipper to focus on spiritual truths.
Artefacts	Items of religious significance to aid worship or meditation, or to remind of Dhamma. Scriptures – may be only one sutra, for example Heart Sutra – representing the speech of the Buddha, i.e. all his teachings. Model of a stupa – representing the mind of the Buddha. Vajra – thunderbolt/diamond – symbolises five wisdoms and five kandhas/poisons. Instruments such as cymbals and bells are present to aid meditation/puja.	Aid to worship. Aid to meditation (as focus). Symbolic nature of each is important. Rupa, scriptures and stupa represent the Three Jewels, i.e. the Three Refuges (Buddha, Dharma, Sangha).
Offerings	Generally: + Flowers = the beauty of enlightenment and a reminder of impermanence as they wither and die. + Candles – light helps us to see where to go – the light of Dhamma in the darkness of ignorance. + Incense – the sweet smell goes everywhere (no barriers) = Buddhism is fit for any place and any person. + Food – gift of thanks to Buddha for the teaching of the Dhamma and to the monks for their religious devotion. + In Mahayana, it is traditional to make seven offerings. Two bowls of water (washing, drinking) symbolise hospitality. Then five others – flowers, candles, incense, food, perfume – represent the five senses.	Dana (giving) is a key element of Buddhist ethics. It evokes Right Action. The symbolic nature of each item allows the worshipper to reflect on religious truths. Making the offerings is a way to focus on worship completely. Giving to the Buddha shows respect and thankfulness for his teachings/example.

Some differences

Mahayana temples usually have three Buddhas/bodhisattvas as the focal part of their shrine, known as a triad, which sit side by side. For example, it may be Sakyamuni Buddha (historical Buddha) with Manjushri (bodhisattva of wisdom) and Samantabhadra (bodhisattva of kindness) flanking that central Buddha. Theravada temples have one central rupa, but often have many other smaller rupa all around that one.

Theravadins make offerings of the four forms (flowers, incense, food and light) and can often buy these four items bundled together for them at the temple. In Mahayana, there are commonly seven offerings, with two water offerings and one of perfume additional to the Theravada four.

Worship – puja

What is puja?

Puja is a formal act of worship or veneration that takes place before a shrine. Before entering the shrine, or the shrine room if in a temple complex, the worshipper will have removed their shoes (humility; people sit on the floor, so this keeps it cleaner). In Buddhist puja, there are three core elements:

+ Bowing to the Buddha – three times to represent the Buddha, Dhamma and Sangha (Three Refuges). This is often done from a kneeling position, with hands together in front of the chest, though it may be full prostration with the worshipper's head touching the floor. This reminds them of their commitment to the ideal set by the Buddha.
+ Making offerings of incense, flowers, food and candles – each symbolic of key teachings. By making the offering, the worshipper becomes mindful of these and that they aspire to become Buddha themselves.
+ Chanting – done when making offerings. It is often a recitation of a set scripture, dictated by the worshipper's form of Buddhism. It may focus on the example of the Buddha, or it may be about the symbolic nature of the offerings, for example.

> **Puja:** Buddhist act of worship.

Some differences

Tibetan Buddhists prostrate themselves fully before the statue, with arms stretched towards the statue. Theravada Buddhists kneel, put their palms together in front of their chest and bow three times to the Buddha.

The words recited will be fixed depending on which form of Buddhism the worshipper follows, for example the Triratna Buddhist Community (formerly known as the Friends of the Western Buddhist Order, or FWBO) recite about the offerings and what they symbolise.

Theravada Buddhists make four offerings; Mahayana Buddhists, especially Tibetans, make seven.

Why do puja?

Puja is an expression of devotion and thankfulness to the Buddha generally, but it may be for a specific purpose, such as becoming pregnant.

Through bowing and making offerings, the worshipper shows humility, which is crucial in the goal to enlightenment and demonstrates determination to achieve enlightenment.

Puja also shows Right Mindfulness as it requires a focus on what is being done and the symbolism behind it. The ritual of puja makes the worshipper engage actively and emotionally with the teachings – it is not enough to just understand the religion, Buddhism is about transforming a person entirely.

In Buddhist countries, most Buddhists attend temple, often daily. Many Buddhists also have home shrines (a space given over to a Buddha rupa, around which are placed items of significance to aid puja and meditation).

> **Key quote**
>
> 'Reverently, I prostrate with my body, speech and mind, and present clouds of every type of offering.' Tibetan prayer

Comparing home and temple worship

Home	Temple
Done on own terms – when, how long, what is recited, etc.	Follows standard routine – enter, bow, make offerings, chant/recite
Effort goes into making shrine	Effort goes into attending temple
Study is personal and usually solitary, self-guided	Monks available to discuss issues, give advice, etc.
Shrine may be very small and simple	Shrines often full of artefacts, and ornate

Chanting

Chanting is a repetition of key scriptures/teachings and can be an aid to meditation. It must be conducted in a single-minded and sincere manner, though it can be done aloud/silently, alone/with others, with prayer beads or not, to music or not. It is always a way of developing devotion.

Mantra recitation

This is a repetition of a set phrase in order to bring about a specific state of consciousness. Tibetan monks are often given mantras personal to themselves by their teachers. Om mani padme hum is a good example, the syllables of which represent the Six Perfections. It could be chanting to call upon the Buddha or a bodhisattva (as in Pure Land Buddhism where Amitabha is called upon). It always shows devotion but is also merit-making.

Use of malas

A mala, a string of prayer beads, is used to count prayers/recitations/mantras. There are 108 beads in total, representing 108 worldly desires and the means to overcome them. These aid focus, but also ensure the worshipper says the requisite number of prayers.

> **Mala:** Buddhist prayer beads.
>
> **Mantra:** set phrase, usually calling on the name of a Buddha/bodhisattva.

Now test yourself   TESTED ◯

1 What is puja? What three elements are there?
2 What do Buddhists chant at puja?
3 What are mantras?
4 What is a mala and why use it?

Activity

Fix It!

Which of these two answers is better? Rewrite both to make them achieve full marks.

Explain two different forms of Buddhist worship.   *(4 marks)*

Answer A - One form is puja, where they go to the temple. Another form is where they worship at home.

Answer B - When Buddhists go to worship, they might chant and use prayer beads. Other Buddhists will bow and make offerings.

Meditation

Meditation is mental concentration in order to achieve a state of mind from which one can eventually attain enlightenment. It is a physical and mental discipline. It is one of the elements of the Noble Eightfold Path, so most Buddhists meditate in some form.

Imagine the mind as a pool of water. Thoughts disturb the surface, so one cannot see clearly into it. Meditation aims to still the surface to allow clear sight and understanding.

How do we know meditation is important/ significant in Buddhism?

Right Concentration is one element of the Noble Eightfold Path, which is the Fourth Noble Truth (magga). Samadhi (meditation) is one element of the Threefold Way. It is considered crucial for attaining enlightenment. Meditation leads to mindfulness, which leads to detachment, which leads to nibbana.

The Buddha is most commonly seen seated in meditative pose in rupas/ images, hence implying its importance. He trained himself in meditation practices and then meditated until enlightenment, so this is his example.

The Buddha taught meditation, and from that so have Buddhist leaders throughout history. All Buddhists meditate.

Key quotes

What the Buddha said

'Hard to restrain, unstable is this mind; it flits wherever it likes. Good it is to control the mind. A controlled mind brings happiness.' Dhammapada 35

'Though one may live a hundred years with no true insight and self-control, yet better, indeed, is a life of one day for a man who meditates in wisdom.' Dhammapada 111

'Not to do any evil, to cultivate good, to purify one's mind, this is the teaching of the Buddhas.' Dhammapada 183

'You yourselves should make the effort; the Enlightened Ones are only teachers. Those who enter this path and are meditative are delivered from the bonds of Mara.' Dhammapada 276

Reading these, it is clear that Buddhists should meditate. Meditation brings the mind under control, which helps a person eliminate unskilful thinking (and, in turn, unskilful words/actions). It brings non-attachment, and from being able to see things clearly, wisdom. Buddhism is a personal journey, and meditation is a crucial practice within that in order to bring success.

Vipassana: meditation for insight.

Visualisation: use of images (actual or in the mind) to meditate.

Zazen: the main form of meditation in Zen Buddhism, practiced cross-legged with the aim of gaining vipassana.

Activity

This answer got six marks – can you spot them?

Explain two reasons why meditation is important in Buddhism. (6 marks)

One reason why meditation is important is because the Buddha meditated. Having studied many forms, it brought him enlightenment eventually. Buddhists see this as the perfect example.

Secondly, the Dhammapada says the teaching of the Buddhas is to 'purify one's mind', which means to meditate. Buddhists meditate to obey the teaching.

Find Now Test Yourself and Exam Practice answers at **https://www.hoddereducation.co.uk/myrevisionnotesdownloads**

Types of meditation

For the course, you have to study four types of meditation.

Type	Information
Samatha (calm/concentration and tranquility)	This aims to develop calmness and 'one-pointedness' of mind (mindfulness). Samatha trains the mind not to be distracted by thoughts.
	Eight 'trance' levels (jhanas) are recognised in samatha meditation, beginning with 'mindfulness of breathing'. This is about being 'in the present moment', still and calm. Each subsequent one is more refined. Nibbana cannot be attained from samatha, as the levels operate within the universe (so are part of conditioned existence).
	Buddhist texts list 40 meditation subjects, including, meditation on breathing, meditation on the Brahma-viharas (sublime states), and meditation on the 32 parts of the body.
	Successful samatha leads to Right Mindfulness.
	Samatha changes a person's outlook and attitudes in daily life as well as while meditating.
Vipassana (insight)	This is specific to Buddhism, developed by the Buddha.
	Focus is on analysing the mind and body and interactions with the material world in order to break attachment. This allows insight to be gained into the true nature of reality, particularly the Three Marks of Existence. From that nibbana can be attained.
	It is a permanent solution to the problem of suffering, given the realisation of the Three Marks.
	Vipassana seems to be more connected to wisdom (panna) than concentration (samatha).
Zazen (meditation in sitting)	This comes from Soto Zen, Japanese Buddhism.
	The meditator sits in a meditative position in a quiet room and tries to attain a state of relaxed attention (being aware but not chasing thoughts, or trying to work things out). It is common for the meditator to have been posed a paradox – **koan** – the answer to which may come in these sessions. These are supposed to train monks to give up on logical reasoning and force sudden intuitive enlightenment.
	Dogen, the founder of Soto Zen, said that zazen in itself could constitute enlightenment.
Visualisation of Buddha or bodhisattva	This involves calming the mind and visualising Buddhas or bodhisattvas to develop the qualities of compassion. It is common to Chinese (Chan) and Tibetan Buddhism.
	It may include trying to recreate an image in one's mind – of a mandala, a tangkha (image of a Buddha in their heaven, e.g. Amitabha), a Buddha, e.g. Guan Yin (bodhisattva of compassion), a Buddha heaven, or a mantra.
	The meditator is trying to see what it would be like to be the subject or in the place being visualised.

Now test yourself

TESTED ◯

1 What is meditation?
2 Why do Buddhists meditate?
3 What is the difference between samatha and vipassana?

Revision tip

A 'differences' question on this topic might well be to explain different forms of meditation, rather than meditation done by different types of Buddhists.

Koan: statement/question intended to pose a mental dilemma ('What is the sound of one hand clapping?'), used in zazen.

Samatha: meditation for mindfulness, concentration.

Death and mourning rituals in Buddhism

Buddhists contemplate death throughout their lives, not only before they are about to die. It was one of the Four Sights. It is just a stage in the cycle of samsara, and an example of anicca (impermanence) so a learning tool. Many Buddhists meditate on death and dying. It is common for Buddhist monks to meditate focused on a skull, reminding them that this is their future as well and that all things will pass.

Funeral rites emphasise the Three Marks of Existence (suffering, impermanence and no permanent self), the hope for a better rebirth, the showing of respect to the dead and to those choosing a religious path. Common to all funerals, monks will recite sutras to/for the dead. Pamsukula robes ('rag' robes) are given to the dead. Cremation is common. Families give alms to the local monastery/temple to transfer merit to the deceased for their rebirth. It is common to hold memorial services 3, 7, 49 and 100 days after the death.

Bardo: in Tibetan Buddhism, the state between death and rebirth lasting up to 49 days – a place of demons, ghosts and terror.

Butsudan: Japanese home shrine.

Matakabhatta: Food offerings given to monks on behalf of the deceased.

Pamsukula robes: 'rag' robes given to the dead (usually placed on the coffin).

Form of Buddhism	Process	Symbolism/significance
Theravada	Sutras recited to the dying/dead.	Trying to direct the thoughts of the dying/dead to the Buddha.
	The coffin with the body in it is surrounded by candles, incense and wreaths.	Tribute to the dead, but also reminders of the Three Marks of Existence.
	Monks visit to chant from Abhidharma scripture; food is given to monks (**matakabhatta**).	Transfer of merit to the dead from reading and giving of alms to aid rebirth.
	At cremation, monks sit facing the coffin; relatives bring lit torches made of candles, incense and a fragrant wood to put under the coffin and start the flames.	Watching death is a meditation on impermanence and no self. Monks are here to bless the dead. The elements of the torch remind of temple offerings.
Japanese	Funeral rites last several days.	Mark of respect.
	Procession to the temple. Coffin placed in front of items to invoke paradise. Mourners give money.	Hope for rebirth in a heaven.

Dana. |
	Priest kneels before the coffin and recites sutras. Family offer respect to the dead.	Reminding all of the Buddha's teachings on impermanence, and especially death.
	Body is burned, while a family meal takes place.	
	Ashes/bones are placed into a box using special chopsticks. This is put out on the family shrine (**butsudan**) before internment in the family grave.	One willow and one bamboo chopstick, representing the bridge between this world and the next.
Tibetan	Book of the Dead read to the dying/dead person to prepare them for **bardo**.	The reader gains good merit for themselves, and helps the recipient.
	In bardo for up to 49 days, beginning with a glimpse of enlightenment, their karma will then take them to it or pull them away from it to rebirth.	The 'being pulled away' is explained as the sense of 'I' being too strong to let go and so rebirth is inevitable.
	'Sky burial' – performed on a hillside. The body is dismembered while a scripture is recited.	Emphasises non-attachment – there is no 'I'. Buddha gave his body to feed starving animals in one rebirth.
	The parts are then left for vultures to eat.	This is a final act of dana by the deceased.

Festivals and retreats

Festivals specifically commemorate an event/person of historical importance. They could be seen as the religion's outward, public face. Retreats are a total focus on the religion, as if going inward away from the public gaze.

Retreats

During the three-month rainy season, the Buddha encouraged monks to seclude themselves in order to meditate more intensely. This retreat has been a practice of monks ever since.

The process involves taking oneself away from the normal concerns/demands of daily life for a period of time and leading a simple, focused life, during which time the main task is to study the Dhamma and/or meditate (i.e. develop one's spiritual practice or understanding).

In the UK this is a chance to fully relax but fully focus – away from busy Western society. It can be considered as a 'spiritual battery recharge'. Participants meet other people, so they can form a sense of community which lasts beyond the retreat.

Parinirvana Day: commemorates Buddha attaining nibbana fully.

Retreat: taking a break from society to focus on spiritual path.

Wesak: festival commemorating full moon in May on which day (in different years) Buddha was born, became enlightened and died.

Wesak

Wesak recalls the birth, enlightenment and death of the Buddha, each of which happened in May on the night of the full moon. The Buddha's teachings help everyone and the Buddhist path is seen as one of peace and so a boon to the world – hence the importance of this festival.

During the festival the laity follows Eight Precepts (the Five Precepts plus refraining from singing/dancing/wearing garlands and perfumes, eating after midday, and sleeping in luxurious beds). They attend temple and make offerings to the temple, but also to the vulnerable of society (Giving), and restate their commitment to the Precepts (Virtue). They participate in chanting scriptures, listening to sermons, and in meditation (Cultivation), as well as doing good deeds (Merit-making). Some Buddhists wear white (novice) robes and spend the whole day/evening at the temple. Many pour water over statues of the Buddha, as if washing them, and put garlands of flowers over them.

Parinirvana Day

For Mahayana Buddhists, Parinirvana Day recalls the day that the Buddha died, so he reached nibbana. For most Buddhists this day is 15 February. It is important because it reminds of final death, ceasing to be reborn – the goal of all Buddhists. Buddhists should reflect on their future death and on any recent deaths.

The day involves attending temple and/or meditation. Some spend the day reading/reciting sutras (especially Parinirvana Sutra). Prayers will be said for the recently deceased to try to send them merit for their journey. Many Buddhists give money and items to support monks at monasteries. It is also a traditional day for pilgrimage in Asia.

Some differences

While Wesak is a social and joyful day, with activities for children and adults in the UK, Parinirvana is a solemn one requiring a certain level of understanding of the faith to be able to attend UK temples (effectively excluding children).

Different countries celebrate the festivals differently. For Parinirvana Day, Buddhists in India may make a pilgrimage to Kushinagar; UK Buddhists will attend temple for an extended period.

2.2 Buddhism: Practices

59

What questions on this section look like:

Buddhism: Practices

This page contains a range of questions that could be on an exam paper. Practise them all to strengthen your knowledge and technique while revising. Check back to pages 11–12 to see the marking grids that examiners use: this will help you to mark your answers.

1 Which of these is **not** one of the Six Perfections?

  (a) Ethics   **(b)** Generosity   **(c)** Not hurting   **(d)** Wisdom   [1]

2 Which of these does the Buddhist festival which is called Parinirvana Day celebrate?

  (a) Buddha's birth   **(b)** Buddha's death   **(c)** Buddha's enlightenment   **(d)** Founding of Buddhism   [1]

3 Give one of the Five Precepts. [1]

4 Give one feature of a Buddhist shrine. [1]

5 Give one teaching about loving kindness (metta). [1]

6 Explain two similar features of Buddhist temples. [4]

7 Explain two different ways in which a Buddhist might meditate. [4]

8 Explain two different forms of worship for Buddhists. [4]

9 Explain two similar features of a Buddhist funeral in two Buddhist traditions. [4]

10 Explain two ways in which belief in kamma (karma) is important in the life of a Buddhist. Refer to sacred writings or another source of Buddhist belief and teachings in your answer. [6]

11 Explain two ways in which temple offerings are important in Buddhism. Refer to sacred writings or another source of Buddhist belief and teachings in your answer. [6]

12 Explain two ways in which retreats might be important for Buddhists in Great Britain today. Refer to sacred writings or another source of Buddhist belief and teachings in your answer. [6]

13 'Buddhists should always attend a temple for worship.' Evaluate this statement. In your answer you should:
  ✦ refer to Buddhist teaching
  ✦ give reasoned arguments to support this statement
  ✦ give reasoned arguments to support a different point of view
  ✦ reach a justified conclusion. [12]

14 'Meditation is more important than good actions.' Evaluate this statement. In your answer you should:
  ✦ refer to Buddhist teaching
  ✦ give reasoned arguments to support this statement
  ✦ give reasoned arguments to support a different point of view
  ✦ reach a justified conclusion. [12]

15 'Compassion without wisdom is not helpful.' Evaluate this statement. In your answer you should:
  ✦ refer to Buddhist teaching
  ✦ give reasoned arguments to support this statement
  ✦ give reasoned arguments to support a different point of view
  ✦ reach a justified conclusion. [12]

Exam tip

Grade 2 students make little use of quotations and/or teachings – 'limited reference to sources of wisdom and authority'. When used, they are the most common but often not the most appropriate for the question so the examiner is left trying to work out how they are relevant (they won't!). Those used are usually not applied to the question – they can just sit there, almost irrelevant. If this is you, get a stock of basic teachings for the religions you study and practise using them.

Grade 5 students use some quotes/teachings, but they can usually be more appropriate or better applied to the question. They are generally accurate, but could be sharper. If this is you, then you need to do more work on learning these teachings and making better use of them.

Grade 8 students make 'well-integrated reference to sources of wisdom and authority', in other words they use lots of quotes/teachings which are specific to the question and which they explain well in relation to the question. They also name their source, e.g. 'The Dhammapada'. It is clear they have a deep understanding of the religion and this is evidence of that.

Key terms from the Specification

As you worked through the guide, you met lots of key terms. A good idea is to go back and create an RS dictionary of your own. On the exam, if asked to define a word, it must come from the Specification, so these are those words/phrases you should know.

Christianity

REVISED

Ascension: Jesus being taken up to heaven on the 40th day of Easter. Page 22

Atonement: the action of making amends for wrong doing. The idea of being at one with the self. Page 23

Baptism: sacrament; a ceremony to welcome a person into the Christian religion. Page 27

Believers' baptism: a ceremony to welcome an adult into the Christian religion using full immersion. Page 28

CAFOD a charity: Catholic Agency for Overseas Development. Page 36

Christian Aid: a charity working in the developing world providing emergency and long-term aid. Page 36

Crucifixion: capital punishment used by the Romans which involves nailing a person to a cross to kill them; Jesus died this way. Page 32

Eucharist: bread and wine ceremony in the Anglican church. Page 27

Evangelism: preaching of the faith in order to convert people to that religion. Page 34

Food banks: charity groups collecting donated food to distribute to people in poverty in Britain. Page 33

Genesis: first book of the Bible; means 'beginning'; includes creation story. Page 17

Grace: unconditional love that God shows to people, even those who do not deserve it. Page 23

Holy Communion: the bread and wine ceremony in the Church of England. Page 29

Incarnation: God in human form; Jesus. Page 21

Infant baptism: ceremony to welcome a child into the Christian religion. Page 28

Iona: an island in Scotland with a fourth-century monastery, used by Christians today as a place of pilgrimage. Page 30

Liturgical worship: a church service with a set structure of worship. Page 25

Lord's Prayer: the prayer Jesus taught his disciples to show them how to pray. Page 26

Lourdes: a town in France where the Virgin Mary appeared; now a place of pilgrimage. Page 30

Messiah: the anointed one who is seen as the saviour by Jewish people and Christians. Page 21

Mission: an organised effort to spread the Christian message. Page 34

Non-liturgical worship: informal structure found in some church services. Page 25

Omnipotent: the idea that God is all-powerful. Page 17

Original sin: belief that everyone born carries the sins of their forefathers. Page 23

Orthodox Church: a branch of the Christian church with its origins in Greece and Russia. Page 25

Persecution: hostility and ill-treatment, usually because of prejudice. Page 35

Protestant: a branch of the Christian church that broke away from the Roman Catholic Church. Page 27

Reconciliation: the process of making people in conflict friendly again. Page 35

Resurrection: the physical return of Jesus on the third day after he died. Page 20

Roman Catholic: the largest Christian group based in Rome, with the Pope as its leader. Page 20

Sacrament: the external and visible sign of an inward and spiritual grace. Page 27

Salvation: the saving of the soul from sin; includes through grace and spirit. Page 21

Street pastors: a Christian organisation of people working on the city streets at night caring for people who are drunk or involved in anti-social behaviour. Page 33

Tearfund: a Christian charity working to relieve poverty in developing countries. Page 36

Trinity: the belief in God the Father, God the Son and God the Holy Spirit. Page 18

Buddhism

Anatta: there is no permanent soul. Page 39

Amitabha: Buddha of infinite light. Page 41

Anicca: belief that nothing is permanent; one of the Three Marks of Existence. Page 39

Arhat: in Theravada Buddhism, a perfected being (the stage before enlightenment). Page 40

Ascetic: a life spent in extreme self-discipline and denying oneself any indulgence. Page 44.

Bodhisattva: a being who has postponed enlightenment after taking a vow to help others. Page 41

Buddha: Siddhartha Gotama; means 'awakened one'. Page 39

Buddha-nature: idea that all beings have the potential within them to become Buddha. Page 40

Buddha rupa: statue of Buddha. Page 52

Buddhahood: the realisation of perfect enlightenment. Page 52

Dhamma (Dharma): the teaching of the Buddha. Page 39

Dhammapada: collected sayings/teachings of the Buddha. Page 45

Dukkha: everything is unsatisfactory. There is pain and suffering in life, some of which is due to the fact that things do not last. Page 39

Enlightenment (nirvana): ceasing to be bound by the wheel of samsara; full realisation of the true nature of things. Page 39

Five Moral Precepts: five guiding principles for Buddhists to follow. They can be followed in skilful (upaya kausala) or unskilful ways. Page 50

Four Noble Truths: the four central beliefs which contain the essence of the teaching of the Buddha: dukkha (suffering), samudaya (causes of suffering), tanha (ending of craving) and magga (Noble Eightfold Path). Page 39

Four Sights: illness, old age, death, holy man: seeing these made Siddhartha begin his search for enlightenment. Page 42

Karma/Kamma: energy created by intentional thoughts, words and actions which shapes lifetimes. Page 49

Mahayana: larger tradition within Buddhism (53 per cent), mainly found in China, Japan, Korea and the Himalayas. Page 40

Magga: the fourth Noble Truth; known as 'The Middle Way,' it includes the way to wisdom. Page 46

Mala: prayer beads, used to aid meditation. Page 55

Mantra recitation: short religious phrases which should be repeated. Page 55

Meditation: practice of focusing; samatha (concentration), vipassana (achieving insight); includes zazen form (self-focus) and visualisation exercises. Page 40

Metta (loving kindness): pure love which is selfless and not possessive. Page 49

Panna (wisdom): insight into the true nature of reality. Page 47

Parinirvana Day: festival to celebrate the enlightenment of the Buddha. Page 59

Paticcasamupada (dependent arising): the belief that everything is interconnected. Page 39

Puja: act of worship. Page 54

Pure Land: form of Buddhism that includes the concept of a heaven. Page 41

Rebirth: belief that the skandhas are reborn into new lifetimes, shaped by the karma of previous ones, until enlightenment is achieved. Page 39

Retreat: temporarily leaving one's everyday life and going to special places to aid spiritual development. Page 59

Samsara: cycle of birth and death; samsara binds the atman to this physical, illusory existence. Page 49

Sila: moral principles that inform behaviour and attitudes; part of the Eightfold Path. Page 41

Six Perfections: six qualities Buddhists (especially bodhisatvas) should try to cultivate within themselves. Page 50

Skandhas: the belief that human beings are composed of five factors - form, sensation, perception, mental formation, consciousness. Page 39

Sunyata: emptiness, void, calmness. Page 40

Theravada: oldest form of Buddhism, based around the Sangha. Page 40

Three Marks of Existence: three aspects common to all existence – anicca (impermanence), anatta (no fixed self), dukkha (suffering). Page 39

Three Poisons: the three causes of suffering: ignorance, greed and hate. Page 43

Threefold Way: a way to develop one's spiritual self, through sila (ethics), panna (wisdom) and samadhi (meditation). Page 39

Wesak: main Buddhist festival celebrating the birth, enlightenment and death of the Buddha. Page 59

General teachings of the six major religions

Use of teachings is very important in this GCSE (in the Religion section as well as the Theme section). It will always be easier to score marks and to make points more clearly if you use teachings that are specific to the topics. The examiner will be able to clearly see the point you are making and the relevance of the teachings; you will be able to make your points in fewer words, more correctly and concisely. You will find many such teachings in this guide. However, in the exam it might be difficult to remember those specific teachings, so this section gives you some general teachings which can be applied to many topics. They form the key beliefs/teachings of the religions – so learn them.

Exam tip

Don't forget – when you write a teaching in an answer – say where it is from. For example, 'Jesus said...', or 'in the Qur'an it says...' and so on. This gets you marks.

Buddhism

+ Karma – our words/actions shape our future.
+ Each of the actions of the Eightfold Path, especially Right Action, Livelihood, Speech.
+ Compassion, the Five Precepts, including not hurting others (ahimsa), not clouding the mind, kind language, not taking what is not freely given, no sexual misconduct.

Christianity

+ Jesus said, Love God, love your neighbour.
+ God created all humans equally.
+ Justice – everyone is equal so we all deserve fairness.
+ Forgiveness, love, compassion.

Hinduism

+ Hindu virtues state compassion, ahimsa and reverence for life.
+ Respect and support for others, service.
+ Self-discipline, wisdom, honesty.

Islam

+ Ummah – the brotherhood of all Muslims that binds them together, and asks for equality and respect.
+ Equality of the Five Pillars.
+ Shari'ah law applied to life's issues.

Judaism

+ Ten Commandments: love G-d, no idols, don't misuse G-d's name, keep the Sabbath, respect parents, don't kill, don't steal, don't commit adultery, don't lie, don't act through jealousy.
+ Equality, love, respect.

Sikhism

+ Sikh values of sharing, sewa, duty, tolerance, chastity, humility.
+ The Khalsa vows, which include meditation and service to God, avoiding intoxicants, fighting injustice and equality of all.

Many of these can be applied to a variety of topics, so you can learn one teaching and use it again and again – less learning! And across religions – less learning!

Exam tip

In the modern world, many religious believers have reinterpreted their holy books in a less literal way. Teachings which might have been seen as rigid 200 years ago, are now reinterpreted in the light of new science and new society. You can use the fact that all religions have groups within them who have 'evolved' their beliefs and practices to help make points in your answers.

Theme A: Relationships and families

Sex

REVISED

People choose to have sex for many reasons, for example love, fun, lust, to create life, money …

Society's attitudes to sex and relationships have evolved over the last 50 years. Homosexuality, for example, is far more acceptable today whereas it used to be illegal to be gay. Nowadays many people do not get married. Also, divorce rates are much higher.

As relationships change, attitudes to sex change, but the religious view remains traditional – you need to know both secular and religious views for this theme.

Contraception

REVISED

Contraception is a precaution taken to prevent pregnancy so that a couple can 'family plan'. Using contraception is seen as a responsible way to bring children into the world – when a couple have decided the time is right for them, they are in a position to look after and provide for the child.

Contraception allows a couple to enjoy a sexual relationship without getting pregnant, and reduces the need for abortion of unwanted pregnancies and the spread of sexually transmitted diseases.

Methods include:
+ artificial devices – these are 'made', such as condoms, the Pill etc
+ natural methods – these are behaviours to limit the chance of pregnancy, such as withdrawal or rhythm methods
+ permanent methods – these are operations to prevent the production of eggs or sperm. For example, sterilisation.

Only the permanent methods are 100 per cent guaranteed.

Relationships

REVISED

People marry for many reasons – for love, sex, to make a marriage legitimate, for children, money, companionship and because it is an accepted way in society and within religions. Others choose not to marry but are still in a solid relationship.

Some people have a free choice about who to marry, some have marriage partners chosen by parents, and some religions advocate marriage to someone in that religion.

Adultery: married person having sex with someone other than the person they are married to – an affair.

Contraception: precautions taken to prevent pregnancy and to protect against contracting or transmitting STIs (sexually transmitted infections).

Homosexuality: a sexual relationship between a same-sex couple (i.e. man/man or woman/woman).

Types of marriage and cohabitation

Cohabitation is living together as if married. The couple have no marriage licence, however, so do not have the same legal rights as a married couple.

Many people in the modern world accept cohabitation and same-sex relationships, believing people should live in a way that makes them happy. Nevertheless, some people still see cohabitation as 'living in sin' and the relationship as 'unofficial'.

As a cohabiting couple have a sexual relationship, this is seen as sex outside marriage and not in line with what many religions teach.

Same-sex relationships are legally protected through civil partnership or a marriage in a registry office. But many religions do not accept same-sex relationships. Under Islamic Shari'ah law, it carries the death penalty. Many religious people, while accepting people are gay, believe they should refrain from sexual relationships.

Sex is for the pro-creation of children and as a same-sex couple cannot naturally have a child then some people would question the need for a sexual relationship. Many same-sex couples now do have children through the aid of medical science as they want a family just as much as other couples do.

Roles in marriage

Marriage vows or promises can help to understand the different roles within marriage. People promise to be good to each other, to be faithful, to love and cherish, to support each other through good and bad times until death – so the intention in marrying is to make a life-long commitment to someone.

Roles have a practical angle focused on looking after the household and finances. Roles have changed in this respect; now it is often about what works best for each couple – they decide their roles for themselves rather than conforming to the expectations of society. Money can also affect decision-making.

The nature and purpose of polygamy

Polygamy is the practice of marrying multiple people, often having children with each. It is illegal in the UK.

Under Shari'ah law polygamy is allowed under certain circumstances. Some British Muslims marry 'Islamically' – no British marriage licence is signed, allowing several marriages. None would be recognised under British law and the couple(s) have no protection under the law.

Prophet Muhammad allowed this system because *at the time* many women were war widows so unable to support themselves. Rather than leave them unprotected, polygamy was condoned.

Today the rules are difficult to implement – the man must seek consent from the first wife, treat the women all the same, spend time and nights with each one, help with bringing up children with each one, and financially support all of them.

Celibacy: abstaining from sexual relations.

Chastity: being sexually pure; in a relationship, waiting to have sex until married.

Civil marriage: a marriage for a couple (or since 2014, same-sex couple) carried out at a registry office.

Civil partnership: the legal registration of a same-sex couple, giving them some legal and financial protection. As of February 2018, civil partnership was extended to include heterosexual couples.

Cohabitation: living together as a couple.

Commitment: a relationship based on a promise to be faithful and supportive.

Contract: binding agreements, such as a marriage contract.

Family planning: planning when to have a family and how big a family to have by use of birth control practices and/or contraception.

Polgamy: the practice of having more than one husband or wife at the same time.

Religious marriage: a marriage service for a heterosexual couple carried out in a religious place of worship. A very small number of religious groups will hold religious marriage services for same sex couples,for example the Metropolitan Church (Christian).

Sex before marriage: a sexual act between two people before a marriage has taken place.

Theme A: Relationships and families

Now test yourself

TESTED

1 What is the difference between 'religious' and 'civil' marriage?
2 Why do people marry?
3 What are the roles in marriage?
4 Explain 'polygamy'.

Religious attitudes to sexual matters

Buddhism

+ Sex is about desire and craving (tanha) – both prevent enlightenment.
+ Buddhism has a strong tradition of **celibacy**. Sex is natural but rewarding as part of a loving relationship, so **chastity** is encouraged. Contraception is allowed to limit family size.
+ The Five Precepts say to avoid sexual immorality, including adultery.
+ **Sex before marriage** or homosexual sex is fine as part of a loving relationship between lay people.

Christianity

+ Generally only married couples should have sex, and only with each other. Many Christians tolerate sex before marriage in a relationship which is leading to marriage. Catholics believe every sexual act must be within the framework of marriage. Chastity is a virtue. Celibacy is practised in monastic life and the priesthood.
+ For some Christians, homosexual sex is considered unnatural (it is against scripture, with no chance of pregnancy). People can be gay but not have sex. Some Christians, such as Quakers in the UK, fully accept same-sex relationships.
+ Responsible parenthood is encouraged, so the use of contraception is accepted. Artificial contraception is against Catholic teaching because it cancels out the chance of pregnancy. Catholics are expected to follow natural methods of contraception as pregnancy should be possible within every act of sex.
+ The Bible says 'Do not commit adultery'; Jesus says that even a lustful look is wrong, so affairs are wrong and a sin.

Hinduism

+ Sex can happen only in the married householder stage. For the other three stages, the man should remain celibate. Sex before marriage is wrong. Hinduism teaches commitment, respect and faithfulness in all relationships. Sex is an essential aspect to building intimacy and wellbeing in the house-holder stage.
+ Chastity is important, with a person's only sexual partner being the person to whom they are married. Hindu virtues are self-discipline and respect – adultery goes against both of these.
+ Hindus encourage contraception. **Family planning** is stressed. Some Hindus believe that a son is required to carry out certain religious rituals. This may lead to less use of contraception to beget a son. Many festivals/holy days are celebrated by Hindus based on their own traditions and beliefs. On some of these days sexual abstinence is encouraged to help spiritual progress and to prevent sex distracting from their focus on God.

Islam

+ Marriage and having children is a religious duty.
+ Prophet Muhammad said sex was special within marriage – pleasurable, and providing the blessing of children, if the couple so wish. Muslims can and should use contraception as part of responsible parenthood.
+ Sex before or outside marriage is prohibited.

Judaism

+ The Torah says a woman is made to be human's companion, so men and women are expected to marry.
+ Sex within marriage is for pleasure and having children. Humans are to be fruitful and multiply. Celibacy within marriage is not recommended.
+ Orthodox Jewish people accept contraception – they often use the Pill because it does not cause the wasting of seed, which is forbidden in the Torah.
+ Over time Judaism has moved away from literal interpretations of the Torah so that even though the Torah might say something is wrong, it is now acceptable in at least some parts of more progressive Judaism (for instance, committed homosexual relationships).

Sikhism

+ Sex is a gift from God but only within marriage. Sex before marriage is wrong. Married life is seen as the norm. Chastity is highly valued before and within marriage as it shows self-control.
+ Although most Sikhs see homosexuality as wrong as it does not follow the example of the Gurus, some accept it as part of what God has created in a person.
+ Adultery is wrong – haumai.
+ Sikhs follow responsible parenthood so allow contraception.

Symbolism within religious marriage ceremonies

Buddhism

- Marriage is a cultural not religious act, but is seen as a social good. There are some common rituals. The vows – to love each other, be kind and considerate, be faithful – set the tone for the relationship. In traditional Eastern Buddhist countries, the wife must perform household duties, be hospitable, protect and invest earnings and the husband must delegate domestic duties and provide gifts to please his wife. In the West, relations between married couples are very different. The fact that Buddhism does not have a standard set of rules for marriage makes this contrast possible.

Christianity

- Marriage is a gift from God and a symbol of Christ's relationship with the Church.
- The vows symbolise the nature of the marriage – full of love and respect, good times and bad times, faithful to each other and life-long.
- The rings symbolise the everlasting nature of the marriage – that love, like God, is eternal and only death can end this contract.

Hinduism

- Marriage is sacred and is considered one of the spiritual stages in life as it is a commitment of two souls to live together and produce children.
- The essence of the Hindu marriage ceremony is that the parents give away their daughter to the man, the man and his family accept the woman as their daughter and the couple take a vow in the presence of people, the sacred fire (Agni), and God.
- The most important part of the ceremony is walking around the sacred fire (Agni) and the seven steps. Each step has an important message for the couple to sustain a stable marriage. For example, the first step is that 'we will nourish each other'.
- Blessings are given to the newly married couple by the parents, the elders, and all those who have come to witness the marriage.

Islam

- Marriage is the joining not just of two individuals but of two families. A successful marriage is the basis of a successful society as the couple treat each other with respect, kindness and love and children will learn this behaviour as normal.
- The dowry shows the respect the groom has for the bride.
- The signing of the contract shows the couple are now together freely and they must be faithful to each other. Marriage is the acceptable place for sex and, in time, children.
- A marriage contract (nikah) is signed which outlines what each person expects of the marriage and what their rights will be.

Judaism

- The veiled bride circles her husband to be a number of times, reflecting the idea that a wife encompasses and protects her husband (Jeremiah 31:21).
- Seven blessings are said over wine, to represent the seven days of creation, and the start of the building of a marriage.
- Rings are exchanged – they are undecorated and unbroken to symbolise the hope of a harmonious marriage.
- The groom crushes a glass under his foot to remember the destruction of the temple in Jerusalem.

Sikhism

- The wedding ceremony is called Anand Karaj or 'ceremony of happiness'. The couple achieve this by becoming 'one spirit in two bodies'.
- Lavan means 'joining together'. This is a hymn with four verses which are read by the granthi. The bride and groom circle the Guru Granth Sahib for each verse and bow to show they have accepted the advice. This is the internal symbol of the two now being together.

Revision tip

While it is unlikely that you will be asked to describe an actual marriage ceremony, knowing the symbolism might help with questions on the roles within a marriage and how to make a marriage successful.

Families and parenting

A nuclear family is a family unit consisting of parents, traditionally mother and father, and children. It is considered the typical family unit in the Western world.

An extended family is the nuclear family plus other relatives, usually including grandparents, who may all live together. This is a common structure in many areas of the world, such as Africa, the Far East, the Middle East and South America. It is also common in many poorer parts of the world and in the Muslim and Hindu traditions.

A single-parent family is a family of one parent and child(ren). A blended family is a family where one or both parents have children from previous relationships.

One of the main reasons for marriage is to have children, and a key role is good parenting. Having children shows commitment and love, fulfils a relationship and is a religious duty. It may well be unplanned or a way to keep the marriage together.

Couples in a same-sex relationship often want to have children. These are usually conceived through artificial means (no sex involved) and cannot have the DNA of both members of the couple, so involve adoption by at least one partner. Methods such as IVF (for lesbian couples) and surrogacy (for homosexual couples) are common. Many religious believers think that children need a male and a female role model as parents. They also think children should be a product of the sexual act, that is, naturally conceived. Hence these religious believers do not agree that same-sex couples should be parents. Others, however, point to the love and care given to the child – who is clearly wanted – saying this is proof that same-sex parenting is acceptable.

Marriage is seen as the correct environment to have children for all couples. The children bring a new purpose and new responsibilities to the relationship. Parents need to provide stability, a consistency in behaviour and life, so that the children feel safe and protected. Part of caring is to educate, enabling children to become successful individuals.

Children should show respect to their parents for their love and commitment.

Educating children in a faith

Educating children is a key purpose of religious families. Religious parents often believe that introducing their children to the faith gives them the best start in life. They believe a religious upbringing will help their children be happy and ready to do well in life. Many have initiation ceremonies to 'officially welcome' the children into that religious group. Growing up, children are taught the beliefs and how to worship.

Religion provides a structure and behaviour code, helping children's development. It provides them with access to supportive people and to involve themselves in activities.

Some say it is wrong to 'force' religion on people, but religious people do not see it that way. Having an identity, being part of something – the benefits far outweigh the negatives. They do accept that some children may reject the faith when they grow up, but many return later in life, too.

Many same-sex couples have the same ideas about bringing up their children in the faith. They also believe it provides the best environment for their child to develop.

> ### Exam tip
>
> The GCSE talks about the **nature and purpose** of marriage and of families. You could be asked about either in the exam. The *nature of marriage* is referring to the roles men and women have, and the value a religion puts on marriage (a duty, a sacred covenant, etc.). The *purpose of marriage* refers to why religious believers marry (duty, procreation, etc.). The *nature of families* refers to what the family is like (nuclear, extended, etc.). The *purpose of families* refers to why religious believers have families (accepting God's gift of a child, to continue the faith, etc.). Make sure you understand the terms, so that you can answer the questions!

> ### Revision tip
>
> This is a good area for discussion. Hence the topic lends itself to not only evaluation (12 marks) questions but also similarities (4 marks) questions. You could be given a statement such as *When couples have children they should always bring them up in their faith* (12 marks) or *Explain two similar religious beliefs about parenting* (4 marks). Could you answer these now from the information on this page, and what you learned in class?

Divorce

Why is there a need for divorce?

Marriage is 'til death us do part' so there will inevitably be difficulties because there are many pressures in life. Some serious issues might be illness, jobs, addictions, affairs and abuse, which are very difficult to overcome, so divorce might be seen as the only solution.

The debate is whether divorce should be allowed or not and if allowed, how easy it should be to get one. Many religious people believe vows are absolute, so divorce is always wrong. Others would agree that it is wrong, though at times necessary, but it should not be an easy option. All marriages should be worked at – marriage is a serious commitment and difficulties should be worked through.

In 1969 the Church of England in the UK was key in getting the divorce laws relaxed because the Church believed that a couple living in a loveless marriage or separated were not being given the chance to move on with their lives. Also, Jesus taught compassion, forgiveness, understanding and second chances – divorce is compatible with that.

What support is available?

Couples will find support from their families, religion, friends, charities, support groups and marriage counselling services. Differences can be overcome if people are prepared to listen, change or alter ways of doing things. Divorce should be the last resort.

Religion would also encourage prayer – asking for God's help.

That divorce rates are high in the UK suggests that people are rushing into marriage or not taking their vows seriously, or that the couple give up too easily – and divorces are too easily obtained.

It must be remembered that some people have no choice – for their own and their children's safety, welfare and life chances. Very few people would disagree with divorce in such cases.

Remarriage

Remarriage can be to a different or the same partner after divorce. Failure of one marriage does not mean another cannot be successful.

What does religion think of remarriage? This really depends upon what the religion's view of divorce is. If the religion disagrees with divorce, then it will disagree with remarriage because it believes the first marriage still exists. Some religions say divorce is not recognised by God so neither is remarriage.

Some might say they see that new happiness has been found but although it is good that people want to remarry, they cannot accept that vows made before God can simply be set aside.

Others would allow a remarriage, just not a religious one. They would support a civil marriage while perhaps offering a blessing to that couple.

Annulment: the Roman Catholic way of ending a marriage – the marriage is set aside as if it were never real. However, a legal divorce must still happen to officially end it as far as the law is concerned.

Divorce: the legal ending of a marriage.

Extended family: the nuclear family plus other relatives, such as grandparents living with the family, but can also include cousins, uncles and aunts.

Nuclear family: basically mum and dad, plus the child(ren).

Remarriage: a person's second (or more) marriage, after a divorce.

Second marriage: this can happen after the death of a partner so the one left marries again.

Now test yourself

1 What is divorce?
2 Give two reasons a couple might divorce.
3 What do religions think about divorce?
4 What do religions think about remarriage?

Religious attitudes to divorce

Buddhism

Vows are a serious commitment which should not be broken easily. Since marriage is seen as keeping society stable, divorce is discouraged. Sometimes divorce has to be seen as the right option as two people causing themselves and others great suffering by staying together breaks the Precepts, creates bad karma and goes against Buddhist principles of compassion and ahimsa.

✚ Keep the Five Precepts.
✚ Be compassionate.
✚ Thoughts, deeds and actions should always be positive because they have a karmic value which shapes our next lifetime(s).

Christianity

For Roman Catholics, divorce is always wrong. Marriage is a sacrament, which cannot be broken. Promises are made to God and each other to stay together 'until death do us part', and these promises are binding.

For most other Christians, divorce is discouraged but accepted as a last resort. It is sometimes the lesser of two evils and also a necessary evil.

✚ God hates divorce (Old Testament).
✚ Whoever divorces … then marries another; it is as if he committed adultery (Jesus).
✚ Forgiveness and love (Jesus).

Hinduism

Hindu teachings do not advocate divorce and until recently divorce was a taboo subject and very rare. Divorce does happen though, and is slowly becoming more accepted as a necessary evil. There is great stigma over divorce and in many societies it is especially difficult for people who have been divorced to remarry, even though this is allowed. If a husband leaves his wife, he is still expected to provide for her.

✚ 'I promise never to abandon her, whatever happens' (wedding vow).
✚ Marriage is one of the spiritual stages in life, therefore it is not desirable to divorce.
✚ Divorce is granted for specific reasons.

Islam

Divorce is a last resort – families are expected to mediate, there is a three-month waiting period, and any outstanding dowry must be paid.

✚ Of all legal things, the one Allah most hates is divorce (Qur'an).
✚ Marry and do not divorce (Hadith).
✚ If you fear a breach between a man and his wife, appoint two arbiters (Qur'an).

Judaism

Marriage is a sacred commitment and union. Although divorce is allowed, it is as a last resort. Time should be allowed for reconciliation to take place.

✚ G-d hates the fact that divorce has to happen (Nevi'im).
✚ When a man puts aside the wife of his youth, even the very altar weeps (Talmud).
✚ A court can grant a woman divorce, if she can show that she can no longer live with him (Maimonides).

Sikhism

Divorce is not the Sikh way, but it is accepted by the faith. Marriage should be a lifetime commitment and a couple should work at it, especially when times are difficult. Families help to mediate for reconciliation.

✚ Marriage is a sacrament.
✚ Marriage is the union of two souls and a life-long commitment.
✚ If the husband and wife are in dispute, their concern for their children should reunite them (Guru Granth Sahib).

Revision tip

Remember not only to use (state) the teachings but also give their source and to apply (explain and relate) them to the question.

Revision tip

Try this formula/sentence structure to help:

In the ……… (holy book) it says ……… (give the teaching) which means ……… (explain the teaching). Therefore ……… (name of the believers, e.g. Christians) would believe ……… (topic of the question) is ……… (acceptable/wrong).

Gender equality and prejudice

Prejudice is the pre-judgement of others based on a characteristic they have, rather than on what they are really like.

In some societies women are not the decision-makers, making them less powerful and seen as less important. This is gender prejudice. It can lead to different treatment (discrimination), so that women are given fewer opportunities – for example, not getting the same promotions at work.

It may be that a culture sets stricter rules for women than for men – for example, where women are not allowed to leave the house, or must be chaperoned, or where girls are not allowed education beyond a certain age. It may be that women do not contribute to decision-making, so a female perspective is never considered. Prejudice within power structures can mean that when women are treated negatively, there is no consequence for the perpetrator, and this further encourages that negative behaviour. Gender discrimination spans from misogynistic comments to murder – it definitely has an impact.

Ultimately gender prejudice makes women (feel) powerless, affecting their confidence and self-esteem. It keeps women less powerful, making society work for men rather than for everyone. The UK has laws to prevent gender discrimination, and employment law looks at equal pay issues between the sexes.

As most religions are very old, it is ingrained for leadership to be assumed by men. In many cases, leadership has been seen as scripturally correct. Some say this has led to inequality between genders within religion, with men having more important and decisive roles, and women reduced to supporting roles. In more progressive forms of most religions, changes in society's approach to status are reflected, but an Orthodox form of a faith, for example, will not have women as religious leaders.

> **Gender discrimination:** acting on prejudices against someone because of their gender.
>
> **Gender equality:** the belief that men and women have equal standing; values, processes and practices are set up to demonstrate this belief.
>
> **Gender prejudice:** pre-judging someone because of their gender; this normally works to negatively affect women.

Theme A: Relationships and families

Activity

Support or challenge?

'Religion treats men and women as equals.' Evaluate this statement. Refer to religious and non-religious arguments. You should agree and disagree with the statement, and come to a justified conclusion. (12 marks)

Use the list of arguments below to help you write a strong answer to this question. They are mixed up though, so first you need to work out which ones agree (support) and which ones disagree (challenge) with the statement. Remember that a conclusion should not just be repeating what you have already written. Read the next page to find some religious arguments. Your conclusion must say which point of view is stronger, and why.

Argument	Supports statement in question	Challenges statement in question
Women aren't allowed to be religious leaders.		
Women are equal but with different roles.		
God created everyone, so all must be equal.		
Women stay at home and have children and look after them; men interact with the world, so have more power.		
Both men and women are needed to keep the religion going.		
Women are considered unclean during menstruation, men are never in that situation so are never unclean.		

Religious attitudes to gender equality

 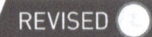

Theme A: Relationships and families

Buddhism

✚ If a man denies the possibility of enlightenment of women, then his own enlightenment is impossible (Lotus Sutra).
✚ The practice of Buddhism in some traditions (such as Mahayana Buddhism) is the same for men and women, showing no inequality of demands on either.

Christianity

✚ There is neither Jew nor Gentile, neither slave nor free, nor is there male and female, for you are all one in Christ Jesus (Galatians).
✚ So God created humankind in his own image, in the image of God he created them; male and female he created them (Genesis 1:27).

Activity

Read the teachings for your religion. Write a short paragraph to state the attitude of your religion(s) to gender equality.

Hinduism

✚ Good treatment of women is seen as a blessing (Laws of Manu).
✚ Where women are honoured, there the gods are pleased (Laws of Manu).

Islam

✚ Men and women have the same spiritual nature, according to the Qur'an.
✚ Prophet Muhammad said, 'I command you to be kind to women.'

Judaism

✚ In Progressive Judaism, women can be rabbis.
✚ The equality of men and women begins at the highest possible level, as G-d has no gender. Both men and women were created equally and in G-d's image (Genesis).

Sikhism

✚ Man is born from a woman … woman is born from woman; without woman, there would be no one at all (Guru Granth Sahib).
✚ Waheguru (God) is neither male or female (Guru Granth Sahib).

Attitudes to the role of men and women

There is a religious debate about the role of women. They are treated differently, yet all religions condemn any kind of discrimination.

✚ In Christianity, women cannot be priests in the Catholic Church.
✚ In Islam, almost all Imams are men.
✚ In Orthodox Judaism, women sit separately and do not take part in synagogue services.
✚ In Hinduism there are still more male priests than female, though Hindu scriptures do not stop women from becoming priests.
✚ Some Buddhist women pray that their reincarnation will be as a man.
✚ In Sikhism, while either gender may read the Guru Granth Sahib at services, it is unusual to see women fulfilling this role.

Religion would argue that as long as women are happy with their roles then it is not discriminatory. Issues arise when women are unable to take on certain roles because they are women.

Activity

Fix it!

Read this answer and suggest ways to improve it.

Explain two different ways in which religions view gender equality. (4 marks)

Religions believe in gender equality because they say men and women are different but equal. Also they don't because Christians don't let women be priests so they can't lead church services.

Now test yourself

1 What is gender prejudice?
2 How do religions treat men and women differently?
3 What is meant by 'different but equal'?

Find Now Test Yourself and Exam Practice answers at **https://www.hoddereducation.co.uk/myrevisionnotesdownloads**

Exam practice

What questions on this section look like:

Theme A: Relationships and families

This page contains a range of questions that could be on an exam paper. Practise them all to strengthen your knowledge and technique while revising. Check back to pages 11-12 to see the marking grids that examiners use: this will help you to mark your answers.

1 Which of the following means to be 'sexually pure'?

   (a) Adultery   **(b)** Celibacy   **(c)** Chastity   **(d)** Contraception   [1]

2 Which of the following terms means to live together as if married?

   (a) Civil marriage   **(b)** Civil partnership   **(c)** Cohabitation   **(d)** Polygamy   [1]

3 Give one reason why religious believers use family planning.   [1]

4 Give one role of a parent in a religious family.   [1]

5 Name one type of family.   [1]

6 Explain two different religious beliefs about homosexual relationships in contemporary British society. In your answer you must refer to the main religious tradition of Great Britain and one or more other religious traditions.   [4]

7 Explain two similar religious beliefs about heterosexuality. In your answer you must refer to one or more religious traditions.   [4]

8 Explain two different religious beliefs about the nature of families. In your answer you must refer to one or more religious traditions.   [4]

9 Explain two religious beliefs about the purpose of families. Refer to sacred writings or another source of religious belief and teachings in your answer.   [6]

10 Explain two religious beliefs about the nature of marriage. Refer to sacred writings or another source of religious belief and teachings in your answer.   [6]

11 Explain two religious beliefs about the sanctity of marriage vows. Refer to sacred writings or another source of religious belief and teachings in your answer.   [6]

12 'Marriage vows should never be broken.' Evaluate this statement. In your answer you should:
- give reasoned arguments in support of this statement
- give reasoned arguments to support a different point of view
- refer to religious arguments
- refer to non-religious arguments
- refer to a justified conclusion.   [12]

13 'Extended families are the best kind of family.' Evaluate this statement. In your answer you should:
- give reasoned arguments in support of this statement
- give reasoned arguments to support a different point of view
- refer to religious arguments
- refer to non-religious arguments
- refer to a justified conclusion.   [12]

14 'Women as well as men should be able to be leaders in their religion.' Evaluate this statement. In your answer you should:
- give reasoned arguments in support of this statement
- give reasoned arguments to support a different point of view
- refer to religious arguments
- refer to non-religious arguments
- refer to a justified conclusion.   [12]

Exam tip

Level 2 students use simple language and simple sentence structures. They generally make mistakes in spellings. If this is you, try using more connectives, and take more care with spellings.

Level 5 students use a mix of simple and complex sentencing. Their use of connectives can be limited (and repetitive). If this is you, become more consistent in writing better sentences and find a range of connectives so that you aren't always using the same (boring!) three.

Level 8 students use complex language and sentencing – they sound very impressive!

Theme B: Religion and life

Scientific truth	Religious truth
Comes from a hypothesis and then repeated testing to confirm a theory	Comes from religions and holy books – from God and personal experiences
It describes the world and how it works	Religion explains why we are here, who is God, what happens at death
It answers the what and how questions – function and process	It answers the why, purpose and meaning questions
It is always developing its truths – as it finds more evidence – so is not absolute but conditional on the testing conditions	It is open to interpretation, but the words stay the same and remain relevant at all times

Origins of the universe

REVISED

Science and religion disagree about how the universe began, but are they actually compatible or conflicting kinds of truth?

The Big Bang Theory says that the universe began 13.7 billion years ago. All the matter in the universe was concentrated at one point and began to expand very rapidly with a big explosion, eventually creating the universe as we know it today. The earliest signs of life appeared millions of years before the land and sea settled. The Earth was hot, covered in primordial soup – a mix of liquids, chemicals, minerals, proteins and amino acids. These fused to give the first life forms and from these all life developed, including humans.

Big Bang Theory: scientific theory about the origins of the universe

Scientific evidence supports this theory. Scientists know the universe is expanding, and they can track the expansion back to a singular point. Background microwave radiation from the explosion can still be detected in space.

However, questions are still asked about how nothing can actually explode. How can a totally ordered and structured world come from an explosion? Don't explosions cause chaos?

Evolution

REVISED

The work of Charles Darwin

Charles Darwin was a natural scientist who through years of research wrote *The Origin of Species*. He suggested the world was a place of change and that the huge variety of creatures is the result of millions of years of adaptation (evolution).

Environment: the world around us.

Evolution: scientific theory which states that life today has evolved from simple forms through a process of natural selection and the survival of the fittest

There is a struggle for survival between creatures through climates, resources and habitat and where species failed to adapt they became extinct. Only the fittest (best suited) survived, which Darwin called natural selection.

Places change creatures because of the environment they are forced to live in, so over millions of years species have evolved.

Environments are different across the world, and creatures live in appropriate places – polar bears reside in the Arctic, not in Africa! As environments change, if creatures don't adapt they die, leading to extinction of species. Adaptation is the key. This theory suggests that it is wrong to think that creatures were designed to look as they do today. A God of creation does not fit with this theory.

However, even Darwin asks: where does all the intelligence in life come from, its complexity or its interdependence? We see design via intelligence and adaptability. Without the guidance of a designer, surely the world would be chaos? Darwin's theory actually makes God an even greater figure of awe and wonder. Perhaps science is just part of God's creation.

> **Awe and wonder**: a feeling of reverence, fear and wonder caused by something majestic or divine, for example the created world.

Now test yourself

TESTED ◯

1 What is science? What is religion?
2 Briefly explain the Big Bang Theory.
3 Briefly explain evolution as a theory.

Activity

Support or challenge?

'It is impossible to believe in both science and religion regarding the origins of the universe.' Evaluate this statement. Refer to religious and non-religious arguments. You should agree and disagree with the statement, and come to a justified conclusion.

(12 marks)

Use the list of arguments below to help you write a strong answer to this question. They are mixed up though, so first you need to work out which ones agree (support) and which ones disagree (challenge) with the statement. Remember that a conclusion should not just be repeating what you have already written, so it is worth keeping back a good argument to use there. You may have to read the next page to find some religious arguments to help with this. Your conclusion must say which point of view is stronger, and why.

Argument	Supports statement in question	Challenges statement in question
No proof of religious stories.		
Religious stories don't make sense to a reasonable person.		
Science can't tell us why it all began.		
Science deals in theories not facts when it comes to the origins of the universe.		
Scientific ideas like the Big Bang seem illogical – how can something come from 'nothing'?		
Religious ideas are what people said before science.		

Genesis

Genesis is the first Book of the Hebrew Bible. The Genesis creation story is believed by Jewish people, Muslims and Christians.

In the beginning there was nothing. Then over seven days God created light and dark, the heavens, land, sea and vegetation, sun, moon and stars, birds and fish, land animals and humans. On the seventh day God rested – it was a 'good' creation.

How is this story understood?

Some people believe it is literally true. God is all-powerful so it is easy to believe that God did all this in literally seven days.

Others believe that it is true but not literally. It is a simplified version of what happened, for example a 'day' is a 'God-day' – so a long period of time. It uses the knowledge and language of the time.

Yet others would say it's about the message – God as the creator deliberately made the world; it was not an accident or chaos. Humans, made in God's image, have a purpose to live, given by God.

Can we believe in science or religion or both?

Some believers would say we only need religion. Genesis is accurate, God created the world in seven days as he can do anything. Humans don't need to understand, they just need to believe. Accepting the scientific view is impossible with this interpretation of Genesis.

Some accept totally the scientific view of the origins of the universe and so see the religious view as nonsense.

Some people believe that God's involvement is what started the Big Bang. So here science and religion go together to explain how it all began.

Some believe that Genesis is simply there to provide a message – that humans have a purpose. So the story is explaining why humans are here whereas science is explaining how we came to be here. Thus together science and religion give humans a more complete answer.

Is science more important than religion then?

Here we must go back to look at the nature of the truths. Depending on the situation, sometimes one is more important than the other. Sometimes we need hypotheses and testing, they help to make sense of how things work and repeated testing shows that things work. It is not enough to simply believe that medicines work, they need to be tested. At the same time religious truths give life meaning and purpose, a sense of well-being, as well as hope of something else after life here. Science and religion simply answer different questions.

There is no absolute proof as to the origins of the universe. Science does challenge religion here, but they both contribute something to our understanding.

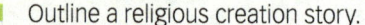

Now test yourself TESTED

1 Outline a religious creation story.
2 What are the three religious interpretations of this?
3 Are science and religion compatible on the origins of the universe?

The value of the world

The world is important, for humans both now and in the future.

Religious people believe they have a duty to look after it (stewardship) and treat it with respect. Life is sacred to all religious believers.

Humans have dominion (power) over nature by permission of God. The world's beauty fills people with awe, making many think of God and so worship him.

Environmental damage

Pollution: damage and solutions

Pollution causes damage to the air, sea (water) and land. In fact, anything can be polluted – there is both light pollution and noise pollution, for example.

Factories and transport cause the most air pollution – CO_2 in the atmosphere is one of the causes of global warming, leading to climate change and extreme weather. Rain picks up the chemicals and falls as acid rain, polluting land, water, crops and buildings. Factories empty waste into rivers and farming chemicals drain from the land into the water sources, killing fish and wildlife.

Pollution is the main reason for global warming – it causes the greenhouse effect as greenhouse gases heat the earth.

Poor air quality causes health problems. Contaminated food and water sources mean animals/fish die. Ecosystems change, becoming unbalanced.

Solutions? We can cut CO_2 levels with government control over factories, reduce the use of fossil fuels and replace with cleaner energy, alter travel habits and be aware of our 'carbon footprints'.

Dominion: the idea that humans have the right to control all of creation.

Global warming: the heating up of the world's atmosphere, causing climate change.

Pollution: the presence/ introduction of something that is toxic to the environment.

Stewardship: duty to look after the world, and life.

Global warming

Global warming causes climate change as the earth becomes hotter. Extreme weather patterns – too hot, too wet, too dry – all lead to floods, droughts, ice caps melting, more deserts and a reduction in rainforests.

The earth heats up and cools off naturally, but scientists say that human activities over the last 100 years have speeded up temperature change. The change alters ecosystems so plants and animals have to adapt or die out.

Solutions? Scientists say we need to change our energy use. Alternative, cleaner energies have to be found. Coal, oil and gas need to be used less and energies such as wind, solar, water and nuclear need to be used more. These are sustainable (they do not run out) and cleaner (so cause less harm) but are expensive. Humans have to be able to meet their needs – heating, lighting, industry and transport – while not damaging the environment (as is currently the case).

World leaders are attempting to address these problems via (inter)national agreements (e.g. Earth Summits) to reduce CO_2 levels. More individuals are becoming aware of the damage their actions cause, so are trying to help fix it.

Revision tip

Make sure you know:
+ definitions of all the topics in this chapter – they make good 1-mark questions
+ for 1/4/6-mark questions, two causes (reasons) and two effects (consequences) for all the environmental topics
+ for 1/4/6-mark questions, two solutions for each problem
+ for 4/6-mark questions, two teachings which relate to looking after the environment, and their source of authority.

Now test yourself

 TESTED

1 Why should religious believers treat the world with respect?
2 What is pollution?
3 What is global warming?

77

Destruction of natural habitats

REVISED

This refers to activities that damage forest and areas of nature beyond repair so that creatures' living space is lost. Pollution is a key cause of this, with acid rain destroying the canopy in rainforest areas, oil spills contaminating the seas and coastline areas, and deforestation (cutting down of huge areas of forest) taking land for grazing, house building, mining and roads, and planting of cash crops like palm oil plantations.

Rainforests are millions of years old and cannot just be regrown; as trees take in CO_2 and produce O_2 we lose the help they give to fighting global warming. Many rainforest plants have medicinal qualities, which we might lose for ever.

Humans seem to believe their needs more important than nature's, hence cutting the forests. Many countries regard building houses and farming land as development to provide for their people.

Solutions? We must protect these areas and provide those countries, which are often poor, with other alternatives to cutting down these areas. Timber is a major money earner, but alternative ways of earning money need to be found.

Use and abuse of natural resources

REVISED

Natural resources include vegetation, minerals and fossil fuels, which have taken millions of years to form. However, humans are overusing them and they are running out because they are limited in quantity and non-renewable. When a coal or oil field is empty, for example, that's it ... gone!

Solution? Humans need to find renewable energies to fuel the world and our lifestyles.

> **Natural resources:** the resources the Earth provides without the aid of humankind.

Caring for the world

REVISED

Sustainable development is the idea that technological advances should be long-lasting and within reach of all nations.

Conservation, meanwhile, is the act of protecting an area or species. Areas of nature need to be returned to their original state of natural beauty, before they suffered the damage inflicted by humans. This could be done by repairing an area through planting trees, creating nature reserves, etc.

Conservation includes breeding of animals, establishing protected areas, even people using their holidays to work for environmental projects.

What can you do to help reduce these environmental problems?

There are many things people can do to help reduce these problems:
+ Make small changes to life patterns.
+ Adopt animals in reserves where their habitats are protected.
+ Recycle.
+ Join an environmental organisation – Greenpeace, for example.
+ Pray for people to work together.

Many religious people believe this is God's world and as its stewards are motivated to care for the earth.

> **Activity**
>
> **Fix it!**
> Read the answer to this question. Work out how it can be improved. Then rewrite it to achieve better marks.
>
> *Religious people have a greater responsibility to look after the world than non-religious people.* (12 marks)
>
> I don't agree with that. Everybody lives in the world, so everybody has a duty to look after it. We all mess it up as well, so we all have a reason to fix it and be stewards.

Animal rights

Animal rights are the rights animals have to live without cruelty and to have good treatment. This means we cannot just do what we want with/to them. They have the right to be treated properly, fairly and with kindness, even when we intend to kill them.

Laws in the UK protect domestic animals (pets) and endangered species by enforcing their care – food, water, shelter and no cruelty.

Animals have many uses:
+ as pets – cats, dogs, birds, mice, hamsters, rats, guinea pigs
+ as helpers – beasts of burden to move heavy loads or do heavy work, for example cattle, horses
+ as work animals – guide, police, customs and hunting dogs, hunting birds
+ as providers – sheep (wool), cows (milk), hens (eggs), bees (honey)
+ as food – lamb, cows, hens, deer, pigs, fish
+ as experimental test subjects – mice, rats, monkeys, dogs
+ as sport – bull-fighting, shooting and hunting.

Hence there are plenty of opportunities to both look after animals and, unfortunately, abuse them.

Animal experimentation

Some animals are bred deliberately for life as an experiment subject. Most experiments test for toxicity, of medicines and medical techniques. Animals are also tested on to improve surgical skills for operations.

There is a big debate over the use of animals for experiments, focusing mainly on the two issues of experimenting for medical products like vaccines and testing for cosmetic products.

Religious people would support medical experiments as they are done for the benefit of human beings, which indicates that there is the belief that humans are more important than animals.

The key issues about these experiments are:
+ Animals can and often do suffer greatly in experiments and any animal used in an experiment is then humanely destroyed, even if the experiment was successful.
+ Many experiments seem unnecessary, for example to test yet another version of a product which has already been tested in the USA.
+ These animals cannot live natural lives in any way.

Scientists have developed other means of testing, without using animals, but they are very expensive.

Use of animals for food

Some religions have rules about the food they can or cannot eat; some simply have guidelines. Most food rules are about the eating of meat.

Many people are vegetarians because they have medical problems, or they do not like the taste, or they disagree with farming or slaughter methods, or they think it is morally wrong to eat meat.

Buddhism

✚ Many Western Buddhists are vegetarian out of respect for all life – animals are also part of the cycle of rebirth. Keeping the First Precept of not taking life would encourage vegetarianism.

Christianity

✚ Many Christians eat no red meat on Fridays; many eat no meat at all during the period of Lent – in both cases out of respect for the sacrifice of Jesus on Good Friday.

Hinduism

✚ Most Hindus are vegetarian out of respect for life and ahimsa (non-violence). The Yajur Veda forbids the killing of animals.

Islam

✚ No pork is to be eaten (the pig is an unclean animal), only meat from an animal which has been ritually slaughtered (halal) so Allah has been thanked and the meat is blessed.

Judaism

✚ Many Jewish people follow the strict rules around food given in the mitzvot, such as not eating meat and milk together, and only eating meat from certain animals that have been ritually slaughtered.

Sikhism

✚ No meat from an animal which has been ritually slaughtered (this is considered cruel treatment); many are vegetarian out of respect for God's creation.

Activity

Match the concepts below to their correct definitions.

Concept	Definition
Pollution	Eating meat and meat products.
Global warming	Human use of what nature produces.
Destruction of natural habitats	To put too much of something into the environment, which spoils/poisons it.
Use and abuse of natural resources	When humans destroy natural areas, so destroying habitats.
Animal experimentation	The heating up of the environment, causing climate change.
Use of animals for food	Experiments carried out for the purpose of toxicity and medicines.

Activity

Fix It!

Read this answer, and work out how it could be improved.

Explain two similar religious beliefs about eating meat. Refer to one or more religious traditions in your answer. (4 marks)

Christians believe that it is fine to eat meat - there are no rules against it. Some Christians don't eat meat on Fridays.

However, Hindus do not eat meat, because of ahimsa (non-violence), and certainly not beef as the cow is a sacred animal.

Activity

Good technique makes your answers sound really good – and makes them easy for the examiner to mark. Have a look at this question and the answer, which is annotated to show you the good technique.

Explain two religious beliefs about the status of animals. Refer to sacred writings or another source of religious authority in your answer. (6 marks)

The Bhagavad Gita says, 'On a Brahmin, cow, elephant, dog – wise men look with an equal eye.'[1] This means that for Hindus all living beings are equal and should be treated with respect.[2] The Brahmin is the most respected in a community, so maybe most important; the dogs are often strays and not looked after, so maybe the least important.[3] However, this teaching says animals and humans are equal.[4]

In the Guru Granth Sahib, it says 'God's light is in every creature'.[5] Sikhs believe all life is sacred because of this. Many Sikhs do not eat any meat at all, and being vegetarian is a rule for Khalsa Sikhs.[6] From this we know the status of animals is high in Sikhism.[7]

[1]Straight away a quote with its source is written to meet the demand in the question. This is a good quote because it is directly relevant to the answer – no need for extended explanations to make it fit, or for the examiner to have to work it out. The mark scheme automatically awards a mark for the source.

[2]The quote is clearly explained, but in a concise way.

[3]The explanation is developed to show how the quote differs from what you would expect.

[4]The last sentence gives the overall point about status (as per the question).

[5]There is a new paragraph to signpost for the examiner you are making a new point. Straight into the next quote.

[6]The quote is explained in a way to answer the question.

[7]The explanation develops the idea, but to make sure the examiner can see it is relevant to the question, a final statement about status is given.

Now read the answer to the question below. What has the student done well in their answer? Use those clues on good technique to help you annotate/highlight it for technique.

Explain two religious beliefs about the use of animals for food. Refer to sacred writings or another source of religious belief and teachings in your answer. (6 marks)

In the Yajur Veda, it is forbidden for Hindus to kill animals. This is because all animals have a soul (atman) just as all life forms have. They are on the start of their journey to enlightenment and should not be killed. By eating meat, they might not be killing the animal themselves, but they are encouraging an industry where animals are killed. They believe this would bring bad karma to them.

A second belief is that violence of any kind is wrong. Hindus are taught to believe in and practise ahimsa (non-violence). It is obvious that violence has to be used to kill an animal for its meat – even when done humanely, it is still a form of violence. Hence, Hindus do not eat meat out of respect for the principle of ahimsa, which in turn brings them good karma.

Now it is your turn to use the same techniques and write your own high-level answer to this question:

Explain two religious beliefs about pollution. Refer to sacred writings or another source of religious beliefs and teachings in your answer. (6 marks)

Revision tip

Two clear paragraphs make it easy for the examiner to spot that you have done exactly what the mark scheme asks for. Reference to scripture in the first sentence is good. There is good explanation of the point – it is clearly understandable.

Religious attitudes to the environment and animals

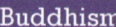

Buddhism

+ All life should be respected. As we will use the earth during many lifetimes, we protect it for ourselves as well as for our children. Ignorance and greed (two of the Three Poisons) lead to most of the pollution being caused – for example, companies building factories in developing countries so they can pay the workers less, have fewer pollution levels to keep to, all leading to bigger profits.
+ The First Precept teaches humans to support the life of all sentient beings.
+ Right Livelihood implies that Buddhists should not work in a job that exploits animals.
+ All living things fear being put to death – let no one kill or cause others to kill (Dhammapada).

Christianity

+ God gave humans the world, entrusting them with this great gift. Humans have the **responsibility** to look after it as stewards. We also have a responsibility to each other, particularly those in need or living in poverty, and our future children to make sure the world is still intact for many generations to come.
+ Animals are part of creation and deserve respect and protection (Assisi).
+ Scientists must abandon laboratories and factories of death (Pope John Paul II).

Hinduism

+ Brahman is in all life. The ideas of sanctity of life and non-violence are built into the religion. All life is interdependent – plants and animals depend on the environment so everyone needs to protect it. Souls will be reborn so we need to live on earth again and if God is in all nature then we show an act of worship by looking after it.
+ Avoid harming all forms of life (ahimsa).
+ Hindu worship includes respect for all and many deities are linked to specific animals.
+ Avoiding harm to animals will make humans ready for eternal life (Laws of Manu).

Islam

+ The world is the work of Allah – humans are khalifahs, trustees of his world. Allah knows who damages his creation and punishment will follow on Judgement Day. The idea of the ummah means we have a duty to pass on the world undamaged to the next generations.
+ Nature is inferior to humans and can be used to improve people's well-being.
+ Showing kindness to an animal is an act rewarded by Allah (Sunnah).
+ Prophet Muhammad (pbuh) insisted animals were well treated.

Judaism

+ G-d gave humans the duty of stewardship. We should respect it. Tikkun olam (repairing the world) is interpreted as tackling environmental issues; tzedek (justice) means justice for the world itself. To 'love your neighbour' you have to not wreck the world.
+ G-d made the world and all in it (Genesis).
+ A righteous man looks after his animals (Proverbs).
+ Do not be cruel to animals (Noachide Laws).

Sikhism

+ The world is a gift from God, existing because God wants it to. Sikhs perform sewa for others so safeguarding the world is essential. The Gurus said God is within everything – so damage the world, damage God.
+ God's light is in every creature (Guru Granth Sahib).
+ Many Sikhs are vegetarian out of respect for God's creation – the langar, for example.
+ Guru Gobind Singh hunted so it is not forbidden.

Revision tip

Remember you need to learn only two of each from the religion/s you have studied. Easy! Just don't forget to be able to mention the source.

The value of human life

Religions would say that human life is the most valuable and special of all life forms.

Religious believers think humans are the highest form of creation and within the highest levels of spiritual development. This means that the value of human life is beyond measure, so it needs protection and care. Most religious believers are 'pro-life' in issues relating to life and death.

The sanctity of life

This is the belief that all life is special as it was created by God, so it needs to be protected.

Everyone believes life is special in one way or another. Christians, Hindus, Jewish people, Muslims and Sikhs all believe life is special because it was created by God. Buddhists and Hindus believe it is special because it strives for enlightenment.

Religions also consider animal and plant life as special, as a creation of God. For the Eastern religions, these are just less evolved forms of life, each of which is also on the journey to enlightenment.

Quality of life

This phrase describes how good a person's life is – how they feel, how comfortable they are, how easy it is for them to live. It is also about whether life is worth living if they have a medical condition.

Sometimes decisions are made about whether someone lives or dies and quality of life is a key factor in this. Abortion and euthanasia are such issues.

> **Euthanasia:** assisting with the ending of life for a person who is terminally ill or has degenerative illness; often known as assisted suicide.
>
> **Quality of life:** how good/comfortable life is.
>
> **Sanctity of life:** life is special; life is created by God.

Activity

Support or challenge?

'Quality of life is more important than the sanctity of life in decisions about the end of life.' Evaluate this statement. Refer to religious and non-religious arguments. You should agree and disagree with the statement, and come to a justified conclusion.

(12 marks)

Use the list of arguments below to help you write a strong answer to this question. They are mixed up though, so first you need to work out which ones agree (support) and which ones disagree (challenge) with the statement. Remember that a conclusion should not just be repeating what you have already written, so it is worth keeping back a good argument to use there. You may have to read the next page to find some religious arguments to help with this. Your conclusion must say which point of view is stronger, and why.

Argument	Supports statement in question	Challenges statement in question
No point living a life of pain with no respite.		
My life, my body, my decision.		
God created all life, so it must be protected.		
Life is so special, it can only be protected.		
The intrinsic value of every individual – regardless of their situation – outweighs the concern for quality.		
How valuable is life if is not enjoyable anyway?		

Religious attitudes to life

Buddhism

+ Life is special and must be protected.
+ The First Precept is to not take life.
+ The heart of Buddhist practice is to overcome suffering (dukkha).
+ The Dalai Lama has said, 'Where a person is definitely going to die, and keeping them alive leads to more suffering, then termination of life is permitted under Mahayana Buddhism.'

Christianity

+ God created life in his own image (Genesis).
+ Do not murder (Ten Commandments).
+ I, your God, give life, and I take it away (Job).
+ The Catholic Church teaches that life must be respected from conception until natural death.
+ Doctors do not have an overriding obligation to prolong life by all means possible (Church of England).

Hinduism

+ Those who carry out abortions are among the worst of sinners (Atharva Veda). This shows fundamental respect for life.
+ Compassion, ahimsa, and respect for life are key Hindu virtues.
+ The result of a virtuous action is pure joy; actions done from selfishness bring pain and suffering.
+ The one who tries to escape from the trials of this life by taking their own life will suffer even more in the next life.

Islam

+ Neither kill nor destroy yourself (Qur'an).
+ No one can die except by Allah's leave, that is a decree with a fixed term (Qur'an).
+ Each person is created individually by Allah from a single clot of blood.
+ Do not take life – which Allah has made sacred – except for a just cause (Qur'an).
+ Euthanasia is zulm – wrong-doing against Allah.

Judaism

+ Do not kill (Ten Commandments).
+ G-d gives life and G-d takes away life (Job).
+ The foetus has the spiritual status of 'mere water' until the 40th day of pregnancy (Talmud).
+ If there is anything which causes a hindrance to the departure of the soul then it is permissible to remove it (Talmud).

Sikhism

+ God sends us and we take birth, God calls us back and we die (Guru Granth Sahib).
+ Life begins at conception.
+ God fills us with light so we can be born (Guru Granth Sahib).
+ All life is sacred and should be respected.

Activity

Fix It!

Explain two religious beliefs about the sanctity of life. Refer to sacred writings or another source of religious authority in your answer. (6 marks)

The Bible said God created life. It is written in Genesis. As God created life, life is special and must be protected.

Now test yourself

1 What is meant by quality of life?
2 What is meant by sanctity of life?

Abortion

The central question here is: when does life begin? The law states it is at birth but the Abortion Act 1967 bans abortion after 24 weeks.

If abortion is after 'when life begins', it can be seen as murder. At any stage from conception the foetus is a potential life.

> **Abortion:** the deliberate expulsion of a foetus from the womb, with the intention of destroying it.

The law in the UK

The law in the UK (excluding Northern Ireland) begins by stating that abortion is illegal, then gives exceptions. Abortion can be carried out only in a registered place before 24 weeks if two registered doctors agree that at least one of the following is true:

+ There is a danger to the woman's mental and/or physical health.
+ The foetus will be born with physical and/or mental disabilities.
+ The mental and/or physical health of existing children will be put at risk.

Breaking the law carries great penalties for all those involved.

The debate

Pro-life: disagree with abortion	Pro-choice: accept abortion
Pro-lifers support the foetus' right to life.	This view defends a woman's right to choose what happens to her body. The arguments are about the woman rather than the foetus.
All life is sacred and must be protected.	A woman should have the right to decide what happens to her body.
God has created life and as stewards, humans have to protect life.	Where the pregnancy is a result of rape or incest, it would be morally wrong to not allow an abortion.
Abortion is murder.	If having a child is going to put a woman's life at risk, then she should have the right to an abortion.
The foetus can't defend itself, so someone else has to do it for it.	The foetus should not be classed as a life in its own right until it could survive outside the womb.
When a foetus will be born with disabilities, we cannot say what the quality of its life would be, so should not decide to forbid it that life.	It is cruel to allow badly damaged foetuses to be born.
Abortion allows women to not take responsibility for lives they have created, and so is wrong.	Banning abortion does not stop it, rather it makes it unsafe. We need to protect women.

What does religion say if the woman's life is at risk?
+ Buddhism: the primary intention is the key – helping to save the woman's life is compassionate even if the foetus dies.
+ Christianity: if the pregnancy threatens the woman's life it is justified (Church of England). Where abortion is a side effect of a medical procedure to save a woman's life it can be accepted (Roman Catholic Church) – this is known as the Principle of Double Effect.
+ Hinduism: the woman's life takes priority, when at risk.
+ Judaism: before birth the foetus has no rights over the mother – actual life has priority.
+ Islam: the life of the mother takes priority as she is a fully developed human being.
+ Sikhism: abortion would be a 'necessary evil'.

Theme B: Religion and life

85

Euthanasia

Euthanasia is mercy killing – helping someone to die if they have a terminal illness. It is done out of compassion and love.

Voluntary euthanasia is a person asking to end their own suffering. It could be active – with the person being given something to end their life so the illness does not kill them – or passive – where medication is refused/stopped so the illness kills them.

Non-voluntary euthanasia is when the patient is incapacitated so their family members decide, maybe to turn off a life support machine or to withdraw medication/food. This is passive as it is allowing the person to die.

A doctor's oath, known as the Hippocratic Oath, says, 'I will give no deadly medicine to anyone if asked or suggest such actions.'

The law in the UK

Euthanasia is illegal in Britain. It is forbidden to help someone to die. Active euthanasia carries a 14-year jail sentence. If viewed as murder, it carries a life sentence.

Doctors do switch off life-support machines (passive) when patients have no sign of brain activity, they do allow patients to refuse treatment or food/water (passive) and they administer drugs to ease pain, which also shortens life. None of these actions is regarded as euthanasia in the UK.

The debate

Arguments for the right to die	Arguments against the right to die
It is the person's body, so they should have the right to decide.	Life does not belong to humans it belongs to God – euthanasia is playing God.
Surely it should be a human right?	To allow euthanasia would be to encourage it – people may force it on others for their own advantage, e.g. making an elderly relative feel a burden.
Only the person can really say when their life is not worth living.	
It is compassionate to put animals in pain to sleep, so we should allow the same compassion to humans to avoid agony and suffering.	People in their last days need care and love rather than being helped to die.
	Doctors and nurses take oaths to protect life, not to end it.

Remember these terms? People say that euthanasia is all about the **quality of life** – that for those who want euthanasia, they are suffering too much, having no quality of life. Others say that, regardless of quality, life must be maintained because the **sanctity of life** means it is too special to end.

Caring for the dying

Hospices are homes for both children and adults dying of an incurable disease. They provide palliative care until death, or respite care.

A basic ethos is that when someone is dying, they cannot be cured, only cared for. If that care covers all aspects of their being, they will not wish for euthanasia.

Now test yourself — TESTED

1 What is euthanasia?
2 Why do some people disagree with euthanasia?
3 Why do others agree with it?

Buddhism

✚ The First Precept is to not take life, therefore generally speaking, abortion and euthanasia are wrong. However, intention is key, so at times it may be the case that an abortion or euthanasia is actually the right action.

✚ Existence is suffering; karma and craving result in suffering. Compassion is a positive response. If we face death with anxiety, anger and upset, our next rebirth is negatively set, so a comfortable death, where the dying accept death, is facilitated. Buddhism supports hospices, which help people to face their death with calmness.

Christianity

✚ Abortion is morally wrong, although some people accept it as a necessary evil. While death might mean going to heaven to be with God, it should not be hastened.

✚ Life should always be protected. Where the mother's life is at risk, most would accept procedures which save her life, which is sacred, even if they lead to the ending of the pregnancy.

✚ Few Christians support active euthanasia, regardless of what a person might themselves wish for. This is seen as killing, so it is wrong. However, in countries where euthanasia is legal some Christians see it as an act of love and compassion and a good use of the medical knowledge God has granted humans.

Hinduism

✚ Life is sacred and must be protected, therefore abortion is wrong in most cases. In each lifetime, a soul creates new karma for the next and 'pays off' karma from previous lives. An aborted foetus is denied these opportunities. Hinduism recognises that many decisions such as the question of abortion should be left to personal conscience. Hence, in cases such as the woman's life being at risk or the serious malformation of a foetus, abortion is seen as a necessary evil.

✚ Passive euthanasia is not encouraged. Families respectfully care for their elderly, suggesting euthanasia should not be necessary. Active euthanasia is considered murder. Hindu principles support care for the dying, not ending life.

Islam

✚ Life is created by Allah, hence abortion is wrong. The issue is when ensoulment takes place: at conception, at 40 or 120 days? Before that time, technically an abortion is acceptable. Where a mother's life is at risk, Islam defends the woman's right to life.

✚ No one knows Allah's plans. Allah has planned for this experience, so it must have some value. Life will end when Allah wills it, so euthanasia is against that. Passive euthanasia would be accepted where there was no hope.

Judaism

✚ Life is sacred. Foetal life has no rights until birth and abortion would be allowed, if, for example, the woman's life was in danger, or for medical reasons. Some rabbis have extended this idea of endangerment to include a woman's mental health being in danger, such as after rape.

✚ Death should be calm. It is important to protect life and to care for the dying, so active euthanasia is wrong. Does euthanasia shorten life or shorten the act of dying? The latter allows a person a 'good death' and so can be acceptable. However, euthanasia can also be seen as throwing life away, which is always wrong.

Sikhism

✚ Life is sacred – every soul is on a journey to achieve liberation. Life begins at conception so abortion is murder; it is destruction of God's creation. Sikhs may contemplate abortion – as a necessary evil.

✚ Sikhs should not harm or end life. Suffering may be seen as working through the negative karma of previous lifetime(s), so must be lived through, not avoided. A Sikh's duty to the dying is to care for them until God decides they die, not to hasten their death.

Revision tip

Many attitudes to abortion or euthanasia in religion are dictated by belief in the sanctity of life. If you can articulate that, you can work out the likely attitude to abortion/euthanasia.

Life after death

Death is when the brain and body stop functioning permanently. Religious people believe that at death the soul/spirit/self leaves the physical body. All religions believe there is a continuation and some other kind of life.

Buddhism

Buddhists believe in rebirth. There is no permanent soul, rather a mix of ever changing skandhas – emotions, feelings, intelligence and so on.

After the death of the body, this mix fuses with a new egg and sperm at conception. The actions and intentions of each life shape the quality of the next. The goal is to achieve enlightenment, and stop being reborn.

Christianity

(See also page 20). Christians believe in the physical resurrection of the body. At death, the body waits until Judgement Day. Catholics call this purgatory. At judgement, the person faces God and Jesus to evaluate their deeds. If they were good in life, they go to heaven (paradise and wonderful forever). If they were bad, they go to hell (eternal punishment).

Hinduism

(See also page 44). Hindus believe in reincarnation. Their atman (soul) lives through many lifetimes, each one shaped by the thoughts, words and actions of their past lifetime(s). Its goal is to achieve enlightenment and become one with the Ultimate Reality, so no longer being reincarnated.

Islam

Muslims believe in resurrection. At death, the body waits in the grave (barzakh) and sees the events of its life. On Judgement Day, people are sorted according to their beliefs and actions. The wicked are cast into hell; the truly good go straight to paradise. All others cross As-Sirat bridge, carrying the book of their deeds (sins make it heavier). The bridge is sharp and so they are purified from sin before going to paradise.

Judaism

Judaism focuses on this life rather than the next. Some teachings mention a heavenly place. Jewish people talk of the 'world to come', which can refer to either the place souls go after death or a Messianic Age when the world will be at peace. Mainly the focus though is on getting this life right and not worrying too much about what comes next.

Sikhism

Sikhs believe in reincarnation. The soul is born into many lifetimes, whose quality is decided by the words, thoughts and deeds of the previous lifetime(s). The point of each life is to serve and worship God, so that eventually the soul can be reunited with God (waheguru) and stop being reincarnated.

Activity

Below are two answers to the same exam question. Neither is perfect, so what is wrong each time? Remember the key rules of needing two teachings, a source and explaining points clearly. Then write your own perfect answer.

Explain two religious beliefs about life after death. Refer to sacred writings or another source of religious authority in your answer.

(6 marks)

Student A:

Buddhists believe after we die, we are born again many times until we get enlightened. Christians believe we get judged by Jesus and if we were good, we go to heaven.

Student B:

The New Testament says that we can have life after death because Jesus was resurrected. He died as a sacrifice for humans' sins, opening heaven to humans. So, after death, our soul is awakened for Judgement Day, then judged by Jesus. If we had been good in our lives, we can go to heaven; if bad, we go to hell.

Now test yourself

1 What is meant by death?
2 Give two ideas used by religions about what happens at death.

Theme B: Religion and life

Exam practice

What questions on this section look like:

Theme B: Religion and life

This page contains a range of questions that could be on an exam paper. Practise them all to strengthen your knowledge and technique while revising. Check back to pages 11-12 to see the marking grids that examiners use: this will help you to mark your answers.

1 Which of the following is not an effect of global warming?

  (a) Climate change   **(b)** Conservation   **(c)** Deforestation   **(d)** Pollution   [1]

2 Which of the following terms means to protect an environmental area?

  (a) Conservation   **(b)** Recycling   **(c)** Stewardship   **(d)** Sustainable development   [1]

3 Give one teaching about the created world. [1]

4 Give one reason a person may be vegetarian. [1]

5 Give one reason why a religious person might feel a sense of awe and wonder for the world. [1]

6 Explain two different religious beliefs about abortion in contemporary British society. In your answer you should refer to the main religious tradition of Great Britain and one or more other religious traditions. [4]

7 Explain two similar religious beliefs about animal experimentation. In your answer you must refer to one or more religious traditions. [4]

8 Explain two different religious beliefs about euthanasia. In your answer you must refer to one or more religious traditions. [4]

9 Explain two religious beliefs about the sanctity of life. Refer to sacred writings or another source of religious belief and teachings in your answer. [6]

10 Explain two religious beliefs about the use of animals. Refer to sacred writings or another source of religious belief and teachings in your answer. [6]

11 Explain two religious beliefs about the Genesis creation story. Refer to sacred writings or another source of religious belief and teachings in your answer. [6]

12 'It is impossible to believe both science and religion about the origins of the universe.' Evaluate this statement. In your answer you should:
   + give reasoned arguments in support of this statement
   + give reasoned arguments to support a different point of view
   + refer to religious arguments
   + refer to non-religious arguments
   + refer to a justified conclusion. [12]

13 'All religious believers should work to end the abuse of the created world.' Evaluate this statement. In your answer you should:
   + give reasoned arguments in support of this statement
   + give reasoned arguments to support a different point of view
   + refer to religious arguments
   + refer to non-religious arguments
   + refer to a justified conclusion. [12]

14 'Religion proves that God created the world.' Evaluate this statement. In your answer you should:
   + give reasoned arguments in support of this statement
   + give reasoned arguments to support a different point of view
   + refer to religious arguments
   + refer to non-religious arguments
   + refer to a justified conclusion. [12]

Exam tip

Level 2 students give unsupported opinions in answers to evaluation questions. This means they often give only their own ideas on something and rarely give two sides. If this is you, try to think of and present an alternate view to your own.

Level 5 students give more than one side in evaluation answers; however, they often do not focus closely enough on the statement. So reasoning is loose and limited. If this is you, underline key words/phrases in the statement and always check back to it with each argument you write.

Level 8 students give more than one side, focus clearly on the statement and develop their reasoning with good detail.

Theme C: The existence of God and revelation

Christian	Islamic	Hindu
One God; three aspects/persons	**One God; no partners**	**One Ultimate Reality; many forms**
One almighty, absolute God.	One God: Allah – Allah has no partner and cannot be split (like the Christian God).	Ultimate Reality – Brahman; pervades the universe in all its aspects.
Trinity – three-in-one: Father; Son; Spirit.	Creator of all.	Tri-murti of three major forms: Vishnu, Shiva and Brahma.
The Father is the creator of the world; the Son was God incarnate (made flesh) as Jesus; the Holy Ghost is God with us now.	Judge.	Many other forms of gods to explain aspects of the Ultimate Reality, such as Ganesha, Lakshmi, Durga – each has specific qualities, e.g. Lakshmi is the goddess of wealth and fortune.
All-powerful, all-knowing, all-loving.	Most compassionate.	
	Most merciful.	
	All-powerful, all-knowing, all-loving.	

Why the different ideas about God?

 REVISED

There are various reasons why people have different ideas about God:
+ Upbringing: their parents describe God in a certain way and that is what they come to believe.
+ What holy books say: they are about God, after all.
+ What religions/religious leaders say: they interpret the holy books, and many people believe they are closer to God or in contact with God, so what they say carries a lot of weight.
+ They inherit a description of God from their cultural viewpoint or from their community.
+ Experiences of God: if you experience God as a loving, kind being when you are in an emotionally difficult period in your life, you will think God is loving and kind. If something bad happens when you are feeling guilty about something, you might think God is vengeful because he has done this to you.

Activity

Explain two similar religious beliefs about God. Refer to one or more religious traditions in your answer. (4 marks)

These answers to the question make common mistakes – can you spot them?

A – Christians and Muslims believe God is very powerful, the most powerful possible. They believe God created the universe, which shows his power, as it says in Genesis and the Qur'an.

B – Christians believe that God is omniscient; that God knows each of us so well he understands humans perfectly. Muslims believe this as well.

Christians believe God is omnipotent; so he could create the world. Muslims believe this as well.

Some differences

+ While Muslims believe there is only One God, who is indivisible, Christians believe that God has three persons (Father, Son and Holy Spirit) in the Trinity.
+ Muslims give 99 names for God, each of which is a quality, but they believe it is impossible to properly know God. Christians believe they can have a personal relationship with God through the power of the Holy Spirit.
+ Hindus believe there is something of God in everything.
+ The Buddha told his followers not to look to a God at all.

Find Now Test Yourself and Exam Practice answers at https://www.hoddereducation.co.uk/myrevisionnotesdownloads

Key characteristics of God

In the beginning was the Word, and the Word was with God, and the Word was God. (John 1:1)

I am that I am. (G-d's response to Moses request for his name – Exodus 3:14)

He is Allah, One, Allah, the Eternal Refuge. (Qur'an 112)

There, where there is no darkness, or night, or day, or being, nor nonbeing, there is the Auspicious One, alone, absolute and eternal. (Shvetashvatara Upanishad 4:18)

> **Revision tip**
>
> There are many characteristics of God, but only six are stipulated by the Specification. It is helpful to be able to refer to others in your answers, so when you meet others in this Theme, learn them.

Omnipotent	Means 'all-powerful'; as powerful as it is possible to be.	**Like!** Makes God very different to humans. Explains how God could have created the world (the Genesis creation story). **But!** If God is so powerful, why not fix the obvious problems in the world?
Omniscient	Means 'all-knowing'; God's intelligence knows no limits.	**Like!** Makes God very different to humans. Explains how God can know what humans will do (Islamic al-Qadr). **But!** If God knows humans so well, why does he not stop 'evil' people?
Personal	Means humans can have a close relationship with God, shown in the prayer 'Our Father …'.	**Like!** Allows humans to feel watched over and protected by God, who must love them because of his personal nature. Means that we can come to some understanding of God as this personifies God, hence 99 names for God in Islam. **But!** Isn't God supposed to be completely different to humans in every way? So how can we relate to God?
Impersonal	Means that God is not something that humans can have a close relationship with or can understand – there is a distance between the two.	**Like!** Emphasises the difference in status between God and humans, which is sensible if we also want to believe in God as creator, absolute, etc. Explains why humans cannot understand God, e.g. as the Ultimate Reality, the divine can only be known through enlightenment. **But!** How can humans have a relationship with this kind of God – something many religions are built on?

Theme C: The existence of God and revelation

91

| Immanent | Means that God is active in the world, e.g. through the life of Jesus, or the Holy Spirit with Christians. | **Like!** Allows a personal relationship. Shows that God will act in the world, e.g. performing miracles. **But!** Does this make God too much like humans? |
| Transcendent | Means God is beyond space and time, controlled by neither. | **Like!** Explains how God could create the world – outside it and not affected by time or space, e.g. all religions say God is eternal and absolute. Explains the gap between God and humans. **But!** How can humans build a relationship with this God, as Christianity encourages? |

Now test yourself

TESTED ◯

1 What does omnipotent mean?
2 What does omniscient mean?
3 What does personal mean in relation to God?
4 What does impersonal mean in relation to God?
5 What does immanent mean?
6 What does transcendent mean?
7 Why might people prefer one idea of God over another?

Revision tip

For these characteristics, make sure you learn:
+ what each word means
+ a quotation or teaching to go with each
+ why that characteristic is helpful to believers
+ why there might be difficulty with each characteristic for believers.

Activity

Support or challenge?

'The most important quality of God is his transcendence.' Evaluate this statement. Refer to religious and non-religious arguments. You should agree and disagree with the statement, and come to a justified conclusion.   (12 marks)

Use the list of arguments below to help you write a strong answer to this question. They are mixed up though, so first you need to work out which ones agree (support) and which ones disagree (challenge) with the statement. Remember that a conclusion should not just be repeating what you have already written, so it is worth keeping back a good argument to use there. You may have to read the next page to find some religious arguments to help with this. Your conclusion must say which point of view is stronger, and why.

Argument	Supports statement in question	Challenges statement in question
This allows God to have created the world.		
Means God is completely beyond humans – exactly what a God should be.		
Better for God to be immanent, as he is with and helps us.		
A personal God who loves us and cares for us is better.		
How can we have a relationship with God if we cannot understand anything of him?		
God must be eternal and absolute to be God.		

Arguments for the existence of God

There are many arguments for the existence of God as well as the ones on this course. It can be helpful to know of some others, to use particularly in evaluation questions. Check out the ontological argument or the argument from religious experience or the argument from morality, for example.

For the course, you need to know the gist of three arguments for the existence of God, something of their strengths and some of their weaknesses. For the exam, you will need to know only a small number of strengths/weaknesses, so that is all you are getting here. However, you could try to work out some of the problems for yourself (which would help you to understand the actual arguments).

> **A posteriori reasoning**: arguing from experience; arguments generated from facts, not from suppositions.
>
> **First Cause argument**: postulates that God is the Uncaused Cause of the universe.
>
> **St Aquinas**: writer of the First Cause argument, which is one of a set of proofs of God's existence.

The argument	Its strengths	Its weaknesses
First Cause argument (cosmological argument) Put forward by Thomas **Aquinas** (13th-century monk), who claimed: ✦ everything natural is caused by something else (e.g. flowers grow because of sun and rain) ✦ nothing natural causes itself (everything relies on something else) ✦ yet, for anything to exist now, there must have been first uncaused cause (something which did not rely on anything else for its existence) ✦ this Uncaused Cause was God.	This is a logical argument – e.g. it makes more sense that something started the chain of existence than that it randomly simply began itself, given nothing else in the world just spontaneously starts. It is an argument we can see evidence for (**a posteriori reasoning**) – we can see the links and chains in nature and in events (think of the cycles you learned about in science); to a human that is our normal experience. So the argument works from something we already know to be true, giving it weight.	Aquinas said that 'all people' recognise the Uncaused Cause to be God – he could not have asked everyone, so this is a sweeping statement and unfounded assertion. Similarly, Aquinas said that 'nothing is self-caused'. While it might be difficult to think of something, that does not mean he is right; again he is making an unprovable statement. He also then uses God as a solution ('there is no uncaused cause … oh, yes there is – God'!).

Activity

Fix it!

Read the answer to this question, then write an improved version of your own.

Explain two religious beliefs about the existence of God. Refer to sacred writings or another source of religious authority in your answer. (6 marks)

One religious belief about God is that there is a God. Christians say the Bible proves it. Another religious belief about God is that God is the Uncaused Cause which started the whole universe off.

The argument	Its strengths	Its weaknesses
Design argument Many versions, this one was put forward by **William Paley**, a 19th-century Christian theologian. He claimed: + objects on earth look like they were designed – he uses the example of finding a watch, never having seen one before + it seems to have a purpose, which means it was thought about and deliberately made + just so, the world looks like it was designed, e.g. ecosystem, seasons, human eye + these all seem to have specific purposes, as if deliberately thought about and designed to be this way + the world must have been designed + it must have been designed by God (no one/nothing else is capable of this).	This is a compelling argument, also a posteriori. We can see amazing things in nature which just seem so perfect for the job they do, so we like to think there is some reasoning behind these things, i.e. that they were deliberate – which means there has to be a mind at work. We can also see the regularity of the cycles and systems within nature – you always have day following night, for example. This a posteriori reasoning allows humans to think there is a co-ordinator behind it all, keeping systems in check (Newton's great watchmaker), which can only be God (a human couldn't do it!).	Evolutionary theory removes the need for something designing and keeping the world in check. We could also say that if there was something, it isn't doing a great job when you consider all the suffering we see ('blind watchmaker' idea). Paley's argument only makes a compelling argument for a designer – is that all God is? Paley's God only designed the world. He might have used stuff which already existed, or might have died after designing - both go against religious beliefs.

Now test yourself

1 Name two arguments for the existence of God.
2 Briefly, what does the First Cause argument say?
3 Briefly, what does the Design argument say?
4 Why are these arguments compelling?
5 Why are these arguments flawed?

Design argument: aka teleological argument; argument which postulates that since the world looks designed, it must have had a designer – God.

William Paley: writer of this particular teleological argument.

Activity

Support or challenge?

'There is no such thing as God.' Evaluate this statement. Refer to religious and non-religious arguments in your answer. You should agree and disagree, and come to a justified conclusion. (12 marks)

Use the list of arguments below to help you write a strong answer to the question. They are mixed up though, so first work out which ones agree (support) and which disagree (challenge) with the statement. Remember, a conclusion should not just repeat arguments, so it is worth keeping back one to use to strengthen your conclusion. Your conclusion must say which point of view is stronger, and why.

Revision tip

Paley's teleological argument is not the only version – you could check out other versions such as Newton's thumb (for design) or the Kalam cosmological argument.

Argument	Supports statement in question	Challenges statement in question
There is no proof of God.		
The teleological argument is compelling because we see evidence all around.		
The First Cause argument is logical.		
There is too much suffering in the world.		
Many people think they are personally responsible and should not look to a supernatural being.		
There are more religious people than non-religious people in the world.		

Arguments for the existence of God from miracles

A miracle is an event contrary to the proper workings of nature, in other words, what is classed as a miracle is something which should not happen in our universe, given the mechanics of it. Some people see as a miracle something which inspires awe and wonder within them, for example the miracle of birth/life. Sometimes people claim a miracle when they 'see' God, such as the seeds in an aubergine looking like the word 'Allah' (God).

The argument	Its strengths	Its weaknesses
Argument from miracles Within an essay debunking any notion of miracles occurring, David Hume, an 18th-century philosopher, actually gave good criteria for being able to label something a miracle. Hume claimed that any 'miracle' should be disregarded if: ✛ there was another (natural) solution ✛ the people claiming it had any links to religion (they would be biased/lying/misinterpreting events) ✛ they are claimed by people with little scientific knowledge. We can use this to reduce the number of events claimed as miracles. However, events claimed as miracles still seem to happen – a person being declared dead, then coming back to life (with no scientific explanation), a plane crash with no fatalities, someone being declared terminally ill with no hope of recovery suddenly being free of a disease (spontaneous regression). God must perform miracles (no one/nothing else explains these occurrences). The **Christological Argument** claims that Jesus rose from the dead (miracle) only because God exists (hence is proof).	There are certainly events which cannot be explained by science. When these events are positive/good, it is compelling to believe that a good force is behind them. If you believe in God, this argument makes sense; we should accept God helps, and not question it. This fits with the idea of Jesus performing miracles, and his resurrection being one.	The random nature of miracles is a big problem – why do seemingly bad, even wicked people have them, and really good people don't? That suggests no thought behind the awarding of a miracle. Jesus said miracles were to showcase God's power – it seems unfair that someone should suffer just to give people a glimpse of a so-called loving God.

Examples of miracles

For the course, you have to know an example of a miracle. There are many in history, and in religious scripture.

John 11 tells the story of Jesus raising Lazarus from the dead. Lazarus had been ill and Jesus did not visit, in spite of requests, until four days after Lazarus had died. Jesus then told the mourners to move the stone from the tomb and called Lazarus out. Lazarus walked from the tomb (alive and well).

A modern-day example is that of Nev, who was dragged into a machine at work. His upper arm was snapped in several places and the nerve was completely severed, rendering him paralysed in that arm. Medical science says a severed nerve cannot be fixed. Following a year of paralysis, sensations and then movement returned. The arm is now almost fully functioning. Doctors cannot explain this, other than 'it is impossible' (so a miracle).

> **Christological argument**: argument stating that Jesus' miraculous resurrection is proof of God's existence.
>
> **Miracle**: an impossible event, contrary to the laws of nature, always good, attributed to a deity.

Arguments against the existence of God

Many people just do not see a reason to believe in a supernatural being. They think that we should just live in a morally good way and live the life we have (not seeking intervention or motivation from a being that cannot be proven to exist). However, many people feel that there is good proof that God does not exist. There are many such arguments, but for the course you could be asked questions directly only about two of them.

The problem of evil and suffering as proof God does not exist

Suffering is mental/emotional/physical pain caused by events in nature (natural evil) or the behaviour of other humans (moral evil). It can be caused directly (e.g. someone thumps me) or indirectly (my parent dies, so I grieve).

Our experience of the world proves that there is suffering. We see/experience evidence of it every day. If God exists and is all-loving, all-knowing, all-powerful, why does he allow this evil/suffering to continue?

No argument to defend God has ever been satisfactory and there is no argument to prove God has enough strength to overcome the doubts caused by our own experience of evil/suffering. That God 'allows' evil/suffering proves there is no God.

Science as proof God does not exist

Science involves making hypotheses which are subject to tests to support their veracity, and the observation of regularity. Science is knowledge based on these.

Science is evolving and so our scientific knowledge increases minute by minute. What was considered to be true hundreds of years ago according to science may have been debunked by modern science (e.g. illness was thought to be caused by bad 'humours' in the body, it is now known to be through viruses, etc.).

Science says there is a logical explanation for every event – even if we do not yet know it, at some point we will. Hence, science does not need to use God to explain things – if anything, God is the 'joker in the pack', a 'god of the gaps' – that is, what we say when we do not know the real answer. God does not actually exist.

> **Moral evil**: human words/actions which cause suffering to self/others.
>
> **Natural evil**: events in nature which cause suffering to sentient beings.
>
> **Science**: systematic study of the natural world through observation and experimentation.

Activity

Develop the notes

A student ran out of time in the exam to write a full answer to the question. Use their notes to write a well-argued, detailed answer. Remember it needs a conclusion.

Science proves God does not exist. *(12 marks)*

Agree
+ Science is logical ideas based on observed evidence.
+ Science grows all the time to explain new things.
+ Science teaches humans not to opt for a being we can't even prove exists over explanations we can work out.
+ We get more science lessons than RS ones!

Disagree
+ Science can't explain everything.
+ Even scientists agree some things are miracles.
+ Science could just be us finding out how God runs the world.
+ If science is so good, why is it always changing (when religion doesn't)?

Revelation

What is revelation?

The term revelation refers to experiencing the presence of God, or the divine. If the revelation is direct, that is, seeing God or hearing God, it is a special revelation. If it is about sensing God's presence rather than directly seeing/hearing God, we call it general revelation.

Special revelation

Many holy books describe examples of this, such as the Qur'an describing Prophet Muhammad's prophethood. Many of these books also claim to be the word of God, for example Orthodox Jewish people believe the Torah was dictated by God to Moses. Many religious leaders claim to have met/spoken with God, which gave them the conviction to spread the word of their religion, for instance Guru Nanak.

One example from the New Testament is basically about how one of the key figures in Christianity, St Paul, became a Christian. Saul was his Jewish name. He spent his time seeking out Christians to be tried by the Jewish courts for blasphemy. Then, on his way to Damascus (modern-day Syria), he was blinded by a light that only he could see. He then heard the voice of Jesus asking why Saul persecuted him. Blind, he was taken to a nearby village. A Christian came to help him, sent by God, and cured his blindness. Saul asked to be baptised, changed his name to Paul and spent the rest of his life converting people to Christianity.

A special revelation provides personal proof of God to the recipient, affirming their religion or life choices. It can be a life-changing experience, so they do new things or behave very differently thereafter. It also gives insight into the character of God, so provides religious truths, and leads to new (interpretations of) religions.

General revelation

This revelation is available to everyone. It is indirect. It is knowledge of God/the divine, gleaned from experience of the natural world. There are many types, but you need to know about two:

+ Knowing God through nature: God created the world, so we can appreciate God through it – we get a sense of amazement, awe and wonder. Maybe the world and the patterns within it make humans think there must have been a designer, who was God. Maybe the beauty of the world – flowers, sunsets, etc. – make humans think of God, or of some supernatural, divine power working behind the scenes. The hymn 'All Things Bright and Beautiful' is a perfect example of this mindset.
+ Knowing God through scripture: 'scripture' is 'holy books' or 'sacred texts'. Many are said to be divinely inspired, or dictated by God. A central theme will be to describe God or aspects of God either directly, such as Psalm 103, or indirectly, for example by describing historical events which God has 'manipulated' (so suggesting justice, or goodness, or wrath, etc.). The reader is reading revealed truths.

A general revelation brings broader knowledge of God, scriptures give a sense of having 'special' knowledge. The person might feel reassured in their religion or life choices. They may feel they have a closer relationship with God.

General revelation: indirect revelation, e.g. through seeing God through nature.

Revelation: when God reveals himself; when God makes himself known to a person either directly or indirectly.

Special revelation: direct revelation, e.g. seeing God in a vision.

Revision tip

For the course, you should have studied one '**vision**' or special revelation. There are many, and you know some from your study of a religion. Get those notes out, and recycle them for this Theme!

Revision tip

Do you know the difference between Special and General Revelation? It can be easy to mix them up, and that would cost you marks! Learn them, and learn examples.

Do you know why revelation is important for believers? It is as much about it being 'personal proof of God' as about how it makes them feel (special, chosen, loved). Make sure you learn that.

Enlightenment as a source of knowledge of the divine

Enlightenment means 'awakening'. You could say it is when someone suddenly realises the truth of something. In this case it could be the grasping of a truth about God. Many religious people throughout history have claimed to have gained an understanding of God/the divine through revelation. It seems that the enlightenment allows a person to see things in a new way.

Many religious people study their sacred scriptures to gain better insight and so become enlightened (if only partially). For Orthodox Jewish people, study of the Torah is very important. Studying and learning about God through reading, debate, meditation/reflection and worship may give insight.

However, if God is absolute, omniscient, transcendent and so on, as described by religions such as Christianity, Islam and Judaism, you could ask whether it is actually possible for our puny human brains to comprehend God at all (even on the lowest level). Does your pet goldfish really understand you?!

In the case of Eastern religions such as Buddhism and Hinduism, enlightenment means full realisation of the truth of life, which leads to escape from rebirth/reincarnation (nibbana).

Hinduism splits life into four ashramas, the final two being devoted to religious study in pursuit of enlightenment. Through this study, and because Hinduism believes in the existence of the Ultimate Reality (divine/God), Hindus believe they can come to understand the nature of God, becoming finally reunited with God via enlightenment. So they can gain knowledge and finally fully comprehend the divine.

Buddhism seeks to realise the true nature of everything – impermanence, no self, and suffering (not just understanding the Buddha's teachings about it). Once this realisation takes place, so does enlightenment. This takes many lifetimes of study. Some Zen Buddhists use koans to gain partial enlightenment – a glimpse of that true nature.

Reality or illusion?

There are other explanations for revelation and enlightenment:
+ Why real?
  + Personal evidence.
  + Life-changing experience.
  + Trust self.
  + Revelation has provided the basis for every religion.
+ Why illusion?
  + It could be a figment of imagination, due to drugs/being drunk/dreaming/being delirious.
  + There is no empirical evidence to prove the event or the realisation to anyone else.
  + Religious people want to see God, so make themselves believe they have done so.
  + There is no such thing as God, so there can be no revelation of God.

> **Enlightenment**: realising a religious truth; attaining nibbana (release from the cycle of samsara).

> **Activity**
>
> **Fix it!**
>
> Below are two answers to the same exam question. Neither is perfect, so what is wrong each time? Remember the key rules of needing two teachings, a source and having to explain points clearly. Then write your own perfect answer.
>
> *Explain two religious teachings about enlightenment as a source of knowledge about the divine. Refer to sacred writings or another source of religious authority in your answer.* (6 marks)
>
> Student A:
>
> Christians have the Psalms in the Bible. Psalm 103 describes God. If a Christian reads this, they learn about God and so can better understand God. Also people like Teresa of Avila used to meditate and communicate with God through this. So she had a better understanding of God and was able to write books about it, like 'Interior Castle'.
>
> Student B:
>
> Christians read about God in the Bible, like in the Psalms where God is shown to be merciful, loving, strong and so on. By reading it, they can gain insight into the nature of God, so they understand him better. Muslims can't know God, because God is too 'God'.

Exam practice

What questions on this section look like:

Theme C: The existence of God and revelation

This page contains a range of questions that could be on an exam paper. Practise them all to strengthen your knowledge and technique while revising. Check back to pages 11-12 to see the marking grids that examiners use: this will help you to mark your answers.

1 What is meant by 'personal' in relation to the divine?

   (a) Able to have a close relationship with God   **(b)** Absolute   **(c)** All-knowing   **(d)** Beyond understanding   [1]

2 What is meant by immanent?

   (a) Absolute   **(b)** Active in the world   **(c)** All-powerful   **(d)** Beyond space and time   [1]

3 Give one alternative explanation to the claim that a person has met God.   [1]

4 Give one reason why scripture helps people to understand God.   [1]

5 Give one reason why some people believe the First Cause argument is weak.   [1]

6 Explain two different religious beliefs about visions in contemporary British society. In your answer you should refer to the main religious tradition of Great Britain and non-religious beliefs.   [4]

7 Explain two similar religious beliefs about ideas about the divine. In your answer you must refer to at least one religious tradition.   [4]

8 Explain two different religious beliefs about science as an argument against the existence of God. In your answer you must refer to at least one religious tradition.   [4]

9 Explain two religious beliefs about enlightenment as a source of knowledge about the divine. Refer to sacred writings or another source of religious belief and teachings in your answer.   [6]

10 Explain two religious beliefs about general revelation. Refer to sacred writings or another source of religious belief and teachings in your answer.   [6]

11 Explain two religious beliefs about God being immanent. Refer to sacred writings or another source of religious belief and teachings in your answer.   [6]

12 'It is impossible to know what God is like.' Evaluate this statement. In your answer you should:
   + give reasoned arguments in support of this statement
   + give reasoned arguments to support a different point of view
   + refer to religious arguments
   + refer to non-religious arguments
   + refer to a justified conclusion.   [12]

13 'The existence of evil proves that God does not exist.' Evaluate this statement. In your answer you should:
   + give reasoned arguments in support of this statement
   + give reasoned arguments to support a different point of view
   + refer to religious arguments
   + refer to non-religious arguments
   + refer to a justified conclusion.   [12]

14 'The design argument is a weak argument for the existence of God.' Evaluate this statement. In your answer you should:
   + give reasoned arguments in support of this statement
   + give reasoned arguments to support a different point of view
   + refer to religious arguments
   + refer to non-religious arguments
   + refer to a justified conclusion.   [12]

Exam tip

Level 2 students often struggle with key terms, which means they miss out questions, simply not knowing what they are being asked. If this is you, start by learning the key terms.

Level 5 students usually know the key terms, but their understanding can be limited. This means answers are often limited. If this is you, you need to work on knowing more detail (e.g. relevant teachings).

Level 8 students know the key terms and use them fluently and well, illustrating to the examiner their clear understanding.

Theme D: Religion, peace and conflict

Buddhism
+ Speaking out about injustice shows compassion (karuna) and could be seen as Right Speech.
+ Justice involves responding with compassion and avoiding violence as it only breeds more violence.

Christianity
+ God requires humans to live in justice and freedom and wars should be fought justly.
+ Wars can lead to conditions no better before the war, but can be fought for the greater good.

Justice: in regards to war has two parts – to put right injustice and to carry this out in a just/right way.

Peace: to live in harmony and without fear with all people.

Reconciliation: the idea of bringing sides together to help resolve issues so people can live in peace. Without reconciliation peace cannot last.

Hinduism
+ Wars are to be avoided at any cost; mediation and compromise is the only way to resolve disputes. War must only be in self-defence, as a last resort and to protect society.
+ Self-defence is justifiable but all actions should be done with a moral approach.

Islam
+ Muslims strive for 'justice', which can mean both an inner religious struggle to be a better person and a collective armed struggle to protect the common good.
+ Islam condemns violence so wars should be carried out in the right way to achieve freedom.

Judaism
+ Justice is key for Jewish people – war is justifiable in self-defence but must be justly carried out.

Sikhism
+ Sikhs will fight for justice in a righteous war. Weapons which kill indiscriminately are wrong.
+ Only minimum force should be used to achieve a goal.

Justice and reconciliation

REVISED ●

Justice as a reason for war means that wars are fought to put right injustices – this could be to help people who are oppressed by the regime that rules their country. Religious people cannot stand by whilst people suffer – they feel duty bound by the teachings of their holy books to act.

Any such action must be carried out in a fair way so that this sets the example and sees people being able to live in peace.

Reconciliation is the act of bringing sides together to help put issues right so that there can be lasting peace. This can in the first place prevent war and in the second bring the victor and the defeated together. War on its own does not bring peace, as issues need resolving through discussion and diplomacy so that all sides can contribute to a peace that they are part of making.

Forgiveness

Forgiveness is a theme that runs through all religions and is taught by religious texts and leaders past and present. It is the idea that after wrongs have been committed, there has to be a way forward for that relationship. Often we accept an apology as the person has seen the error of their actions and put the wrongs in the past. After war-time atrocities, some forgive unconditionally (without an apology) as it is the only way they can get on with their lives. Their example has led to enemies actually coming together – an example would be concentration camp guards meeting camp survivors. Forgiveness can lead to understanding of what happened for both the perpetrators and the victims. Often people can never forget, and nor should they, but people can still forgive. Often the benefit of forgiveness is of more value to the person doing the forgiving then to the person being forgiven. Forgiving does not mean 'letting someone off for what they did' – Christians believe people should be punished justly as well as forgiven.

All religions teach that their God is one who will forgive. God forgives everyone, as long as they are truly sorry. God's nature is to be loving and just, hence God forgives. Religious believers think they should try to show forgiveness as God does – it is a virtue.

> **Forgiveness**: willingness to not blame a person any more for the wrongs they have done.

Religious attitudes to forgiveness

1. The Buddha suggests that anger is 'like holding a hot coal – intending to throw it at someone –but you are the one who gets burned' (anger eats away at people so forgiveness prevents more hurt).

2. Jesus said, 'Love your enemies' (a person must forgive to love, leaving no one to be the enemy).

3. Gandhi said, 'Forgiveness is the attribute of the strong' (the stronger person is the one who is able to forgive despite what may have happened to them).

4. The Qur'an says, 'Those who pardon and maintain righteousness are rewarded by God' (forgiveness is a higher quality that Allah will reward after being faced with injustice).

5. Rabbi Joshua Liebman said, 'We only achieve inner health from forgiveness' (not forgiving can eat people away inside and make them 'ill').

6. Guru Amar Das said, 'Dispelled is anger as forgiveness is grasped' (here forgiveness is the healer for the victim – allow people to move on with a peaceful mind).

Now test yourself

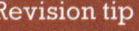 TESTED

1. What is justice when speaking about war?
2. Why might justice be needed after war?
3. What does 'reconciliation' mean?
4. Why might reconciliation be difficult after war?

Revision tip

Remember these key words – justice and reconciliation – are religious principles that can be applied to many topics. So learn them and use them widely.

Theme D: Religion, peace and conflict

101

Violence and violent protest

Religious people have a duty to fight/protest against injustice to create freedoms and peace. Wars can result from injustices. Religious believers have to try to stay true to and indeed balance the beliefs that they hold with the conflicts they face. Most religious teachings focus on peace, yet sometimes peaceful means do not work. When violent protest and violence seem to be the only way to achieve a common good, they become a 'necessary evil'. Human nature can compel people to ignore key religious teachings of non-violence in order to bring about justice, i.e. some sacrifice these beliefs for the greater good (principle of utility).

> **Conflict**: disagreement which can lead to fighting.
>
> **Violence**: aggression in language or action towards another person.
>
> **Violent protest**: voicing disagreement in a violent/aggressive way.

What do religions say?

Buddhism

+ Generally not accepting of violence (not ahimsa, causes dukkha, unskillful action).
+ Speaking out about injustice is compassionate and can be seen as Right Speech.
+ Peace can happen only with mutual respect (Dalai Lama).
+ There have been rare instances when Buddhists have used violence in protests, for example in Vietnam during the Vietnamese War against the government.

Christianity

+ Teaches against violence as Jesus said 'Blessed are the peacemakers'.
+ Christians are told to love their enemies; oppose or challenge them, but in a loving way.
+ Violent protest has been infrequently used in fighting unjust laws, as some Christians accept that force may be a necessary evil, e.g Dietrich Bonheoffer plotted to assassinate Hitler.
+ Some Christian activists have used violence to get their message across, for example anti-abortion campaigners in the USA.

Violence or not?

Hinduism

+ Non-violence is the only way to achieve anything long term.
+ Ahimsa is key, but injustice should not be tolerated – protest can be a religious act if done in the right way.

Islam

+ Action should be peaceful but violence can be used in self-defence.
+ Unfairness must be protested against and violence avoided
+ Sometimes protests do occur, e.g. in the UK there have been protests over wars and issues in the Middle East, Islamophobia and racism.

Judaism

+ Jewish people should protest against injustice peacefully.
+ Jewish people have suffered persecution throughout their history so many of them want to help others facing a similar situation.
+ Sometimes civil disobedience is used, but violence is not.

Sikhism

+ Teaches not to harm others but at the same time may be prepared to use force to resist injustice.
+ Sewa means Sikhs will defend the persecuted, always with peaceful intention.
+ For example, peaceful protests about the desecration of a copy of the Guru Granth Sahib in Faridkot, India.

Is violence ever justifiable?

Yes

+ When all other efforts to resolve an issue have failed, then violence may be the only remaining solution, especially where injustice prevails, especially if there is severe provocation.
+ In self-defence.
+ In fighting for God.

No

+ Most religions hold non-violence as a guiding principle.
+ Violence leads to hatred and violence, so perpetuating a cycle of hatred, fear and death; in this, people get hurt, including many innocent people.
+ Violence makes a cause seem less worthy, nullifying the positives of a protest, for example, and being used as a reason to ignore the point of the protest.

> **Now test yourself** TESTED ◯
>
> 1 What is violent protest?
> 2 Why might religions be reluctant to use violent protest?
> 3 Why might religious people choose to protest violently?

> **Activity**
>
> **Support or challenge?**
>
> *'Religious people should never protest violently.' Evaluate this statement. Refer to religious and non-religious arguments in your answer. You should agree and disagree, and come to a justified conclusion.* (12 marks)
>
> Use the list of arguments below to help you write a strong answer to that question. They are mixed up though, so first work out which ones agree (support) and which ones disagree (challenge) with the statement. Remember, a conclusion should not just repeat arguments, so it is worth keeping one back to use to strengthen your conclusion. Your conclusion must say which point of view is stronger, and why.
>
> | Argument | Supports statement in question | Challenges statement in question |
> |---|---|---|
> | Most religions believe in non-violence, e.g. Hindus and ahimsa. | | |
> | Jesus was a man of peace – he stopped his disciples from fighting when he was arrested. | | |
> | If all else fails and there is still injustice, protest violently. | | |
> | Non-violent protest does not carry any weight with bad people, e.g. Hitler did not stop the Holocaust when faced with protests. | | |
> | Violent protest makes you as bad as what you are protesting against, so is self-defeating. | | |
> | Religious people should respect life always, so violence shows disrespect and is wrong. | | |

Terrorism

The UN Security Statement

Terrorist acts are 'acts intended to cause death or serious bodily harm to civilians with the purpose of intimidating a population or compelling a government or an international organisation to do or abstain from doing any act'. In other words, terrorists do terrible things to some people in order to intimidate other people, making them scared in their ordinary lives. The intention is to get their own way with one or more governments or to gain power illegitimately. These acts are considered criminal. This separates acts of war (which if done properly are not criminal) from acts of terrorism.

Terrorism in the world today

Today terrorism is a word used widely. The early 21st century has seen acts of terror come to the fore, either because of attacks carried out or attacks being threatened, and of course counter-terrorist measures and all the money and people these involve.

Terrorism is not new, but media coverage has brought it more to people's attention. Suicide attacks have taken terrorist acts to a new, perhaps more frightening, level. The media reports many incidents so that we are more aware of acts of terror, their toll and impact.

The terrorism of today targets anyone: ordinary people, buildings, businesses, the internet, historical sites, sports events and market places – anywhere people gather.

Reasons for terrorist attacks

Terrorists often claim they are:
+ fighting for God or to defend the faith
+ fighting for social justice and against political injustice
+ fighting poverty
+ asserting their religious beliefs
+ fighting because their wishes will not be heard any other way.

Why others disagree

All acts of terror because of their nature are wrong:
+ Those targeted are innocent, with no direct link to the actual issue.
+ Religion is wrongly associated with such acts – murder is wrong under all religious law.
+ Terrorists are power driven rather than religious activists.
+ Their causes are illegitimate.
+ Murder, beheadings, kidnaps, rapes – all used in 21st-century terrorism – are never justified.
+ Places that are terrorist strongholds are places of fear for ordinary people.

> **Terrorism**: an act of violence intended to create fear.
>
> **Terrorist**: a person who plans or carries out acts of terror.

Some religious teachings

Buddhism: no one should kill, nor incite others to do so.

Christianity: those who live by the sword die by the sword.

Hinduism: the pursuit of truth does not permit violence being inflicted on one's opponent.

Islam: the greatest sin is to take another man's life.

Judaism: when siege is laid – surround only three sides so that those who want to escape to save their lives can.

Sikhism: peace through justice is the ideal.

> **Revision tip**
>
> Terrorism is a difficult topic to ask questions about. This is because it is a very emotive topic. If asked about it, treat it sensibly and objectively.

Religious responses to the reasons for war

War is a major issue in the world today – wars between nations, civil wars, the war on terror, futuristic wars such as nuclear and cyber wars. The world has enough weapons to destroy the planet many times.

Many reasons have been used to justify wars, but not all people agree or disagree with these.

> **Retaliation**: payback for harmful action.

So why do wars start?

Wars are fought over land, in self-defence, for power, to keep agreements (treaties) and in support of other nations. These factors can also be interpreted as greed, self-defence and retaliation. These are the reasons you could be asked about in this course.

Greed

+ This is war to gain more land, more power and more resources.
+ In general, most religious teaching would not support this as a reason.
+ Greed comes from selfishness – both not approved of by religions. Considering the numbers of people who die in war, greed is not justifiable as a reason for war.
+ Greed is one of the Three Poisons in Buddhism, keeping humans bound to the wheel of samsara; it is haumai in Sikhism.

Self-defence

+ Religious holy books/texts describe wars. The Hebrew Bible, the Qur'an, the Bhagavad Gita, the Guru Granth Sahib all suggest that war may be necessary in self-defence.
+ If a country or religion is under attack then conflicts can happen. It would be seen as entirely right and proper to defend your country against attack.
+ The problem comes when the response is disproportionately large and self-defence turns into aggression for its own gain.

Retaliation

+ At times, a country will be attacked in a way that provokes retaliation. For example, one of the causes of the First World War was retaliation against a political assassination.
+ The problem with retaliation is that it is often a knee-jerk reaction which leads to the escalation of a situation into war. Religions would all say that peaceful negotiation and discussions to resolve issues are better than simple retaliation – they defuse rather than explode issues.

Religion and belief as a cause of war

Religion or religious teachings do not cause war. Many teachings are ambiguous, so interpretations cause the problems. However, some teachings are unclear, leaving the door open to use violence/war in the name of religion.

Declaring religion as the reason for war gives it support from members of that religion. But people directing war might be using religion to increase their own power – the real but hidden point of the war, and against religious teachings.

Points to note are:

1 It is true that religion is involved in war if two different countries with different religions are in conflict. However, the causes may well be more political or economic than religious.
2 It is true that religious beliefs divide people and when splits in religions have occurred, violence has often erupted.
3 Religions often try to show the differences between themselves whereas actually there are more similarities than differences. Religious beliefs can bring people together, solve crises and bring peace.

True religious beliefs do not cause war – they bring people together when viewed in the right way.

> **Exam tip**
>
> Whilst the specification only has greed, self-defence, retaliation and 'religion and belief' as reasons for war, there are many more. Can you think of any? It might be helpful, especially in evaluation questions, to be able to discuss other reasons as well.

Religious attitudes to war

Buddhism

+ The First Precept, to refrain from taking life, is ahimsa and is a core principle of Buddhism.
+ Hatred does not cease by hatred, hatred ceases by love (Dhammapada).
+ He should not kill a living being, nor cause it to be killed, nor should he incite another to kill (Dhammapada).
+ Buddhism does not believe in war – it leads to greater problems than it solves. It is often the result of the Three Poisons, while also encouraging these in people.

Christianity

+ Put away your sword. Those who live by the sword die by the sword (Jesus).
+ Blessed are the peacemakers (Jesus).
+ Love your enemies, and pray for them (Jesus).
+ Christianity teaches peace and love, though many fight in wars to defend against invading forces. There has to be a just cause, a last resort and peace restored after.

Hinduism

+ Even an enemy must be offered appropriate hospitality if he comes to your home (Mahabharata).
+ War is not in keeping with Hindu virtues of ahimsa, tolerance, peace, compassion and respect.
+ Hinduism sees that if war is a just one, it is a duty to fight and not doing so brings bad karma. In protecting others, fighting may be the only way.

Islam

+ Lesser jihad refers to the shared struggle to uphold justice and protect the faith, which in certain situations may include armed defence.
+ To those against whom war is made, permission is given to fight (Qur'an).
+ Those who die in the name of Allah will be rewarded with paradise (Qur'an).
+ Hate your enemy mildly; for he may become your friend one day (Hadith).
+ Muslims have a duty to fight in self-defence or in defence of Allah and the weak and oppressed, but only as a last resort.

Judaism

+ Get ready for war. Call out your best warriors. Let your fighting men advance for the attack (Joel, Nevi'im).
+ The sword comes to the world because of the delay of justice and through injustice (Ethics of the Fathers, Talmud).
+ When siege is laid to a city, surround only three sides to give an opportunity for escape to those who would flee to save their lives (Maimonides).
+ Judaism has previously regarded war as a religious duty. The Tenakh describes battles fought with G-d on the side of the righteous. War today is still acceptable but only as a last resort in self-defence and against injustice.

Sikhism

+ The Sikh khanda includes two swords and Sikhs wear the kirpan, showing a willingness to fight when necessary.
+ When all other methods have failed it is permissible to draw the sword (Guru Gobind Singh).
+ A true warrior is one who fights for the downtrodden, the weak and the meek (Guru Granth Sahib).
+ Sikhism allows war in self-defence and for justice. The Gurus suggested military training for all, went into battle against oppression and an army was set up after the Khalsa. Many Sikhs fought in the British Army in the First and Second World Wars. Sikh men and women still join their nations' Armed Forces today.

Now test yourself

1 Give some causes of war.
2 Why do some people say that religion causes war? Use examples from this page.
3 Why do some people say religion encourages pacifism (not war)? Use examples from this page.

Revision tip

Remember, don't just learn the teachings, know how to use them. That means being able to interpret them in the light of the issues today.

Just war

Within some religions' tradition there are guidelines on the rules for a legitimate war. Those guidelines attempt to control the decision to go to war and then how it is fought, making it somehow just or fair. These sets of rules have allowed religious people to fight, even when their religion purports to be one of peace.

Holy war: war fought in the name of God; believing God has sanctioned the war; in Islam, there are criteria for this kind of war.

Just war: war fought under the auspices of the just war criteria, relates to Christianity and Sikhism; believing it is right to fight a legitimate war in the interests of justice and peace.

Christian just war

Proposed by St Augustine, written in detail by St Thomas Aquinas in the 13th century, these rules have still been referred to and used as a guiding principle in modern warfare:

+ Controlled by just authority – elected government.
+ Just cause – must not be for revenge.
+ Clear aim – promote good over evil.
+ Last resort – all diplomatic methods have been tried first.
+ Winnable – it is wrong to risk life if the war cannot be won.
+ Fair conduct – reasonable force must be used and civilians protected.
+ Good outcome – the benefits of war outweigh the evil of war.

The **just war** suggests that if you do not fight, you allow a greater evil to happen than the war would have caused. In other words, the war is the lesser of two evils, or a necessary evil.

Sikh just war

Outlined by Guru Gobind Singh when he set up the Khalsa:

+ Sikhs refer to just war as dharam yudh: 'in defence of justice'.
+ War is the last resort.
+ The cause must be just – a Sikh defends himself, his nation and the weak.
+ War should be fought without hatred or the wish for revenge.
+ Territory must not be taken.
+ All soldiers must behave justly and civilians must not be harmed.
+ Only the minimum necessary force should be used.
+ When aims are met, the war should end and peace be established.

Activity

Fix it!

Read the answer to this question, then try to improve it.

Explain two different religious beliefs about war. Refer to sacred writings or another source of religious authority in your answer. (6 marks)

Some people think that any war is acceptable if the government can give a good reason for it, like fighting the Iraq war when they thought Saddam Hussein had weapons of mass destruction.

Religious people, on the other hand, believe a war is only acceptable if it meets the just war criteria, because then it is allowed by God.

Holy war

Theme D: Religion, peace and conflict

Christian holy war

✚ A war fought for God or faith.

✚ An example is the Crusades – a series of wars during the Middle Ages between Christians and Muslims. Both sides believed they were fighting for God and God was on their side.

✚ Must be authorised by a religious leader with great authority.

✚ The purpose is to defend the faith from attack.

✚ Most Christians today do not agree with the idea of holy war.

Muslim holy war

✚ A holy war is a just war with rules based on the Qur'an and Hadith.

✚ It can be fought only as a last resort and not against another Muslim nation.

✚ Muslims have a duty to join the army and fight if a just leader begins a war.

✚ Not all Muslims have to fight. Prophet Muhammad said one man from each two should fight, so that there are still men to defend and look after the towns and villages.

✚ Sane Muslim men, not boys, whose families will cope without them fight.

✚ Soldiers on the battlefield must fight – running away is wrong because that makes it more difficult for other soldiers.

✚ If a town is attacked, everyone – men, women and children – has to fight back.

✚ It may begin only when the enemy attacks and it ends when the enemy shows they want peace.

✚ Civilians must not be harmed, attacked or mistreated. Crops should be left alone. Holy buildings especially should not be damaged.

✚ Prisoners of war should be treated well. Money collected for zakat can be used to pay for food for them.

✚ When people regain their rights, the war ends.

Now test yourself

TESTED

1 What are the conditions for just war?

2 What is the difference between just war and holy war?

3 What are the conditions for holy war?

Activity

Spot the problem!

Read the answer to this question. Work out how it can be improved, then rewrite the answer to achieve the marks.

Explain two different beliefs about just war. Refer to sacred writings or another source of religious authority in your answer. (6 marks)

Muslims say Allah allows these wars – sanctioned by Allah. The Qur'an gives the rules for fighting these wars, so if Muslims keep to the rules, they are right with Allah.

Secondly, they believe that not everyone has to fight in a holy war. It is important that some people stay behind to protect civilians and keep things going. If the battle comes to their town, then everyone has to fight the aggressor.

Revision tip

Think about whether these ideas can be applied in the modern world today.

Remember, not all religions make reference to just wars or holy wars. If the exam question is about either of these, you may need to refer to other world religions you are not using as your main focus – it's the only way!

Explain two similar religious beliefs about just war. (4 marks)

Explain two different religious beliefs about holy war. (4 marks)

Victims of war

War results in many victims through injuries and death, destruction of buildings and land, contamination of land and water, refugees, famine and disease, captivity and the defeated. There are organisations that try to help the victims of war, both when war is happening and after it.

It is part of all religions to help those in trouble and defend those who cannot defend themselves. To help the victims of war fits with the basic teaching of the Golden Rule: treat others as you would be treated, which every religion subscribes to.

Christian Peacemaker Teams (founded in 1984) covers a wide range of Christian denominations. The organisation sends small teams to work on peacemaking in conflict zones – this is an example of third-party non-violent intervention.

The Buddhist Peace Fellowship (founded in 1978) works by applying Buddhist principles to resolve issues in the world. It raises awareness of issues, tries to strengthen leadership in the troubled areas, and acts with other groups to make change happen. It supports victims of war by helping bring peace back to an area and doing relief work for victims of war.

Khalsa Aid (set up in 1999) bases its work on the Sikh principles of selfless service (sewa) and universal love. It provides relief assistance to victims of war, funded through donations from Sikhs all over the world, as well as other disaster and relief work.

Individual religious believers can help by joining an organisation to strengthen its work through contributions, taking a job which directly works with victims of war, campaigning politically and encouraging others to do so, and praying for peace.

> **Peacemaking:** activities intended to bring or keep the peace.
>
> **Victims of war:** those who are negatively affected by war.

Peacekeeping: how is religion involved in wars today?

There are three key areas for answers:

+ Is religion the defining factor in wars?
    + Yes – as communities are divided by war, religion often comes to the fore.
    + No – religion is often misused just to try to explain who is fighting who. Religion is drawn in but war is more about land and power.
+ Does religion play a part in ending war?
    + Yes – many religious leaders call for peace, including employing peace negotiators. The majority of believers want peace and should be able to bring into line those who don't.
    + No – religious people call for peace but they are ignored. Religious extremists will always find excuses for war.
+ Does religion keep the peace?
    + Yes – all religions have a central message of peace, expressed through key principle sayings: ahimsa, do not kill, love enemies, etc.
    + No – teachings talk about peace but religious believers may not want it; indeed, some want war. Even with their best peace efforts there are greater overriding factors, such as the craving for power, etc.

> **Revision tip**
>
> The above are the types of questions that could be the basis of questions in any exam, so learn the for and against points. It would also be useful to have a couple of teachings from your chosen religions to show that peace and not war is what religions strive for.

> **Now test yourself** TESTED
>
> 1 Who are victims of war?
> 2 How do religious organisations help victims of war?
> 3 How might individuals help them?

Weapons of mass destruction (WMDs)

 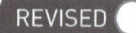

Most religious people disagree with weapons of mass destruction (WMDs) and many have joined protests against them. They disagree because:

WMDs are capable of killing and maiming large numbers of people.

It is almost impossible to only target military operations as their area of impact cannot be controlled or limited.

WMDs are controlled from far away, so whoever releases the weapon does not experience or see the effect directly.

Types of WMDs

WMDs use conventional (i.e. ordinary) weapons with a warhead with the WMD-type load. The explosion of the weapon causes widespread scattering of the contents/effect of the warhead.

Nuclear weapons – atomic bombs – cause immediate destruction of all life and structures within their range. The radioactive fallout will have long-term effects, contaminating land for long periods.

Biological warfare – germ warfare – uses live disease-causing bacterium or viruses such as anthrax to bring death or serious illness.

Chemical warfare uses non-living toxins such as nerve agents and mustard gas to cause death, incapacity or illness.

Radiological weapons – dirty bombs – are weapons using conventional explosives to disperse radioactive material. As well as killing people, they contaminate the impact areas for long periods (potentially years).

Religious attitudes

+ Use of WMDs is wrong because of uncontrollable/extreme effects.
+ It is against just war and holy war theories.
+ It is against the principles of peace, justice and sanctity of life.
+ Some believers accept that a nuclear deterrent needs to be maintained.

Should countries have nuclear weapons?

Nuclear weapons are often seen as the acceptable side of WMDs. They are held by a finite number of governments and are subject to international regulation. They are seen as 'defensive weapons', being held to keep the peace (working on the principle 'if I have this weapon, you will not attack me').

Reasons for proliferation (increase in nuclear countries) are:
+ they discourage attack – have a deterrent value
+ they maintain peace
+ use of other WMDs is made less likely.

Reasons for disarmament (removal of nuclear weapons) are:
+ there is no moral justification for their use
+ WMDs waste of valuable resources (nuclear is extremely costly) which could be used more effectively
+ it encourages other countries to develop them and use them.

> **Nuclear deterrence:** holding of nuclear weapons for the purpose of deterring others from acts of aggression against them.
>
> **Nuclear weapons/war:** a weapon/war of mass destruction.
>
> **Weapons of mass destruction (WMD):** a weapon that is capable of killing many people and/or destroying buildings and land indiscriminately. The internationally legal example is nuclear, other forms (chemical, biological, 'dirty bombs' are illegal under international law).

> **Revision tip**
>
> This question could come up as follows:
>
> *Explain different religious beliefs about WMDs in contemporary British society.*
>
> *In your answer you must refer to the main religious tradition of Great Britain and one or more other religious tradition.* (4 marks)
>
> Remember, the rider of the question is really important to read on the 4-mark question so that you answer it using the correct religions. 'Main religious tradition of Great Britain' is Christianity.

> **Now test yourself**   TESTED
>
> 1 What are WMDs?
> 2 Why do some people support the holding of WMDs?
> 3 Why do many religious believers reject WMDs?

Religious attitudes to peace and pacifism

 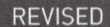

Buddhism

+ Peace can exist if everyone respects all others (Dalai Lama).
+ The Buddhist message is one of peace, not war. It is wrong to take life (First Precept).
+ Golden Rule: 'I will act towards others exactly as I would act towards myself.'

Christianity

+ Everyone must commit themselves to peace (Pope John Paul II).
+ The Christian message is one of peace. Jesus taught a message of love and Christians have a strong pacifist tradition.
+ Golden Rule: 'Treat others as you wish to be treated.'

Hinduism

+ Key Hindu virtues include ahimsa (non-violence), tolerance, compassion and respect, as well as protection of others.
+ The Hindu message stresses that justice can be achieved only through non-violence. Since all life is sacred because Brahman is within all, the atman, war destroys this ideal.
+ Golden Rule: 'This is the sum of duty: do nothing to others which if done to you could cause the pain.'

Islam

+ The Muslim greeting is salaam alaikum ('peace be upon you').
+ One meaning of the word Islam is peace. One of Allah's names is As-salaam, which means 'the source of peace'. It is said that if all people followed the Muslim way of life, there should only be peace.
+ Golden Rule: 'None of you truly believe until he wishes for his brothers what he wished for himself.'

Judaism

+ It shall come to pass ... nation shall not lift up sword against nation, neither shall they learn war any more (description of G-d's Kingdom).
+ The Jewish message is tikkun olam – to heal the world. For this to happen, peace must be at the centre of all that people do.
+ Golden Rule: 'What is harmful to yourself do not do to your fellow man.'

Sikhism

+ The Lord is the haven of peace (Guru Granth Sahib). Peace is believed to come from God.
+ The Sikh message of peace obtained through justice is the ideal for all.
+ Golden Rule: 'As you value yourself, so value others – cause suffering to no one.'

Pacifism is the belief that all war and killing are wrong and that peace is the only way. Pacifists oppose war, regardless of the reasons for the war. Conscientious objectors are often pacifists who refuse to fight directly but will assist in relief work, or act as medics or mediators – all seen as peacemaking roles.

The Quakers are a Christian group with a peace testimony never to use violence. They believe they follow the true teachings of Jesus, opposing all wars, and love should be the key between nations.

Gandhi, the Hindu leader, used non-violence for all his political actions – speeches, sit-ins, marches – showing it could be used effectively and be just as powerful as any physical force.

Bonhoeffer, a German Christian pastor, used pacifism to oppose the Nazis. He believed helping the oppressed was a test of faith. In the end he did sacrifice his principles for the greater good – he planned to assassinate Hitler but was arrested and executed for treason.

> **Pacifism**: belief that all war and killing is wrong, that peace is the only way.

Now test yourself

TESTED ◯

1 What is peace?
2 What is the Golden Rule and how does it influence people towards peace?
3 Explain a religious attitude to peace.

Exam practice

What questions on this section look like:

Theme D: Religion, peace and conflict

This page contains a range of questions that could be on an exam paper. Practise them all to strengthen your knowledge and technique while revising. Check back to pages 11–12 to see the marking grids that examiners use: this will help you to mark your answers.

1 Which of the following is the meaning of 'justice'?

(a) Fairness   (b) Greed   (c) Retaliation   (d) Happiness   [1]

2 What does WMD mean?

(a) Weapons causing most death   (b) Weapons of major destruction

(c) Weapons of mass destruction   (d) Weapon of mass devastation   [1]

3 Give one reason why forgiveness is important to religious people.   [1]

4 Give one effect of conflict.   [1]

5 Give one reason why some religious believers support the keeping of nuclear weapons.   [1]

6 Explain two different religious beliefs about violence in contemporary British society. In your answer you should refer to the main religious tradition of Great Britain and one or more other religious traditions.   [4]

7 Explain two similar religious beliefs about forgiveness. In your answer you must refer to one or more religious traditions.   [4]

8 Explain two different religious beliefs about holy war. In your answer you must refer to one or more religious traditions.   [4]

9 Explain two religious beliefs about just war. Refer to sacred writings or another source of religious belief and teachings in your answer.   [6]

10 Explain two religious beliefs about helping victims of war. Refer to sacred writings or another source of religious belief and teachings in your answer.   [6]

11 Explain two religious beliefs about reconciliation. Refer to sacred writings or another source of religious belief and teachings in your answer.   [6]

12 'All religious believers should be pacifists.' Evaluate this statement. In your answer you should:
   + give reasoned arguments in support of this statement
   + give reasoned arguments to support a different point of view
   + refer to religious arguments
   + refer to non-religious arguments
   + refer to a justified conclusion.   [12]

13 'War can never bring peace.' Evaluate this statement. In your answer you should:
   + give reasoned arguments in support of this statement
   + give reasoned arguments to support a different point of view
   + refer to religious arguments
   + refer to non-religious arguments
   + refer to a justified conclusion.   [12]

14 'Greed is the greatest cause of war.' Evaluate this statement. In your answer you should:
   + give reasoned arguments in support of this statement
   + give reasoned arguments to support a different point of view
   + refer to religious arguments
   + refer to non-religious arguments
   + refer to a justified conclusion.   [12]

Exam tip

Level 2 students do not make it easy for the examiner to give marks. Their writing can be confused, too brief and too vague. If this is you, you just need to learn the content better – start by making notes that work for you.

Level 5 students use a mix of clear and vague ideas. Often the examiner has to look for where new ideas start. If this is you, try giving more clues – a new idea means a new paragraph, and you say 'Firstly' and 'Secondly' before your points.

Level 8 students write clearly and use – as the norm – clear signals for the examiner to work with.

Find Now Test Yourself and Exam Practice answers at **https://www.hoddereducation.co.uk/myrevisionnotesdownloads**

Theme E: Religion, crime and punishment

Laws

Most religions also instruct their followers to keep the laws of the country in which they live. They should break a law only in certain circumstances – to protect life, for example, or if they are being challenged to break a key principle of their own religion.

Religions recognise that laws are for our own and society's good and safety, so must be right. Most laws are not unlike religious ones anyway.

Religion and rules

Religions have their own rules and laws that believers are told to follow, giving people a framework and guidance to help them live their lives correctly to achieve their spiritual aims. For example, the Ten Commandments apply to Jewish people and Christians, and Sikhs follow a code of conduct called the Rahit Maryada.

When a believer breaks one of their religious laws they commit a religious offence (sometimes called a sin). Just as in society when someone breaks a law, they are punished; there is also the belief that people who sin will be punished in some way. Ultimately their afterlife could be affected, meaning they are going to hell or being reborn in a lower life form.

To decide what is right and wrong, religious people have several sources of authority to guide them. Nevertheless, they should always be guided by their conscience, sometimes described as the voice of God inside your head telling you what is right or wrong.

Religious traditions accept that everyone makes mistakes, but they also teach the ideas of punishment for the wrong-doing, repentance by the individual and compassion from the victim, which then allows them to forgive. A victim can offer forgiveness even if the criminal shows no remorse.

Some people believe that forgiveness is the best way for both criminal and victim to rebuild their lives. Punishment, though, is a clear part of the process. Jesus discusses forgiveness on many occasions but that does not mean to the exclusion of punishment. When Jesus was on the cross his comments about the two criminals being crucified with him can be interpreted as forgiveness; however, there was no reference to their punishment being stopped or cancelled.

Conscience: the voice in our heads that teaches right from wrong.

Forgiveness: letting go of anger towards someone for a wrong they have done to us.

Law and order: rules of our society, and how they are enforced.

Morality: a person's or religion's beliefs of what is right and wrong in behaviour and action.

Sin: an act which goes against God's will; a religious offence.

Revision tip

Learn these key terms, they form good 1-mark questions and underpin the whole topic in general. If you know their meaning you will be able to apply them in 4-, 6- and 12-mark questions.

113

Crime

Which crimes do you think are the worst? Always have two or three reasons to be able to explain why, with examples. Can any crime ever be justified?

Types of crime

When someone breaks the law they commit a crime. Most people experience the effects of crime at some point:

+ Crimes against the person: directly harms a person, e.g. hate crime, murder
+ Crimes against property: damages or deprives people of their property, for example arson, burglary.
+ Crimes against the state: potentially endangering everyone or affecting the smooth running of society, for example terrorism, selling state secrets.

Causes of crime

There are various factors that may lead to crime:

+ Upbringing: the morals of family/friends/neighbourhood are a factor.
+ Mental health problems: a person's state of mind – for instance, having no understanding of right or wrong, or are the victim of an abusive upbringing.
+ Poverty: there is no alternative way to survive – a person may have no money, no job, they cannot provide for themselves or their children.
+ Addiction: a person may need money to fund an addiction.
+ Greed/hate: these emotions are often responsible for crime.
+ Opposition to existing laws: crimes may be committed in protest about laws that are considered either unfair. Sometimes laws have to be broken to get them changed.

Evil: what is it and is it linked to crime?

Evil is immoral and wicked; good is virtuous and righteous. There are those who suggest that people who commit the worst crimes are evil. Look at these possible 12-mark questions statements:

'All humans are born with the ability to be evil.'

+ Outside religion, some believe that evil is part of our mental make-up. Our upbringing and the influences in our lives bring the evil out in us – hence, bad influences, can trigger or sow the seeds for evil actions. That is, evil is not a force but rather a psychological phenomenon, with everyone having the potential to be evil. The level of the crime depends on how much evil has been triggered.

'People are not evil, they just do evil things.'

+ Others say actions are evil, not the person themselves. However, we still have to punish a person for committing the wrong/evil deed. Most religious people believe that even those who do evil things can be brought back to good ways. This then affects how people view punishments too.

'All evil has to be punished severely.'

+ Evil, disturbs people's sense of well-being and safety, so has a great impact. Victims have to be helped, evil-doers punished and everyone else reassured.

> **Crime:** breaking the law; this can be against a person (e.g. assault), property (e.g. arson) or the state (e.g. terrorism).
>
> **Evil:** an act which is very wicked or immoral.
>
> **Evil intention:** morally wrong thinking which can lead to what is considered wicked behaviour; often linked to the idea of a malevolent force, e.g. the devil.
>
> **Greed:** unreasonable desire/hunger for something.
>
> **Hate crime:** a crime committed because of prejudice.

> **Revision tip**
>
> These paragraphs can be used in answer to any of the three evaluation statements – providing you with a two-sided argument. Look at the next page for the religious arguments you would also need to include in your answer. Simply put all the ideas together and hit Level 4: 10–12 marks!

> **Now test yourself** TESTED
>
> 1 What is meant by 'crime'? Give examples.
> 2 Why do people commit crimes?
> 3 What is meant by 'evil'?

Find Now Test Yourself and Exam Practice answers at **https://www.hoddereducation.co.uk/myrevisionnotesdownloads**

Good and evil

Religious ideas about the origins of evil

Buddhism

✚ Evil actions are those strongly motivated by greed, hatred and delusion (the Three Poisons). An act is not of itself evil – what makes it evil is the **intention** behind it or the outcome.

✚ Evil arises from delusion/ ignorance and is overcome with wisdom/ awareness. Evil does not come from original sin. Instead each person is responsible for the evil they cause, because it comes from their intentions or ignorance.

✚ No one is ever entirely evil because all have the capacity to change and learn to do good, purify the mind and become enlightened.

Christianity

✚ Evil is the abuse of the free will God gave humans, allowing them to choose right from wrong.

✚ Many Christians believe in a figure called the devil or Satan, an evil power, though less powerful than God. This devil tries to tempt and encourage humans to behave badly.

✚ So, evil is a combination of internal and external factors.

Hinduism

✚ There is a constant struggle in the universe, in the world and in ourselves between light and dark, good and evil.

✚ Good and evil are natural parts of the creation.

✚ Humans commit evil deeds as they are ignorant of their divine nature (Atman). Desires and selfishness encourage them to forget their true divine nature and go in the wrong direction.

✚ By our thoughts/words/actions we create karma – if evil, we will have to make up for that in possibly many future lifetimes.

Evil?

Islam

✚ The Qur'an says that there is a devil (Iblis) who was announced as an angel. Allah had ordered the angels to bow to Adam, but Iblis refused.

✚ Iblis was expelled from paradise, but was able to cause Adam and Eve's expulsion from Eden.

✚ Iblis continually tempts humans to be wicked. Humans fail to show self-discipline and give in to Iblis' temptations.

✚ Evil is a mix of a temptation by Iblis and the weakness of humans.

Judaism

✚ Adam and Eve were tempted by the serpent to disobey G-d, resulting in their expulsion from Eden.

✚ The serpent represents a malevolent force, which continues to subvert the behaviour of humans.

✚ Humans have free will, so there has to be evil - this allows them to exercise their free will for good or bad. Observing mitzvot (laws), a Jewish person avoids evil.

Sikhism

✚ Selfishness (haumai) is the root of evil.

✚ It prevents people from following their religion, encourages them to break rules and hurt others. The more selfish a person, the more evil they are capable of.

✚ Evil lies within the consciousness of any person, and the level of selfishness we have makes it more or less controlling of our actions.

Now test yourself
TESTED

1 For any religion, try to explain their idea of where evil comes from.

2 Use your own intelligence to work out where you think good comes from and how a person might stay good.

The aims of punishment

There are many aims of punishment – this course requires you to study three of them. However, you could refer to any others in answers which are not exclusively about the three specified.

Knowing a fuller range of aims helps you better understand why punishments are given by judges. So here are some other commonly used aims:

+ Protection: the key aim is that the law must protect society from the criminal and the criminal from society – to keep everyone safe. When someone is locked up in prison, they cannot cause harm in society so people are safer.
+ Vindication: the law has to be tough enough for people to live by the rule of law. People must feel that the punishments given mean the law is upheld. In effect, punishments justify the existence of laws.
+ Reparation: the criminal can 'repair the damage done', either with direct contact with the victim of their crime to physically put something right, or by doing something to benefit the local community. They are 'making up for' by 'repairing'.
+ Compensation: the criminal pays back something (usually with monetary value) to compensate the victim for the damages done – whether physical, emotional or financial, or damages to items/property.

Deterrence

This deters (puts off) the criminal from doing the crime again because the punishment is harsh. It also deters other people from committing crimes in the first place because they are put off by the punishment given to others.

Key point: if people were deterred from criminal acts, there would be no crime to punish. Harsh punishments like the death penalty are used as a deterrent in some countries – there is no chance then of repeated crime. Christianity and Sikhism agree with deterrence but not always through very harsh punishments (which may make criminals worse). Buddhism does not agree with harsh punishments as they could themselves cause harm, which is against the Precepts. Deterrence can be created in many ways, but there is no guarantee that deterrence will be effective.

Retribution

This is the idea that the punishment 'should fit the crime', almost to the point where it can be seen as taking revenge. The law of course is not actually vengeful – it provides justice by seeing the criminal pay for their crimes and ensuring that they have not got away with them.

The 'death penalty' or a 'life sentence' for a murderer would be retribution – for example, the death penalty ensures a 'life for a life'. It ensures justice and no repeated crimes. Some people would say that a whole life sentence is better as it 'takes away the freedom of life' rather than the law carrying out an act as bad as the criminal's murder. Revenge is not an appropriate response, coming as it does from hatred. However, justice is done, and it is costly for a whole life sentence and prison is not always considered harsh enough.

Reformation

Many punishments are given to try to change the behaviour of the criminal – to be able to safely put them back into society, having seen the error of their ways. They realise they were wrong, or see the effect on their victims and reform, so change.

Deterrence: aim of punishment; where the punishment puts someone off committing the crime.

Death penalty: capital punishment; execution as a lawful punishment.

Justice: a belief in what is right and fair.

Reformation: aim of punishment; helping the person see how and why they should behave better.

Retribution: aim of punishment; getting back at the person for what they have done.

Revision tip

Learn the definitions – they make good 1-mark questions.

Learn two examples of punishments for each aim. Look at the religious attitudes to punishment to be able to answer 6-mark questions, such as 'Explain two religious beliefs about … reformation/retribution/ deterrence … as an aim of punishment.'

For 12-mark questions, jot down ideas about why one punishment could be said to be more important than another or why they are all equally important. Also the religious teachings will be useful to construct your answers.

A criminal can be reformed through a harsh punishment or through a positive punishment with education, rehabilitation and counselling programmes. Most religions support reformation as an aim of punishment. Many want to see work done with criminals, such as education and counselling programmes, so they change their moral outlook and see the inappropriateness of their ways. Reform cannot be guaranteed though and criminals do reoffend.

Activity

Support or challenge?

'Reformation is the most important aim of punishment.' Evaluate this statement. Refer to religious and non-religious arguments in your answer. You should agree and disagree, and come to a justified conclusion. (12 marks)

Use the list of arguments below to help you write a strong answer to that question. They are mixed up though, so first work out which ones agree (support) and which disagree (challenge) with the statement. Remember, a conclusion should not just repeat arguments, so it is worth keeping one back to use to strengthen your conclusion. Your conclusion must say which point of view is stronger, and why.

Argument	Supports statement in question	Challenges statement in question
It changes people's moral outlook for the better, so changes them for ever.		
Protection is necessary from murderers and those who hurt other people.		
Jesus believed in second chances, and reformation helps people appreciate a second chance.		
A victim would prefer to be compensated for what has happened to them – if someone has vandalised my house, I would rather it be fixed.		
Not all people can be reformed because their behaviour is too ingrained.		
There is something of God in everyone, so everyone can be reformed, and then they would contribute positively to society.		

The principle of utility

The 'principle of utility' means doing what brings the 'greatest good for the greatest number'. It comes from a philosophy called 'utilitarianism'.

This can be applied in several of the Themes, but is a specific part of this Theme. You can apply it to the aims of punishment, types of punishment, and capital punishment.

When considering the aims of punishment, the utilitarian view might be that reformation is best because when the criminal comes back to society (the many), if they are reformed, they will cause no more harm to society, but instead will help society. Another use of the principle of utility is to believe that any criminal should be imprisoned, because protecting society (the many) is more important than that one person spending some time in prison. In the case of capital punishment, the state is ensuring the safety of all by taking the life of the offender.

Religious attitudes to crime and punishment

Buddhism

✚ Buddhists recognise the need for a justice system to punish offenders and protect society. The best system would encourage an offender to recognise the harm they have caused, so that they change their ways for the better. This means a system which promotes reform, and so spiritual growth is best.

✚ Buddhism emphasises compassion, which is the opposite of cruel punishments including corporal punishment or the death penalty. Many specific crimes go against the Moral Precept of non-harming, or of not taking what is not given. Buddhism recognises that the intention behind the crime can make it worse - not only does this lead to a greater punishment, but it also makes for more bad karma for the criminal.

Christianity

✚ The law has responsibility to punish and care for the criminal while trying to reform them. While prison removes freedoms/rights and separates offenders from their families, it is also concerned that they be reformed and can rejoin society as 'good' citizens. Therefore there can be conflict between severe punishments and the Christian belief in help, love and reform.

✚ However, some Christians want more of an emphasis on 'justice' based on the 'an eye for an eye' teaching from the Bible, for example a proportionate response when punishing for crime. Most believe in people being treated humanely and fairly, giving them the chance to face up to their crime, serve a fair punishment and have a second chance to turn their lives around.

Hinduism

✚ Scripture says punishment is a ruler's right and through fearing the threat of punishment, all beings should follow their dharma. Punishment maintains social order.

✚ In the past, punishments allowed for compensation rather than for retribution. This allows for society and criminals to be reconciled and social justice to be restored. In modern law, punishments are given by the state and victims need to be compensated too.

Islam

✚ The Qur'an emphasises the justice of Allah and the idea, of accountability for one's actions. Also it teaches of mercy and forgiveness. The legal system prescribes punishments for crimes such as murder, rape and theft.

✚ Most Muslim countries have modern prisons and principles of fair treatment of criminals.

Judaism

✚ There is a strong belief in repentance and while a person can repent to G-d, this is pointless if they try to avoid the punishments from society.

✚ One of the seven laws of Noah states that there is a need for a proper legal system to establish a moral society. Treatment of offenders must be just and fair, with a focus on reform. Revenge as in retribution according to the Talmud is not a Jewish principle.

Sikhism

✚ Sikhism teaches punishments should be just, fair and allow for reform. Sometimes community actions are given for correction, based on sewa, such service in the gurdwara. These have an emphasis on penance, humility and renewal.

✚ Some Sikhs agree with capital punishment to keep society safe, but many believe only God has the right to take life.

Suffering and forgiveness

Religious beliefs about suffering

Religions condemn suffering caused by human action and all have rules/principles which are there to try to prevent suffering. Teachings tell us it is wrong to cause suffering and that those who do so should be dealt with.

Buddhism believes suffering is everywhere – we all have to look within ourselves to stop this suffering. Other religions want God to help them overcome suffering or be forgiven for causing it.

Religion gives humans the path to righteous actions, but this path is difficult to follow at times. All religions stress how our emotions – love, hate, greed and desires – easily lead to suffering and provide teachings to keep these in check.

Religions support the law to prevent suffering, believing law-breakers should be punished fairly and with justice, and that victims must be helped.

Helping those suffering from crime: the victims

Victims (and witnesses) are supported by the justice system. They are offered emotional and practical support and practical tips to keep safe. There is specific support in certain areas, such as for abuse or rape victims, victims' rights, help for young victims and help for foreign language speakers.

Forgiveness for the criminal

It is very important to forgive and this is a key religious quality. Forgiveness is more about the victim than the criminal, and often has more impact on the victim, allowing them to let go of the negative ideas of revenge to move on and let the criminal move on too. It does not mean the victim condones, accepts, excuses or forgets the crime, however.

Some criminals repent, earning forgiveness; some do not but are forgiven anyway. Society deals with criminals with punishment, whereas victims can deal with them with forgiveness.

For Buddhists, forgiving practises compassion and Right Understanding. Without it the world remains vengeful and troubled. For Christians, Jesus said we should forgive 'not seven times but seventy times seven'. Hindus see forgiveness as one of six cardinal virtues. Islam states, 'whosoever forgives and makes amends, his reward is upon Allah'. In Judaism, the Torah explicitly forbids Jewish people to take revenge or to bear grudges. Sikhs believe 'forgiveness is as necessary to life as the food we eat and the air we breathe'.

Most religions believe that forgiveness is a quality of God, to be copied by the believer.

> **Activity**
>
> Giving yourself timed tests is a great way to boost your exam readiness. So, for a 4-mark question, give yourself 5 minutes. Go!
>
> *Explain two different religious beliefs about the punishment of criminals.* (4 marks)

> **Repentance:** being truly sorry for what you have done.
>
> **Suffering:** a feeling of pain, harm, distress or hardship which is caused by the actions of others when they commit crime.

> It is not the law's business to forgive. The law deals with the criminal as it has to. It can be described as a process: crimes committed; criminal caught and punished; time served; **repentance** shown (maybe), and new start. The crime is not forgotten, but the criminal has the chance to move on.

> **Activity**
>
> Use the information on this page, and the checklist below, to answer the following:
>
> *'All criminals should be forgiven rather than punished.'* (12 marks)
>
> + The key words are 'all' and 'rather'. Can you think of different crimes which could be forgiven and those which might not be forgivable?
> + Think about two/three reasons criminals should be forgiven, maybe using some examples to demonstrate your points, and then two/three points showing why punishment is necessary too.
> + In these types of questions arguing that both are required often makes a good conclusion.

Prison

Prison is the secure confinement of a criminal to deprive them of their liberties. They have a regime to follow day in day out. Most prisoners will be released back into society having completed no more than half their original sentence, as they become eligible for release on parole at that point.

Aims prison fulfils:

+ Protection: keeps society safe from the criminal and the criminal safe from society.
+ Deterrence: prison itself should deter the criminal and would-be criminals.
+ Retribution: length of sentence fits the crime committed.
+ Reformation: work is done in prison to change the criminal for the better.
+ Reparation: the criminal might be encouraged to meet their victim and make up for what they have done.
+ Vindication: sentences are lengthy for serious criminals so that the law is respected.

Concerns about prison:

+ The conditions in which prisoners are kept are not conducive to reform.
+ There is debate over which crimes should result in prison.
+ How can putting bad people with bad people reform any of them?
+ Most prisoners reoffend, so prisons are not effective, but they are costly.
+ Crime carries on in prisons – drug use, gangs, assaults, violence, threats.
+ Separation from families, detachment from society, readjustment on release are all the source of problems.

Community service

This punishment is given for less serious crimes to repair the damage caused, with a set number of hours spent 'paying back' the community by working on projects. It is more positive than prison so has better outcomes. It can be done around working hours and there is no separation from families. Community service offers help to avoid criminal activity.

Aims community service fulfils:

+ Reformation: a positive change can come about in the criminal through a positive contribution to society.
+ Deterrence: the orange jackets make people highly visible when on community service and they do not want to be seen doing this again.
+ Retribution: the project matches the crime – graffiti clean-up. Society is getting them back.

Concerns about community service:

+ There are not enough projects available – many not suited to the crimes committed – so it is not helpful.
+ It is seen as too soft an option and often does not bring reform.
+ Monitoring and management are often poor, so those sentenced to community service do not complete hours or are badly behaved, without any punishment or reprisal.

> **Revision tip**
>
> The Specification requires you to study two punishments used in the UK: prison and community service. You can refer to others in answering non-specific questions though, to support the points you make.

> **Community service:** doing unpaid work for the community as a legal punishment.
>
> **Prison:** deprivation of liberties as a legal punishment.

Corporal punishment

Corporal punishment is illegal in the UK, and in most democratic countries. All religions in the modern world (except Islam) would disagree with its use.

> **Corporal punishment:** inflicting physical pain as a legal punishment.

Historically, many religions allowed the use of corporal punishment, but most modern teachings no longer support it.

The Qur'an sanctions corporal punishment for certain crimes so it is included in the laws of some Islamic countries.

Corporal punishment is seen as an effective deterrent because no one wants pain. It is retribution, but it is also inhumane and barbaric.

Criminals can become hardened, so the lesser forms of corporal punishment have no deterrent value.

Religious teachings about corporal punishment (CP)		
Buddhism Crimes come from intention – this is what needs to be dealt with, but CP does not target this. CP is not a loving action, breaking the First Precept.	**Christianity** The Old Testament says 'An eye for an eye', but Jesus taught 'You heard it said, an eye for an eye … I say if someone hits you offer the other cheek.' This challenges the idea of using CP.	**Hinduism** In modern Hinduism corporal punishment is considered to be abhorrent and is not acceptable.
Islam 'As for a thief, male or female, cut off their hand' (Qur'an). In spite of Shari'ah law allowing for it, many Muslims today don't believe in CP though; they emphasise and believe that Allah is merciful and forgiving.	**Judaism** Torah law permits CP, though it was only used very rarely in early Judaism. In reality few Jewish people support the use of CP.	**Sikhism** 'Fareed, do not turn around and strike those who strike you with their fists. Kiss their feet, and return to your own home' (Guru Granth Sahib).

Is it ever good to cause suffering?

Yes

+ People learn their lesson because they are made to suffer.
+ It allows retribution – the punishment 'should fit the crime'.
+ CP deters people from committing crime, which helps the community.

No

+ Causing a person pain can make them more angry/resentful.
+ Religions teach that love conquers all – hurting someone does not fit with this.
+ Religions encourage believers to be loving as God is – causing suffering is not a loving act.

Now test yourself	TESTED

1 What is prison?
2 What is community service?
3 What is corporal punishment?
4 What is good/bad about each of these types of punishment?

Activity

Support or challenge?

'Punishments in the UK are not harsh enough.' Evaluate this statement. Refer to religious and non-religious arguments in your answer. You should agree and disagree, and come to a justified conclusion.

(12 marks)

Use the list of arguments below to help you write a strong answer to that question. They are mixed up though, so first work out which ones agree (support) and which disagree (challenge) with the statement. Remember, a conclusion should not just repeat arguments, so it is worth keeping one back to use to strengthen your conclusion. Your conclusion must say which point of view is stronger, and why.

Argument	Supports statement in question	Challenges statement in question
Community service is too easy to get out of and no one works hard.		
Corporal punishment would make more people think twice – physical pain has the harshness to deter. The UK doesn't have this.		
Prison is very difficult, depriving of freedoms and keeping a criminal from their family.		
Punishment should be about deterrence and reformation, not harshness – which sounds like revenge and is against religious teachings.		
Many criminals reoffend after they have been punished in the UK.		
Jesus taught forgiveness – even when he was being punished in the harshest way. It is good the UK does not have this kind of punishment.		

Activity

Read the question and both answers. Which answer is better? Use a highlighter and annotations to show why it is better. Then, write your own perfect answer.

Explain two different beliefs from modern British society about the death penalty. In your answer, refer to the main religious tradition in Great Britain and one or more other religious traditions.

(4 marks)

Student A:

Christians agree with the death penalty because they believe in an eye for an eye. This means murderers should be put to death. Muslims also agree with the death penalty because the Qur'an says it must be carried out for certain crimes.

Student B:

Muslims have the death penalty as Shari'ah Law. The Qur'an says which crimes are punishable by death, but also says that life cannot be taken except by way of justice (so the death penalty can only be used for the most serious crimes). Judaism – on the other hand – allows for the death penalty, but never uses it. The Torah gives situations for which the death penalty may be used, and Jewish law defines how capital punishment should be carried out.

Exam tip

The 4-mark question that has 'In your answer, you should refer to the main religious tradition in Great Britain…' as its second half is easy to do badly on. The reference to 'main religious tradition of Great Britain' means you MUST write a Christian response as part of your answer. Fail to do that, and you have lost two marks instantly!

The death penalty – capital punishment

In the few countries where the death penalty is legal, it is reserved for the most extreme offences, usually murder. Crimes such as blasphemy, adultery, drug offences, corruption, fraud, treason and war crimes are also capital offences (they carry the death penalty).

Why the need for such an extreme punishment?

Where the death penalty is used, the crimes are seen as being so bad that no other punishment would be suitable. Society must take revenge on the individuals who commit such heinous acts and deter others from committing such offences.

This meets the biblical ethos of 'an eye for an eye' and also the Islamic teaching of equal retribution. A murderer shows no respect for human life, so the state has none for theirs.

Many holy books name certain offences as being punishable by death.

Arguments for CP:
+ An 'eye for an eye, life for a life'.
+ Deterrence – to put people off committing horrendous crimes.
+ Justice for the victims and their families.
+ Life sentences do not mean life – prisoners might at some point be set free.
+ Terrorists murder indiscriminately, they cannot be reformed.
+ It is a waste of resources housing criminals for their entire life.
+ The death penalty has been used for centuries around the world.
+ It demonstrates that society will not tolerate some crimes.

Arguments against CP:
+ Retribution is uncivilised – two wrongs don't make a right.
+ Most murders are 'spur of the moment', so capital punishment would not deter.
+ Killing the murderer does not end the pain of loss for the victim's family.
+ It makes executioners seem as bad as criminals.
+ Executing terrorists would make them martyrs.
+ Innocent people can be executed after an unfair trial.
+ The sanctity of life, that all life is sacred, including that of murderers.
+ It is inhumane and degrading to put anyone through the mental torture of death row.

> + There are 85 countries that retain the death penalty; only 21 use it routinely.
> + Since 2000, approximately 1,000 people per year worldwide have been recorded as executed by their governments.

Now test yourself

TESTED ○

1 What is capital punishment?
2 Why do some people support the use of capital punishment?
3 Why do other people disagree with the use of capital punishment?

Activity

In her exam, Jenni wrote this answer. You can see she focused on aims of punishment rather than the pros and cons of the death penalty. Notice how she underlines her key points to make them leap out for the examiner (clever!).

Use the bullet points from arguments for and against the death penalty to write a stronger answer to this.

The death penalty does not solve the problem of crime.

(12 marks)

To solve the problem of crime, I think we have to get the punishment right. The death penalty is a good <u>deterrent</u> – who wants to get killed? So it puts people off. It also <u>protects</u> society from that criminal hurting anyone else. So it does solve the problem.

However, it is <u>only useful for some crimes</u>, so it doesn't solve the problem really. Jesus talked about <u>forgiveness</u> – the death penalty is definitely not that!

Religious beliefs about capital punishment

REVISED

Buddhism

+ Buddhists do not agree with punishments that are unduly severe – and the death penalty is.
+ The death penalty goes against loving kindness (metta) and compassion (karuna).
+ The First Precept is about not taking life.
+ The death penalty is a form of revenge, so comes from bad intentions (Three Poisons).

Hinduism

+ In ancient times, some laws allowed for the death penalty for murder and treason.
+ Gandhi said: 'An eye for an eye and we shall all soon be blind.'
+ Punishment should allow for the offender to reform.

Judaism

+ 'The Lord does not enjoy seeing sinners die. He would rather they stop sinning and live' (Nevi'im).
+ If anyone takes the life of a human being on purpose they could potentially be put to death (Torah).
+ 'G-d created the world with justice and mercy so that it would last' (Midrash).

Would religion agree with capital punishment or not?

Christianity

+ 'An eye for an eye' (Old Testament).
+ 'Do not murder' (Old Testament).
+ 'God gives life and takes life away' (Job).
+ Capital punishment would deny the sanctity of life – 'all life is sacred'.

Islam

+ 'The greatest sin is to take another person's life' (Qur'an).
+ 'The penalty for murder is death' (Qur'an).
+ 'Take not life except by way of justice and law' (Qur'an).

Sikhism

+ Many do not support the death penalty because of their belief in the sanctity of life.
+ Some would see it as a useful deterrent and just punishment for some crimes.
+ 'If someone hits you, do not hit him back, run after him and kiss his feet' (Guru Granth Sahib).

Revision tip

Remember that not all believers will agree with the death penalty, even if teachings suggest it is acceptable. Most holy books have teachings to support and to challenge the use of the death penalty. Generally, within most religions, the attitude to the death penalty is negative.

This is a popular topic, having been on the exam most years and fits into all the question styles. It could be a definition or reason for 1 mark, similar or different beliefs for 4 marks, religious beliefs for 6 marks, or a 12-mark evaluation. In other words, there is plenty of scope for the examiner to ask it on your exam.

Midrash: 'story telling', written by rabbis to interpret the Tenakh, or answer questions arising from it.

Find Now Test Yourself and Exam Practice answers at https://www.hoddereducation.co.uk/myrevisionnotesdownloads

Exam practice

What questions on this section look like:

Theme E: Religion, crime and punishment

This page contains a range of questions that could be on an exam paper. Practise them all to strengthen your knowledge and technique while revising. Check back to pages 11-12 to see the marking grids that examiners use: this will help you to mark your answers.

1 Which of the following is not an aim of punishment?

    (a) Deterrence   **(b)** Reformation   **(c)** Retribution   **(d)** Justice   [1]

2 What is meant by corporal punishment?

    (a) Death penalty   **(b)** Deprivation of liberties

    (c) Paying compensation   **(d)** Physically hurting someone   [1]

3 Give one reason why religious believers agree with the use of prison as a punishment.   [1]

4 Give one religious teaching about justice.   [1]

5 Give one reason why some religious believers support capital punishment.   [1]

6 Explain two different religious beliefs about forgiveness in contemporary British society. In your answer you should refer to the main religious tradition of Great Britain and one or more other religious traditions.   [4]

7 Explain two similar religious beliefs about justice. In your answer you must refer to one or more religious traditions.   [4]

8 Explain two different religious beliefs about the aims of punishment. In your answer you must refer to one or more religious traditions.   [4]

9 Explain two religious beliefs about whether it can ever be good to cause suffering. Refer to sacred writings or another source of religious belief and teachings in your answer.   [6]

10 Explain two religious beliefs about the need to follow the law. Refer to sacred writings or another source of religious belief and teachings in your answer.   [6]

11 Explain two religious beliefs about people who break the law because of mental health problems. Refer to sacred writings or another source of religious belief and teachings in your answer.   [6]

12 'Opposition to an unjust law is the only good reason to commit a crime.' Evaluate this statement. In your answer you should:
   + give reasoned arguments in support of this statement
   + give reasoned arguments to support a different point of view
   + refer to religious arguments
   + refer to non-religious arguments
   + refer to a justified conclusion.   [12]

13 'Murder is not the worst crime a person can commit.' Evaluate this statement. In your answer you should:
   + give reasoned arguments in support of this statement
   + give reasoned arguments to support a different point of view
   + refer to religious arguments
   + refer to non-religious arguments
   + refer to a justified conclusion.   [12]

14 'Severe punishment can maintain law and order.' Evaluate this statement. In your answer you should:
   + give reasoned arguments in support of this statement
   + give reasoned arguments to support a different point of view
   + refer to religious arguments
   + refer to non-religious arguments
   + refer to a justified conclusion.   [12]

Exam tip

Grade 2 students show little knowledge of the diversity within or between religions. If this is you, you need to get notes that are better for you to work with.

Grade 5 students show some knowledge of diversity and an understanding of how this influences different people. If this is you, focus your notes and revision on specific groups within religions so that you can write clearly and knowledgably.

Grade 8 students show good knowledge and understanding of the diversity within and between religions. They demonstrate this clearly in detailed answers.

125

Theme F: Religion, human rights and social justice

Social justice

REVISED

This is justice which tries to more fairly distribute wealth, where the law is fair to all, and there are equal rights and opportunities for all. Society must be fair to all, regardless of race, age, gender, sexuality and disability, and it has to be open to all with education, healthcare, housing and social welfare – social justice aims to bring this about.

Social justice is a reason why religions fight for human rights and against prejudice and exploitation, including fighting for people who are vulnerable. There are always people in society who can look after themselves despite political systems, but there are always those who cannot. Those in poverty may need preferential treatment and a society is judged on how it treats its most vulnerable. Others believe too much help can make people reliant on that help, however, so they do little to help themselves.

Equality: everyone is equal in value and worth.

Gender: the state of being male or female.

Justice: bringing fairness back to a situation.

Social justice: justice in terms of wealth and opportunities in a society.

Key religious ideals

+ Buddhism: selflessness – Right Action, Livelihood, speech, effort and intention should, if carried out properly, lead to social justice.
+ Christianity: the teachings of Jesus used in terms of liberation from unjust economic, political or social conditions.
+ Hinduism: Dharma is found in everything and everyone has an atman, so that means everyone is equal. Compassion is a key belief.
+ Islam: social justice with zakah and almsgiving are central to the faith.
+ Judaism: the concepts of simcha (gladness), tzedakah (charity and justice), chesed (deeds of kindness) and tikkun olam (healing the world) lead to social justice.
+ Sikhism: the message of equality of all beings shows believers should deal with all humankind with the spirit of universal brotherhood and equality.

Exam tip

In any question on this topic, *respect for others* is a very important underpinning concept. For example, all human rights come from the point of view that others deserve respect, so deserve these rights. Prejudice is the opposite of respect for others. If we show respect for those in poverty, we will not exploit them and we will help them.
Use this principle in all your answers – religions all teach/value it.

Now test yourself

TESTED

1 What is meant by stewardship?
2 What is meant by responsibility?
3 What is social justice?

Human rights: what are they?

These are the rights humans should be able to expect as a minimum because they are human.

The UN Declaration of Human Rights (1948) and the UK Human Rights Act (1998) include basic rights and freedoms. Some examples are right to life, to not be persecuted by others, to have a fair trial, to free speech, and also the right to have food, shelter, education, healthcare and work.

The UN claims that adopting and following the Human Rights Act is part of the way to build freedom, peace and justice in the world. In other words, where a country commits to human rights, its people enjoy better lives.

Rights bring responsibilities to the self and others through the medium of respect. Being a citizen brings rights within a country, but also confers the responsibility to respect and follow the rules of that country.

> **Responsibility:** duty towards something.

Activity

Support or challenge?

'Religious believers should accept all the rights in the Human Rights Act.' Evaluate this statement. Refer to religious and non-religious arguments in your answer. You should agree and disagree, and come to a justified conclusion. (12 marks)

Use the list of arguments below to help you write a strong answer to that question. They are mixed up though, so first work out which ones agree (support) and which disagree (challenge) with the statement. Remember, a conclusion should not just repeat arguments, so it is worth keeping one back to use to strengthen your conclusion. Your conclusion must say which point of view is stronger, and why. Phrases like 'more persuasive', 'easier to accept', 'make more sense for me' are good for the final evaluation you do in a conclusion.

Argument	Supports statement in question	Challenges statement in question
Human Rights Act covers all aspects of life.		
Human Rights Act ensures fairness for everyone in every aspect of life.		
Some rights go against what a religion teaches, e.g. who you can marry.		
Human rights are decided by secular groups, whereas religious people follow religious law.		
Human rights are abused all the time everywhere, so are meaningless anyway.		
Human rights are something to aspire and work to for a better society - everyone should agree with them.		

Now test yourself

1 Give examples of two human rights.

Freedom of religious expression

What do religions teach about this?

Buddhism believes all religions are valid spiritual paths to the universal truth. People should decide for themselves after hearing/learning the teachings – no persecution and religious freedom is the right path.

Many Christians believe the only way to eternal life is through Jesus, so this excludes all other faiths. Hence they try to convert others to the word of Jesus – discrimination should not be shown to peoples of other faiths and neither should persecution be perpetrated.

Hindus believe in `Vasudhaiva Kutumbakam', which means the whole world is one family. Hinduism is a way of life and not a prescriptive religion so it is tolerant to other faiths.

Islam accepts Christians and Jewish people as 'People of the Book'. Prophet Muhammad built relationships with those of other faiths and taught peace and tolerance, inclusiveness and acceptance of other religions. The morally good will be rewarded in paradise, so discrimination and persecution are wrong.

Judaism is seen as the best way to live, but Jewish people allow others to live as they wish. How people live their lives is the important factor, not who they worship – no intolerances should be shown.

Sikhs must not offend other religions – all are the same flesh and creations of God. Guru Nanak often rejected the exclusiveness of other faiths – no persecution should be shown.

Freedom from persecution because of religion: the right to be legally protected if someone targets you because of the religion you follow. They would have committed a hate crime, which is a criminal offence.

Freedom of religious expression: the right of any person to follow the religion of their choice and to be open about what they believe. In the UK, you cannot be told (legally) that you are not allowed to follow a particular religion – none is banned.

Tolerance: accepting of difference.

Activity

Fix It!

Read this answer and work out how to improve it.

Explain two similar religious beliefs about the freedom of religious expression. In your answer, refer to one or more religious traditions. (4 marks)

One religious belief is a Christian one. They believe the only way to eternal life is through Jesus - so you have to believe in Christianity. But a Christian shouldn't be horrible to people who aren't Christians.

A second religious belief is Hindu. They believe all religions are ok to believe in.

Should religious people express their beliefs openly?

Some people openly express their faith: by the morally good life they live, through clothing, wearing a specific item like a cross, talking to others about their faith, through the media or through gestures such as sportspeople openly praying before an event.

UK society is enriched by religious beliefs and culture, which promotes diversity with understanding, tolerance and harmony. Laws also allow all this to happen freely. It is a person's right to express their religion and this right must be respected as long as no one is being harmed by it.

For some religions, there is the expectation to 'bear witness', that is to let others know what their faith is, and even to try to convert people to the faith (proselytise/evangelise). Members of these groups will certainly be open about their faith.

However, there are other opinions:

+ Some take offence at religion if they are non-religious, seeing any expression as unacceptable, and sometimes even that just expressing your religion is an attempt to proselytise.
+ It could make people targets of hate crimes as they make themselves known, hence some stay quiet out of fear.
+ Religion divides people rather than bringing them together, for example where two religions differ in attitude to something.
+ Some religions include practices which are not legal in the UK, or which are stricter than UK law, for example the clash between Shari'ah and UK law on how to deal with adultery, or the acceptance of polygamy. These often lead to negative publicity and discrimination of those perceived to be in that religion.

Activity

Fix it!

Read the answer to this question. Work out how it can be improved, then rewrite the answer to achieve the marks.

Explain two religious beliefs about freedom of religious expression. Refer to sacred writings or another source of religious authority in your answer. **(6 marks)**

One belief is by Christians who say that Jesus told them to go and make everybody into a Christian. So for Christians, they have to convert people. Second belief is by people who aren't religious and they don't want to know about it. They think people should keep their religion to themselves not force it on people.

Revision tip

Watch out for this topic as a 12-mark evaluation, for example *Religious people should be open and proud about their beliefs*. It could focus around whether it is right to express religious beliefs or whether people should just keep their beliefs to themselves. Find examples both of expression and of discrimination to support your arguments.

Prejudice

Introduction

There are many types of prejudice – against colour, religion, age, nationality, sexuality, disability, appearance. The Specification names racism only. It also lists freedom of religious expression and the status and treatment within religion of women and homosexuals.

Prejudice is about what we think. It is true to say everyone can be prejudiced at times, even by accident – however, not all people then discriminate.

Prejudice and discrimination can have a great effect on a person's life. In Britain, discrimination is against the law.

Causes

These are the reasons/experiences which create the thoughts that may then be manifested in actions:

1 Bad experience
2 Upbringing
3 Media
4 Ignorance
5 Scapegoating.

Role and status of women in religion

Most religions allow women supporting but not leadership roles. (See page 93).

In Catholic Christianity women cannot be priests or higher. In the Church of England women can be vicars and in 2016 the Church had its first woman bishop (in Stockport). Orthodox Jewish leaders are all men but the Reform Jewish movement has a woman as its Chief Rabbi.

As religions try to keep pace with modern society, the role of women is undergoing changes.

Role and status of homosexuals in religion

(See also page 87.) Homosexuals are fully accepted within the Christian Quaker tradition and in the Metropolitan Church as leaders and they are allowed marriage services. In other religions gay people are accepted but they should remain celibate, that is not have same-sex physical relationships. Sex is for procreation.

Buddhism accepts homosexuality as part of a loving relationship. In Islam, homosexuality is seen by many to be against God's will and is forbidden by Shari'ah law; the punishment for same-sex relationships can be as severe as the death penalty. Sikhism also disagrees with it as it is seen as an act of selfishness because sex is for procreation.

Discrimination: to put prejudiced ideas into action.

Positive discrimination: to promote opportunities for minority groups so they are better represented.

Prejudice: to pre-judge something or someone, usually without any real evidence for that judgement.

> **Revision tip**
>
> There are many kinds of prejudice. Do you know what the following are – homophobia, disability prejudice, gender prejudice? It is a good idea to learn the terms, how religious attitudes to prejudice apply to them, and how religious believers could work to reduce these forms of prejudice or support victims.

> **Now test yourself** TESTED
>
> 1 What is meant by prejudice?
> 2 Give two types of discrimination.
> 3 Give two causes of prejudice.
> 4 Explain religious beliefs about racism.
>
> NB: The core of this answer would be the same if the question were about prejudice or discrimination generally or specific forms of discrimination.

> **Revision tip**
>
> Think about qualities that religions preach about: tolerance, harmony, respect and equality. These are handy words to use to support answers as well as specific teachings.

Racism

Racism is the belief that the colour of a person's skin, or their ethnicity, affects their ability; that some races are better than others.

> 'All human beings are born free and equal … should act in a spirit of brotherhood … everyone is entitled to all the rights and freedom.' *Universal Declaration of Human Rights*

Religious attitudes to racism

Buddhism

+ Believes discrimination leads to *dukkha (suffering)* so it must be wrong and avoided.
+ Encourages Buddhists to not harm others and to develop metta (loving kindness).
+ We are all unique as individuals, but we share in the capacity for suffering and for awareness and compassion.
+ Prejudice creates bad karma and has a negative effect on rebirth.
+ The Dalai Lama stated that the best way to live life was to 'always think compassion'.

Christianity

+ Believes that all forms of discrimination are wrong.
+ 'God created everyone equally.'
+ 'There is neither Jew nor Gentile, slave nor free man, male nor female. We are all equal in Christ' (New Testament).
+ Jesus said to 'love our neighbour' and to 'treat others as we wish to be treated'.
+ In the Good Samaritan story the man is helped because of his need, not because of who he was or wasn't (in fact, the victim and helper were from enemy nations).

Hinduism

+ Hindu Dharma is that Brahman is found in everything, therefore any prejudiced thoughts or discriminatory actions are wrong.
+ Hindus believe in non-violence (ahimsa), love and respect for all things.
+ Compassion is a key belief – needing to improve things for others, not persecute them.
+ Hurting others can lead to bad karma, which negatively affects future reincarnations.
+ The true self is the atman and as everyone has one, this must mean everyone is equal.

Islam

+ Believes that Allah created everyone as equal but different, so discrimination is unjustified.
+ Allah loves the fair-minded (Qur'an), which makes discrimination wrong.
+ Prophet Muhammad chose a black former enslaved person to do call prayers in Madinah and he welcomed anyone regardless of wealth, status or creed.
+ The Muslim Declaration of Human Rights states that everyone is equal.
+ On Hajj everyone, rich or poor, dresses in the same white sheets, equal before Allah.

Judaism

+ Believes that prejudice and discrimination are incompatible with Jewish law.
+ God created everyone equal – prejudice is seen as an insult to God.
+ Jewish people should welcome and not persecute strangers – practise justice, love and kindness (Torah).
+ Treat others as you wish to be treated (Torah).

Sikhism

+ Believes in the principle of justice and to fight for justice where it does not exist. Equality and sewa (service to others) would clearly indicate that discrimination is wrong.
+ 'Using the same mud, The Creator has created many shapes in many ways' (Guru Granth Sahib).
+ Those who love God love everyone (Guru Granth Sahib).
+ God created everyone, therefore all are equal and so deserve the same treatment and respect.
+ 'God is without caste' – Guru Nanak.

Revision tip

Racism is a topic that is listed in the Specification, meaning that questions can be asked directly about it, unlike homophobia or disability prejudice. So it is a good idea to know teachings which are specific to racism, not just ones which can be used for both general and specific questions. Having specific teachings makes your answer sound stronger to the examiner – the link to the question is obvious.

Theme F: Religion, human rights and social justice

Wealth

How do people become wealthy? They:

✚ earn it: they are highly educated, get a well-paid job
✚ win it: perhaps on a talent show, or gambling
✚ inherit it: from a rich family, as a gift
✚ achieve it undeservedly: through crime, etc.

Revision tip

Learn a couple from the two religions you have studied plus two from Christianity. Remember it is one of the 'differences topics' and it is necessary to be able to write about Christianity.

Religious attitudes to wealth

Buddhism

✚ Believes that there is essentially nothing wrong with having wealth but rather how it is used.
✚ Riches ruin the foolish ... through craving for riches, the foolish one ruins himself (Dhammapada).
✚ Greed for wealth is associated with the Three Poisons and is a form of craving.
✚ Unskilful thoughts from greed keep humans circling in samsara, in an endless round of repetitive, habitual attachment (Kulananda).
✚ Buddhism teaches Right Action, Right Thought, Right Intention and Livelihood – for the wealthy to see poverty and ignore it would be wrong.

Christianity

✚ Christians believe that there is nothing wrong with wealth in itself; it is how we use it that matters. Wealth is seen as a gift from God. Our money should come from lawful means. In the Bible there is the warning that the wrong attitude to money could lead people away from God.
✚ The love of money is the root of all kinds of evil (New Testament).
✚ No one can serve two masters ... You cannot serve both God and money (Matthew).
✚ Be on your guard against all kinds of greed: a human's life does not consist in the abundance of his possessions (Luke).

Hinduism

✚ It is important to create wealth (artha) to provide for family and maintain society. The wealthy should not hoard wealth but use it in a stewardship role.
✚ Money causes pain when earned, pain to keep and pain to lose as well as to spend (Panchatantra).
✚ Happiness arises from contentment; uncontrolled pursuit of wealth will result in unhappiness (Laws of Manu).
✚ Look after everyone and act as if everything belongs to you, but know in your heart that nothing does (Ramakrishnan).
✚ Life is all about good deeds here and now. This helps the receiver and the giver's own rebirth in the next life.

Islam

✚ All wealth is a gift from Allah – humans are caretakers of Allah's wealth and will be judged by their use of it to benefit humanity.
✚ Wealth is sweet for him who earns it lawfully and spends it rightfully. He who obtains wealth wrongfully is like one who eats but is never satisfied. (Hadith).
✚ Earning a lawful livelihood is an obligation – no one has eaten better food than what he can earn by the work of his own hands (Hadith).
✚ It is not poverty which I fear for you, but that you might begin to desire the world as others before you desired it, and it might destroy you as it destroyed them (Hadith).

Judaism

✚ Wealth earned in the right way is a gift from G-d and can be used for the self and others. If the heart is filled with the desire for money then there is no room for G-d.
✚ Do not weary yourself trying to become rich (Proverbs).
✚ He who loves silver cannot be satisfied with silver (Ecclesiastes).
✚ He who has a hundred, craves for two hundred (Midrash).
✚ Money should not be craved but it is necessary in life.

Sikhism

✚ Anyone possessing riches has been blessed by God as they are able to help those in poverty. Livelihoods should be made by honest means. Anything that is earned dishonestly is seen as the 'blood of the poor'.
✚ One who lives by earning through hard work, then gives some of it away to charity, knows the way to God (Guru Granth Sahib).
✚ Be grateful to God for whose bounties you enjoy (Guru Nanak).
✚ Those who are too greedy for money have anxiety (Guru Granth Sahib).

Poverty

Causes

Reasons for poverty vary depending on where in the world people live. In LEDCs, poverty is often a fact of life outside people's control – it is not their fault. Poverty is a way of life for many in these countries.

Other reasons for poverty may be family background and upbringing, one's self (addiction, idleness, attitudes to education), or external factors such as high unemployment, unfair trade and lack of opportunities.

Issue – fair pay

+ Fair pay includes issues of fair pay between men and women for the same job.
+ Pay is based on different things, such as hours worked, qualifications needed and type of job.
+ Some people are low paid (minimum wage); others earn excessive (too high) wages.

Reflecting on the issue

+ Are jobs fairly valued and paid – carer (low pay), elite athlete (highly paid)?
+ Low-paid jobs require few qualifications but are still needed by society.
+ People have completed long and difficult study/training to get highly-paid jobs – for example, lawyer – so deserve more.
+ Lowest paid workers often work the most hours, to earn enough.

Issue – excessive loans

+ Excessive loans – borrowing money for what they need, as long- and short-term loans.
+ Loans are made available instantly but with very high rates of payback.
+ They are often used for emergency money people need but haven't got.

Reflecting on the issue

+ People often pay back weekly at the minimum rate so the amount of interest still increases, meaning the debt becomes higher.
+ People in poverty often fall behind on payments, so increasing the debt.
+ Companies exploit their needs, their inability to pay and their lack of understanding of how the system works.
+ Some people feel forced to take out new loans to resolve the problem of falling behind with an existing one, hence getting further into debt.

Issue – people trafficking

+ The person pays a price for this 'opportunity' of a 'better life'.
+ Often families pay huge amounts to give one member the hope of a better life
+ Poverty and war in a country increases people trafficking.

Reflecting on the issue

+ People end up 'belonging' to these gangs as enslaved people, sex workers/prostitutes because the gangs demand extra money in return for their freedom.
+ Many end up as illegal immigrants, living in fear of violence and drugs.
+ Some children are sold into enslavement to earn for their families back home.
+ This practice preys on the desperation of those in poverty.

Excessive interest on loans: massive interest rates on loaned money that lead to more debt.

Fair pay: to be paid a rate appropriate to the work done.

Interest: money paid back on loans in addition to the original amount borrowed.

People trafficking: the illegal trade of humans to exploit them through sexual exploitation and/or forced labour.

Poverty: having less than the basic needs of life, so that life is a struggle.

Revision tip

'Fair pay', 'excessive loans' and 'people trafficking' are three distinct parts of the Specification, so you need to know the definition of each in case you are asked specifically about one of them. For each one, it is good to know why it is an issue and how it breaks religious principles. Since 'excessive loans' and 'people trafficking' mean exploiting those in poverty, they break principles of justice and of compassion in every religion. They also are a challenge for beliefs about the sanctity and dignity of life. Learn those and use them in your exam.

Responsibility to those in poverty

Who	Why	How
The government – we elect a government to look after the best interests of society, including those in poverty. They provide for the needs of the country as a whole and as individuals.	They have the means to help: they collect the taxes to finance the running of public services. People will not vote them into power if they don't help.	Provide health/educational/welfare services and links to business – they can bring all these into play to help those in poverty. They have money, expertise and access to co-ordinate help. Their policy decisions on saving and spending directly affect the wealth of individuals, e.g. cutting benefits or spending more on the homeless.
Charities – a charity by nature is set up to help someone/something. It collects money to help its cause and therefore has the means to help.	To help is the reason they exist. They are set up on religious or humanitarian principles, i.e. compassion and wanting to reduce suffering.	They fundraise through organised events, national charity shops, donation collection. Through experience they then decide how the money raised is best spent.
Religions are about communities and helping each other. The worship of God has to be seen in action as well as words.	The teachings of holy books tell them it is their duty to do God's work. Famous leaders in history and today put those in poverty at the heart of their work. It shows loving kindness to bring social justice to the world. God rewards such action.	Religions organise community events, donate to religious charities, work with people in poverty here and abroad, pray for them and simply be there for people in their times of need.
People in poverty themselves – they need to want to help themselves or at least want help from others, otherwise the help is wasted.	People in poverty should not want to remain so, they should want to improve their situation rather than staying reliant on society and charity. Some people are living in poverty due to their own action (e.g. drugs) or inaction (e.g. not gaining qualifications) so they do have a responsibility to themselves to change this.	They have to believe things can improve, take the help that is on offer, work hard to become independent again. Many have made efforts to get out of poverty but have been knocked back, e.g. job applications ignored many times, so it is up to society to make it possible for those in poverty to help themselves.

Charities

Each religion has its own charities working with people in poverty around the world. Examples include the International Buddhist Relief Organisation, Christian CAFOD, Hindu Sewa International, Muslim Aid, World Jewish Relief and Sikh Khalsa Aid.

In the UK, most are run with volunteers and professionals working in conjunction with the Disaster Emergency Committee (UK Government organisation) to co-ordinate emergency, short- and long-term aid.

Poverty in the UK

Secular charities like Shelter and religious charities like the Salvation Army focus on helping people who are homeless or living in poverty in the UK today. They provide food and shelter and help people to rebuild lives. Shelter does it out of a sense of compassion, and religions out of compassion and to follow religious teachings.

Issues with giving to charity

Should we give to charity or directly to the individual? Should we give money or buy them food? Does the money we give actually help the people who need it? How much of each £1 we give to a charity is actually spent on people in poverty?

> **Revision tip**
>
> Learn two similar religious beliefs behind the work of charities for your 4-mark questions.
>
> The work of charities is always a good topic for an evaluation 12-mark question.

Religious attitudes to helping people in poverty

Buddhism

+ Karuna – compassion – wishing others freedom from suffering.
+ 'Today everyone is looking for personal happiness. So, I always say, if you wish to be happy and aim for self-interest, then care for others. This brings lasting happiness' (Dalai Lama).

Christianity

+ If anyone has material possessions and sees his brother or sister in need, how can he love God? (New Testament).
+ If a brother or sister has no clothes or food, what good is it to wish him well without caring for his physical needs? (James).

Hinduism

+ Hindus believe strongly in charity to help those in poverty and at all festivals people donate for various causes.
+ Some believe by helping those in poverty they can improve their own Karma and rebirth.
+ It is taught 'it is the same God shining out through so many different eyes. So helping others is no different than helping ourselves'.

Islam

+ He who eats and drinks whilst his brother goes hungry is not one of us (Hadith).
+ For a debtor, give him time to pay – but if you let it go out of charity this is the best thing to do (Qur'an).

Judaism

+ You shall not burden your heart or shut your hand against your poor brother (Torah).
+ The Torah forbids charging a fellow Jewish person interest on money.

Sikhism

+ A good person always seeks the welfare of others (Bhai Gurdas).
+ A place in God's court can only be attained if we do service to others in the world (Guru Granth Sahib).

+ There is always someone poorer than you, therefore we are all wealthy enough to be able to help others.
+ Some people are wealthy enough and have positions where they can deal with some of the greater issues such as loan interest or fair pay.
+ We might help for religious reasons or simply out of compassion, but in a modern world with the wealth there is, we could argue that until poverty does not exist we all have work to do.

Revision tip

When learning teachings, keep in mind that you need them for 4/6-mark questions. In each of these you need to give the teaching and be able to explain how it applies to the question. A good way is to start with the teaching, explain what it means and then how it applies in practice to the individual believers today. Then add an appropriate example.

Activity

Explain two religious beliefs about tackling poverty. Refer to sacred writings or another source of religious authority in your answer. *(6 marks)*

In the Qur'an, Muslims are told 'for a debtor give him chance to pay'.[1] This means that when lending money to those in poverty, then a fair chance should be given to pay, not to keep putting the person further into debt.[2] So, for example, they should not be charging excessive loans with massive interest that people in poverty can never pay back.[3]

[1]Stating the source first, a teaching is used in first sentence.

[2]Teaching is explained and applied.

[3]Example is used to develop the point.

Read the answer above. It is half of a 6-mark answer. Write the other half, using the same structure. This will help you to get used to how to answer these types of questions for your exam.

Now answer this one in the same way.

Explain two religious beliefs about excessive loans. Refer to sacred writings or another source of religious belief and teaching in your answer. *(6 marks)*

135

Exam practice

What questions on this section look like:

Theme F: Religion, human rights and social justice

This page contains a range of questions that could be on an exam paper. Practise them all to strengthen your knowledge and technique while revising. Check back to pages 11–12 to see the marking grids that examiners use: this will help you to mark your answers.

1 Which organisation created the Human Rights Act?

   (a) Amnesty International   **(b)** NATO   **(c)** The G7   **(d)** The United Nations   [1]

2 Racism is a form of prejudice against what?

   (a) Age   **(b)** Colour   **(c)** Gender   **(d)** Religion   [1]

3 Give one religious teaching about poverty.   [1]

4 Give one way religious believers can fight prejudice.   [1]

5 Give one way those in poverty may be exploited.   [1]

6 Explain two different religious beliefs about the status of women in religion in contemporary British society. In your answer you should refer to the main religious tradition of Great Britain and one or more other religious traditions.   [4]

7 Explain two similar religious beliefs about freedom of religious expression. In your answer you must refer to one or more religious traditions.   [4]

8 Explain two different religious beliefs about charity. In your answer you must refer to one or more religious traditions.   [4]

9 Explain two religious beliefs about tackling poverty. Refer to sacred writings or another source of religious belief and teachings in your answer.   [6]

10 Explain two religious beliefs about social justice. Refer to sacred writings or another source of religious belief and teachings in your answer.   [6]

11 Explain two religious beliefs about the status and treatment of homosexual people in religion. Refer to sacred writings or another source of religious belief and teachings in your answer.   [6]

12 'People trafficking is the worst form of exploiting people in poverty.' Evaluate this statement. In your answer you should:
   + give reasoned arguments in support of this statement
   + give reasoned arguments to support a different point of view
   + refer to religious arguments
   + refer to non-religious arguments
   + refer to a justified conclusion.   [12]

13 'Equality for all is impossible in today's world.' Evaluate this statement. In your answer you should:
   + give reasoned arguments in support of this statement
   + give reasoned arguments to support a different point of view
   + refer to religious arguments
   + refer to non-religious arguments
   + refer to a justified conclusion.   [12]

14 'Respect for others is the most important of the human rights.' Evaluate this statement. In your answer you should:
   + give reasoned arguments in support of this statement
   + give reasoned arguments to support a different point of view
   + refer to religious arguments
   + refer to non-religious arguments
   + refer to a justified conclusion.   [12]

Exam tip

Level 2 students write very simple, limited answers. If this is you, try to give two answers to every question (bar the first two!), so you pick up a few more marks.

Level 5 students write solid answers, which make sense but lack sparkle. If this is you, try getting a deeper understanding of the subject content to give yourself more personal knowledge to write from.

Level 8 students write answers with a 'wow factor', their answers flow so the reader has no sense of vagueness/confusion after reading.

Key terms from the Specification

As you worked through the guide, you met lots of key terms. A good idea is to go back and create an RS dictionary of your own. If asked to define a word, it must come from the Specification, so these are those words/phrases.

Theme A: Relationships and families

Cohabitation: living together as a couple. Page 65

Contraception: precautions taken to prevent pregnancy and to protect against sexually transmitted infections. Page 64

Divorce: legal dissolution (ending) of a marriage. Page 69

Extended family: the nuclear family plus other relatives, such as grandparents living with the family, but can also include cousins, uncles and aunts. Page 68

Family planning: the planning of when to have family using birth control/contraceptives. Page 66

Gender discrimination: acting on prejudices against someone because of their gender. Page 71

Gender equality: the idea that men and women are of equal worth. Page 71

Gender prejudice: the idea that men and women are not equal. Page 71

Homosexuality: being physically attracted to the same sex. Page 64

Nuclear family: basically mum and dad, plus the child(ren). Page 68

Polygamy: the practice of a man having more than one wife at the same time. Page 65

Procreation: the biological process of a couple producing children. Page 67

Remarriage: marriage a second time after divorce (not usually to the person originally divorced from). Page 69

Theme B: Religion and life

Abortion: deliberate termination of a pregnancy, with the intention to prevent life. Page 85

Animal experimentation: use of animals to test for toxicity and validity of medicines. Page 79

Awe and wonder: sense of amazement. Page 75

Big Bang theory: the scientific view of the beginning of the universe. Page 74

Dominion: the idea that humans have the right to control all of creation. Page 77

Environment: the world around us. Page 74

Euthanasia: mercy killing; ending life for someone who is terminally ill, or who has degenerative disease; this can be voluntary (a person deciding for themselves) or non-voluntary (being decided by others as the individual is incapable). Page 83

Evolution: scientific theory which states that life today has evolved from simple forms through a process of natural selection and the survival of the fittest. Page 74

Natural resources: the resources the Earth provides without the aid of humankind. Page 78

Pollution: to put too much of something into the environment, causing an overload. Page 77

Quality of life: how good/comfortable life is. Page 83

Responsibility: duty to do something. Page 82

Sanctity of life: life is special; life is created by God. Page 83

Stewardship: duty to look after the world, and life. Page 77

Theme C: The existence of God and revelation

REVISED ○

Design argument: the idea that the world is designed so God exists as the designer; teleological argument. Page 94

Enlightenment: realising a religious truth; attaining nibbana (release from the cycle of samsara). Page 98

First Cause: the idea that the world was the result of something causing it. Page 93

General revelation: indirect revelation, e.g. through seeing God through nature. Page 97

Immanent: at work in the world, e.g. performing miracles. Page 92

Impersonal: beyond human capacity to understand; distant (in intellectual and emotional terms). Page 91

Miracles: events which are considered impossible so should not have been able to happen and cannot be explained by science. Page 95

Omnipotent: all-powerful. Page 91

Omniscient: all-knowing. Page 91

Personal: relatable; humans can meet and connect with God. Page 91

Revelation: God revealing himself. Page 97

Science: the collection of knowledge from observation and testing. Page 96

Special revelation: direct revelation, e.g. seeing God in a vision. Page 97

Transcendent: beyond space and time, controlled by neither. Page 92

Ultimate Reality: the idea of a God with total power. Page 90

Vision: seeing something which is non-physical, usually of a holy person. Page 97

Theme D: Religion, peace and conflict

REVISED ○

Conflict: disagreement which can lead to fighting. Page 102

Forgiveness: willingness to not blame a person any more for the wrongs they have done. Page 101

Holy war: rules around fighting a war acceptable to Islam. Page 107

Just war: rules around fighting a war acceptable to Christianity and Sikhism. Page 107

Justice: making things fair again. Page 100

Nuclear deterrence: holding of nuclear weapons for the purpose of deterring others from acts of aggression against them. Page 110

Nuclear weapons/war: a weapon/war of mass destruction. Page 110

Pacifism: the belief that all violence is wrong. Page 111

Peace: the opposite of war; harmony. Page 100

Peacemaking: activities intended to bring or keep the peace. Page 109

Reconciliation: making up between two groups after disagreement. Page 100

Retaliation: payback for harmful action. Page 105

Terrorism: use of violence and threats to intimidate, especially for political purposes to create a state of fear in a population. Page 104

Victims of war: those who are negatively affected by war. Page 109

Violence: aggression in language or action towards another person. Page 102

Violent protest: voicing disagreement in a violent/aggressive way. Page 102

Weapons of mass destruction (WMDs): weapons which cause uncontrollable and untold damage, e.g. nuclear weapons. Page 110

Theme E: Religion, crime and punishment

REVISED ●

Community service: punishment; the criminal has to do a set number of hours' work in the community as their punishment. Page 120

Corporal punishment: physically hurting the criminal as their punishment. Page 121

Crime: breaking the law; this can be against a person (e.g. assault), property (e.g. arson) or the state (e.g. terrorism). Page 114

Death penalty: capital punishment; execution as a lawful punishment. Page 116

Deterrence: aim of punishment; where the punishment puts someone off committing the crime. Page 116

Evil intention: morally wrong thinking which can lead to what is considered wicked behaviour; often linked to the idea of a malevolent force, e.g. the devil. Page 115

Forgiveness: letting go of anger towards someone for a wrong they have done us. Page 113

Greed: unreasonable desire/hunger for something. Page 114

Hate crime: a crime committed because of prejudice, e.g. beating someone up because you think they are gay. In UK law, it can mean the doubling of a sentence if found guilty. Page 114

Law (law and order): the rules which govern a country to keep people safe. Page 113

Prison: being locked up and deprived of one's liberties as a lawful punishment. Page 120

Reformation: aim of punishment; helping the person see how and why they should behave better. Page 116

Retribution: aim of punishment; getting back at the person for what they have done. Page 116

Theme F: Religion, human rights and social justice

REVISED ●

Charity: giving in order to alleviate problems, in this theme, of poverty. Page 134

Discrimination: actions based on prejudice, often negative. Page 130

Equality: the idea that everyone is equal, of equal value and worth. Page 126

Excessive interest on loans: borrowed money which has to be paid back with unfairly high levels of interest. Page 133

Fair pay: payment that is appropriate for the work done. Page 133

Freedom of religious expression: the right of any person to follow the religion of their choice and to be open about what they believe, without discrimination or punishment. Page 128

Gender: the state of being male or female. Page 126

Human rights: the rights a person is entitled to simply because they are human. Page 127

Interest: additional money paid back on loans, on top of the original amount borrowed. Page 133

Justice: bringing fairness back to a situation. Page 126

Loan: an amount of money borrowed. This is usually paid back in installments with interest added on. Page 133

People trafficking: the illegal trade of humans to exploit them through sexual exploitation and/or forced labour. Page 133

Poverty: having less than the basic needs of life, so that life is a struggle. Page 133

Prejudice: prejudging someone based on a characteristic they have, e.g. their looks. Page 130

Racial prejudice: prejudice based on a person's racial/ethnic origins. Page 131

Responsibility: duty, e.g. the responsibility to work to earn money. Page 127

Social justice: justice in terms of wealth and opportunities in a society. Page 126

Wealth: a person's money and possessions. Page 132

Revision strategies

Revision is what you should be doing when you read this book. However, just reading isn't enough – you need to find ways to make what you read stick. Then you need to find ways to improve your exam effectiveness – timings and technique. The following are some strategies you may like to try so that you can find out what works for you. Each strategy has been effective for students at GCSE. Try to make your own revision stuff though – don't just beg from your teacher. Making your own stuff is a form of revision, so it is worth the effort.

Strategies for recall

Creating revision cards

These are small cards which have the key details on them – key words and definitions, reasons/causes, relevant teachings, examples and so on. The idea is that you would have reduced your own notes to this brief detail – being able to do this demonstrates your understanding of the topics. The words/ideas on the cards are meant to trigger the much more detailed knowledge that you have. So you use them to remind yourself.

You can also put images on the cards – visual images help our brains to recall.

A twist on this is to swap sets with other students. This allows you to check what you know because they may have put in some things which you have missed. Read through the cards and if there is something you feel vague or clueless about, you know you have to go back to a bigger set of notes and start from there.

Charismatic worship
- Informal.
- Evangelical worship (hymns, prayers, sermon, readings).

'spirit inspired' – speaking in tongues.

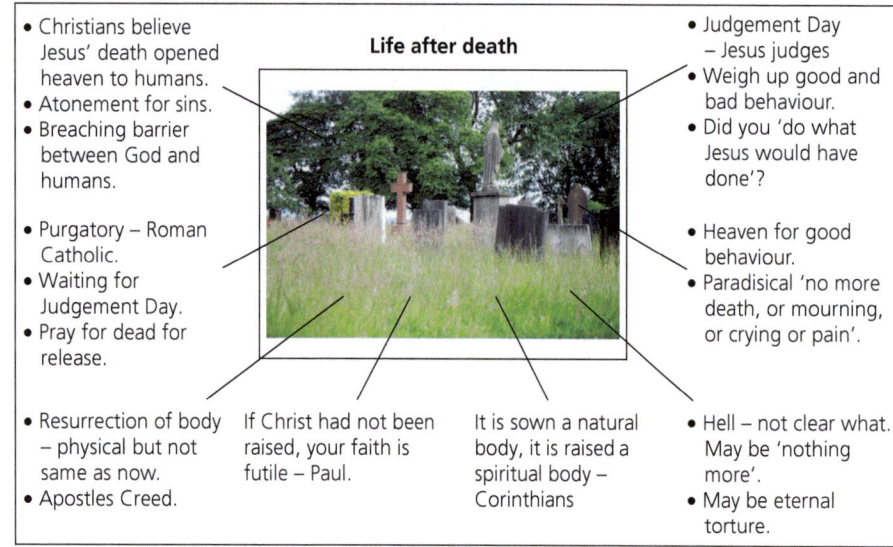

Life after death

- Christians believe Jesus' death opened heaven to humans.
- Atonement for sins.
- Breaching barrier between God and humans.

- Purgatory – Roman Catholic.
- Waiting for Judgement Day.
- Pray for dead for release.

- Resurrection of body – physical but not same as now.
- Apostles Creed.

If Christ had not been raised, your faith is futile – Paul.

It is sown a natural body, it is raised a spiritual body – Corinthians

- Judgement Day – Jesus judges
- Weigh up good and bad behaviour.
- Did you 'do what Jesus would have done'?

- Heaven for good behaviour.
- Paradisical 'no more death, or mourning, or crying or pain'.

- Hell – not clear what. May be 'nothing more'.
- May be eternal torture.

Creating image cards

These are cards which have as their focus an image – for example, of the Christian belief about life after death. Around the image, you make notes – what it is, key words, symbolism, importance/cause/reason, diversity of practice, teachings. The exact nature of the notes depends on the topic, of course.

So, why an image? Well, your brain likes images and finds them helpful for recall. Most people think visually, so this strategy is effective. Even making the cards is a good form of revision – you have to analyse images, and create an effective set of notes which fits to the card, covering all aspects of the topic.

Creating flash cards

Flash cards are simply cards with a statement or question on one side and information on the other. You can take exam-style questions as the questions, or just general ones. We suggest you might use these as questions starters:
+ key word definitions ('holy war =')
+ what a believer believes about …
+ what is the importance of …
+ how is a believer influenced by …
+ similar beliefs about …
+ different beliefs about …
+ reasons to agree with a given statement
+ reasons to disagree with a given statement.

You will notice they are close to the questions AQA has said it will use, so the idea is to make you think that way already in your revision, to tailor the way you revise so that it helps you more effectively in the exam.

Of course, they are your flash cards, so put what you want. Get someone to test you with them.

Creating audio files of notes

Any notes you have made or acquired (like the ones in this book) are a prime target for using as audio files. Just record yourself reading them aloud, then play the recording back any time. You can just listen, or listen as you read the notes. You could play low-level music in the background – choose your preferred artist for the topics you find most difficult, so that the positive feel you get from the music helps make the topic more palatable.

You could team up with others and swap files so that you associate a topic with a person, helping your brain to keep the elements of that topic together as one.

These are good to listen to when doing other tasks – walking to school, doing the dishes, and so on.

141

Making mindmaps/thoughtmaps

How do you revise? Do you read page after page and hope it soaks in? If you do, I've got bad news for you. That is one of the most inefficient ways to revise – sorry!

Would you like to be able to put everything about one topic onto one sheet? You can learn here. Some people like to use these at the start of their revision, giving them an overview of what they have to learn. Others use them as a checklist at the end. I'd recommend both ways.

You will need A3 paper, lots of different colour pens and your notes (just in case!).

Look at the chart below – we'll call it a thoughtmap.

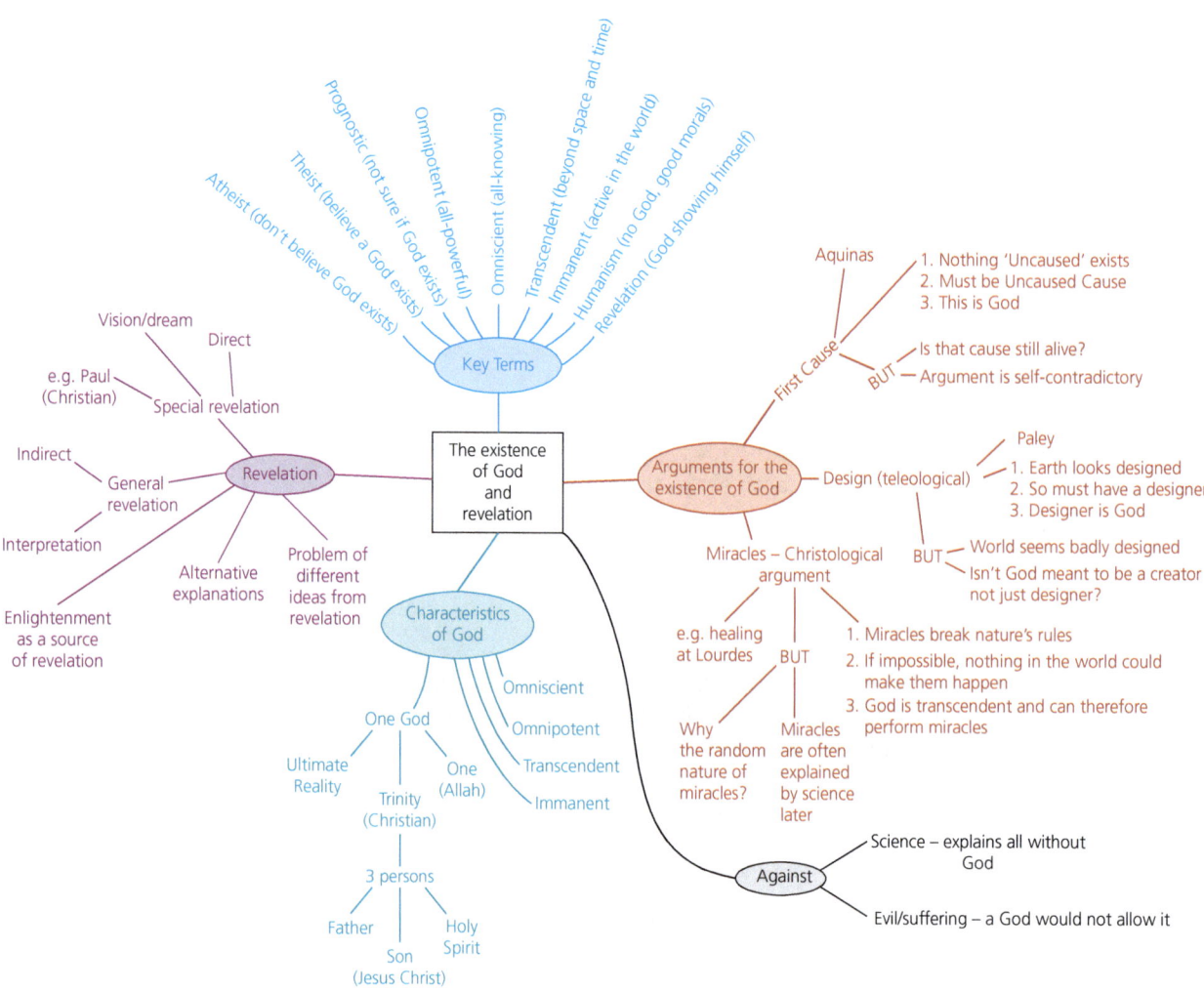

In the centre, in big letters, is the topic name. It needs to stand out, so you know what the page is about. Here it is THE EXISTENCE OF GOD AND REVELATION, but it could be any topic you choose IN ANY SUBJECT (not just RS).

Around it at the first level are the chunks that make up that topic. These are the general issues that the exam questions will be based on, for example questions about how we look after our world. Each chunk has its own colour. When you try to remember the bits of the chart, those colours will help your brain to organise the ideas.

Find Now Test Yourself and Exam Practice answers at **https://www.hoddereducation.co.uk/myrevisionnotesdownloads**

Around each element are the relevant sections. They continue the colour of their element. These make up the foci of the questions, for example saying characteristics of God in this mindmap. You can add the details for each of those sections. They are what your answers will include. For example, where you have key words, you give definitions. You can also add images (if you can draw!).

This chart isn't finished; loads more can be added – try to do that for yourself.

Do this for any topic. Use a sheet of A3 size paper. Stick it on your bedroom wall – you'll read it both deliberately and by accident there. What details you don't remember, check back in your notes. Add any that won't stick.

Strategies for exam effectiveness

Doing time tests

The number of people who run out of time in the exam is astonishing. You need to be able to manage your time well so that you get your best chance at the best marks. You need to train yourself to write everything you need to in the time given. So practise a lot – give yourself these approximate timings, get some questions from your teacher or from books or the AQA website, and try to write an answer in the time you set. For a 12-mark question, give yourself 14–15 minutes; for 4- and 6-mark questions, give 5 and 7 minutes respectively; 1-mark questions need to be done in seconds. You will get better if you practise, so don't just leave it to chance or give up if you find it difficult at first.

Exam question practice

You can get exam papers from the AQA website, from textbooks or your teacher. You can even make them up yourself if you get a good idea of the way the questions have to be worded. It isn't difficult to do this because of the fixed nature of the question sets. Look at any of the Exam Question pages in this book to get a good idea of that fixed wording - just swap a new topic for the one on the question, and then answer it. The more questions you practise, the more familiar you will be with the wording and the requirements, with a resultant improvement in your technique, speed and marks.

The thing about papers is that you have the range of question types you would meet in the exam, and can do them in the exam time. Authenticity is key here to help you feel comfortable and this familiarity helps reduce exam anxiety. You aren't just checking what you know, or whether you can answer questions – you are also helping yourself develop a positive RS exam mindset.

Learning to be the examiner

If you know how the examiners mark answers, you can shape your answers in a way that makes it easier for the examiner to mark them. So find out about the mark schemes, how marks are awarded, the style which makes your writing clearer. Do this by taking chances to learn and to mark – your teacher probably does this with you in class, so pay close attention.

143

Index

145

Find Now Test Yourself and Exam Practice answers at **https://www.hoddereducation.co.uk/myrevisionnotesdownloads**